CW01283744

Spine = A severe scoliosis, complete S-curve with the convexity to the right in the dorsal & to left in lumbar regions. The line traced by the tips of the post. Processes is not sharply curved by the rotation & the consequent deformity is very severe. In front the sternum is concave & the function of the sternum with ensiform cartilage forms a projecting point like the prow of a ship. This "prow" is directed a little to the left corresponding with the deviation of the spine to the right. The ribs, deformed as they are, are capable of free movement & fairly good expansion. Resonance is good; no rales are heard. The area of the heart occupies normal size & relation from the chest wall. Apex impulse is in the 5th space in the mid-clavicular line. Sounds are regular, no murmurs.

Abdomen = falls sharply away from the rib margin. No spasm, no tenderness. Inguinal glands pea-sized. External genitalia negative.

Extremities: Left leg in Thomas splint fully extended. Suspension attached to ring of splint. ... foot lies in valgus which can ... corrected. Extreme flattening of the ... head of the astragalus. ... present but weak. Quadriceps ... overcome gravity.

Divine Femininity

*A collection of poetry
about her,
from my point of view*

Also by Angela Solis

What Lies in the Wolf's Heart (2019)

MANIC. (2021)

Divine Femininity

*A collection of poetry
about her,
from my point of view*

BY

ANGELA SOLIS

2023

Divine Femininity
Copyright © 2023 by Angela Solis.

All rights reserved. This book or any portion thereof may not be reproduced or used in any manner whatsoever without the express written permission of the author except for the use of brief quotations in the context of reviews.

Written in the United States of America.

ISBN: 979-8-218-17582-5 (paperback),
979-8-218-17584-9 (hardcover)

Book design & layout by Rachel Clift.
rcliftpoetry.com

First printing edition, 2023.

Angela Solis
@gurdy1998

Devoted to working on each other together, separately. Always.

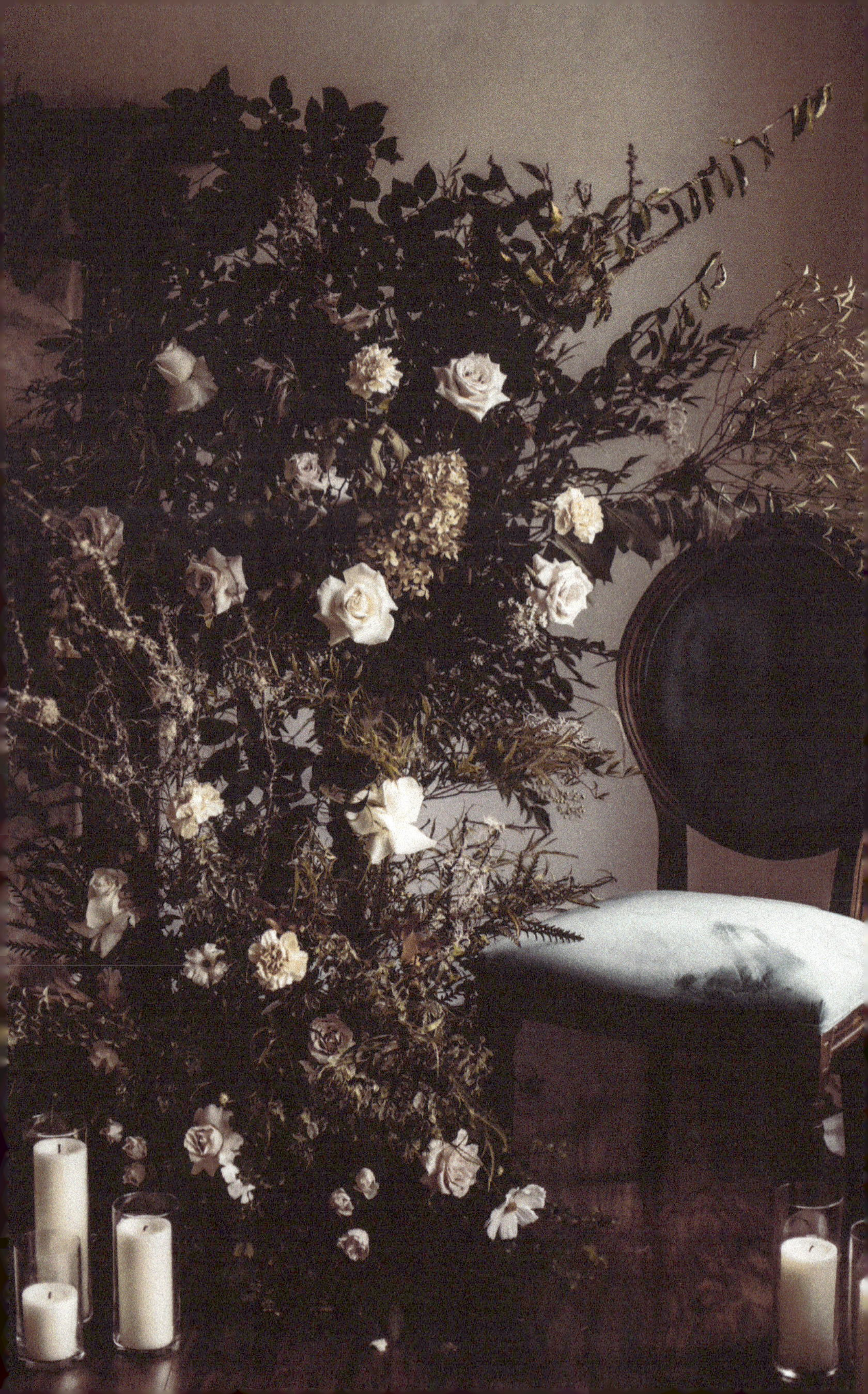

Foreword

by R. Clift

"I asked myself—
What, Sappho, can
you give one who
has everything,
like Aphrodite?"
— *Sappho, c. 600 B.C.*

I have known Angela for several years now, and I'm lucky to call her a dear friend. I've had the honor of helping her bring her first two books to life. Now, you hold the third installment of releasing her poetry into the world. This book is unlike anything she has written or published before, for it is more than simply pages bound together with glue— it is the essence of a lover. Of someone so dear to this author, she could write of her for decades to come.

What is the relationship between poet and inspiration, *artist and muse*, if not an innate and most intimate love? Angela features this kind of love in each poem woven together to create this collection.

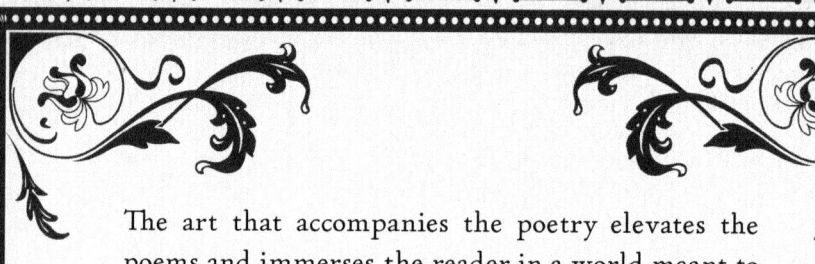

The art that accompanies the poetry elevates the poems and immerses the reader in a world meant to hold you in safety and warmth, as one would hold a partner.

While reading, it is lines like "*I think of you even in the unseen.*" and "*I could recognize her by touch alone.*" that gives the reader a hint of the adoration a poet can capture when she is inspired by the love of her muse. Take this book with you, and witness the kind of magic that can be unearthed and brought to light when one surrenders themselves to such passion. This book reads, more than anything, as a heartfelt and ardent love letter.

To answer Sappho's question— *what can one give to a muse like Aphrodite— one who has everything*? I believe Angela has answered that question here in these pages. She's shown us— one may give our own Aphrodite the promise of unending devotion, the understanding that she is intricately known and adored all the more for it, and of course, poetry. Above all, Angela has shown us time and time again, one must give those we love poetry from the heart.

— R. Clift
POET, AUTHOR
March 2023

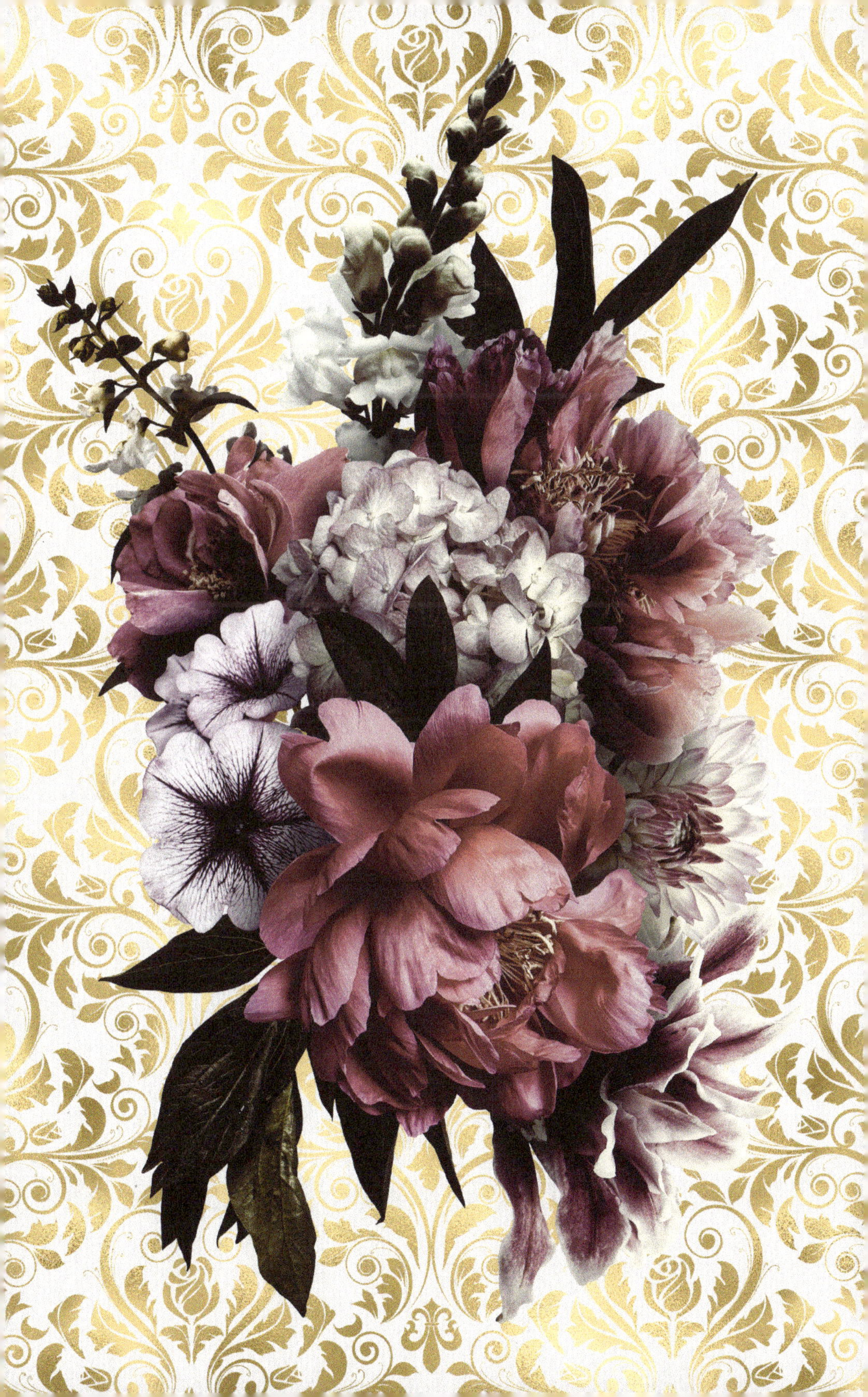

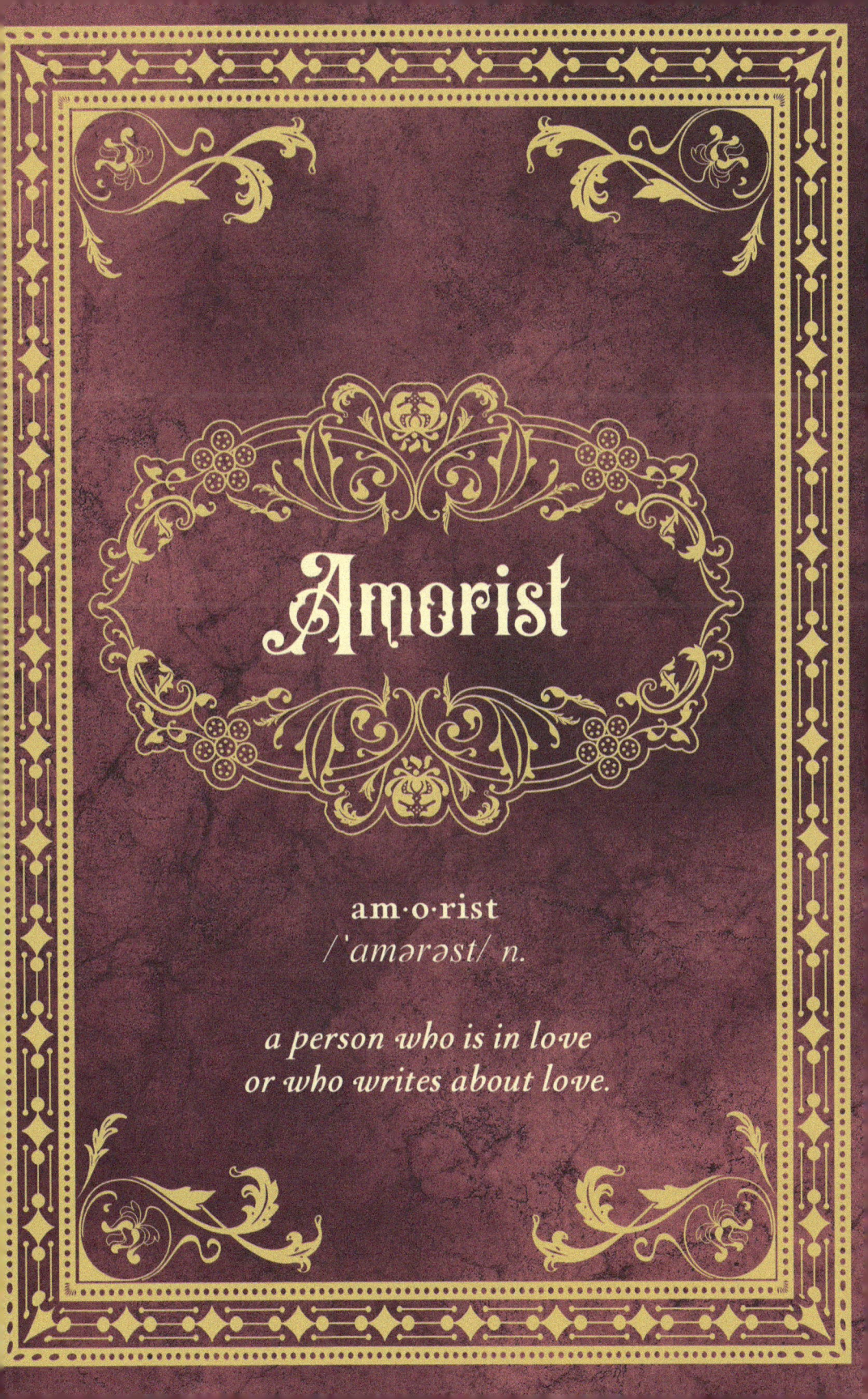

Amorist

am·o·rist
/ˈamərəst/ n.

a person who is in love
or who writes about love.

Logophile

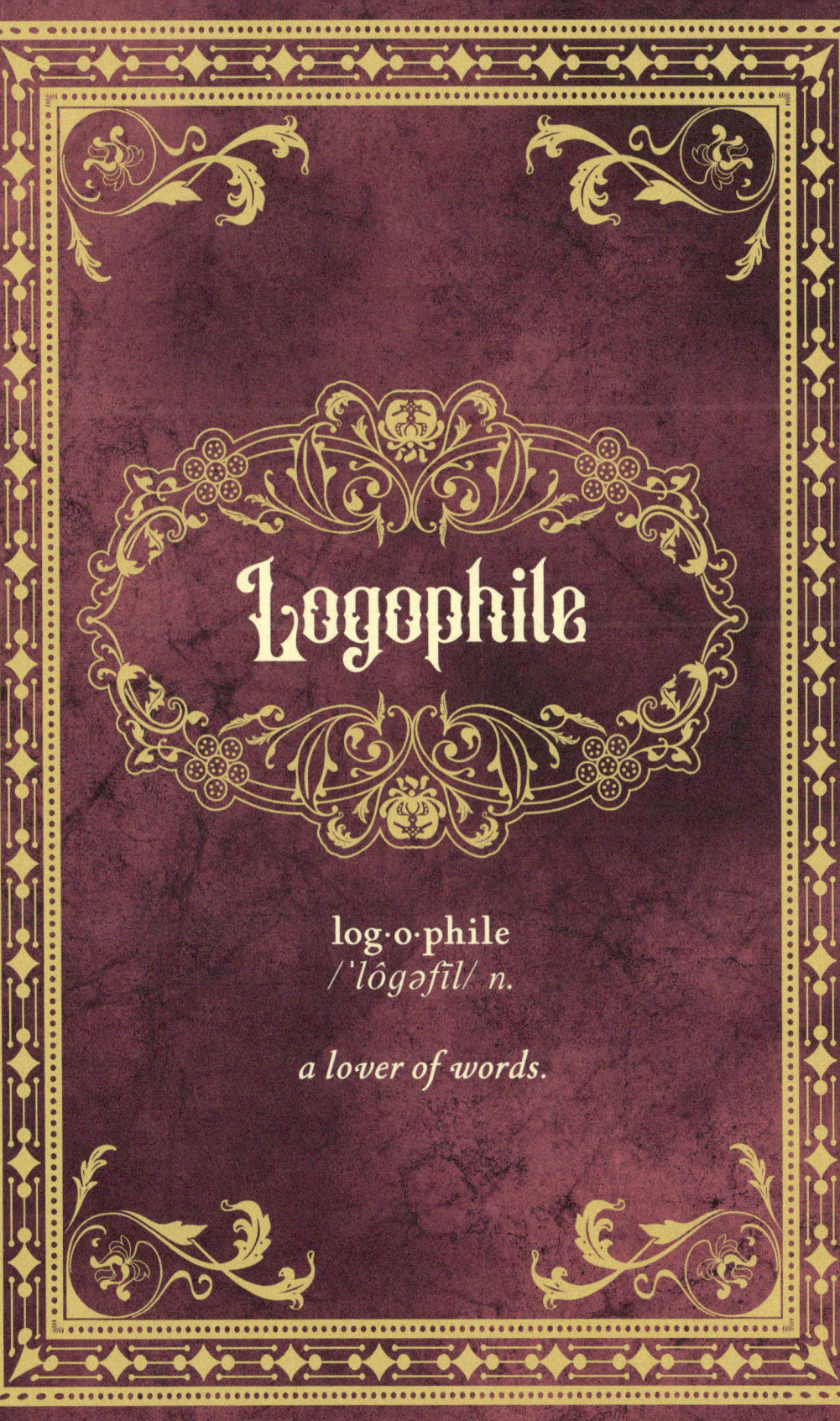

log·o·phile
/ˈlôgəfīl/ *n.*

a lover of words.

SCAN ON SPOTIFY

Часть первая

ГЛАВА 1

Скарлетт О'Хара не была красавицей, но мужчины вряд ли отдавали себе в этом отчёт, если они, подобно близнецам Тарлтонам, становились её жертвами её чар. Очень уж причудливо сочетались в её лице утончённые черты матери — местной аристократки французского происхождения — и крупные, выразительные черты пышущего здоровьем ирландца-отца. Широкоскулое, с точёным подбородком лицо Скарлетт невольно приковывало к себе взгляд. Особенно глаза — чуть раскосые, светло-зелёные, прозрачные, в оправе тёмных ресниц, сбегающих вразлёт со слегка приподнятых к вискам бровей. И белая кожа — ах, эта белая кожа, которой так гордятся женщины американского Юга, бережно охраняя её шляпками, вуалетками и митенками от жаркого солнца Джорджии! — две безукоризненно тёмные лепестки магнолии, в оправе тёмных ресниц, сбегающих вразлёт...

19

April 29th, 2021

*"Your eyes are warm,
I never noticed them how I do now,
I guess that's why I stare more."*

M,

I never intended for my inner monologue of interminable love letters dedicated to you from my iPhone notes to catalyze into ink filled pages or to mature into a tangible spine encapsulating pages of you from my point of view. It would feel like an injustice to not only myself but to you if I kept all of this work hidden. For three years, I know you have been uncomfortable with compliments, and you may consider yourself undeserving of this gesture or that it's too much, but I assure you, even this isn't enough. You deserve to experience me and all of the love that I can provide. You deserve to feel safe, seen, heard, and comprehended. I can only hope you enjoy my overt but passionate love and adoration for you.

To my muse: My thoughts, ever-devoting love, gratitude, and admiration expressed in this tangible love letter to you are indelible not only within these pages but in the foremost memory of my soul. You are embedded in my spine; you walk with me ubiquitously. I have yet to meet a soul as idiosyncratic and vigorous as yours. One who is capable of possessing this magnitude of warmth—it's ineffable. I can only hope and pray that I can make you feel the same in this lifetime. Thank you for furnishing my heart of a home with a gift of love that is so evergreen.

Indubitably yours,

Angela Solis

Table of Contents

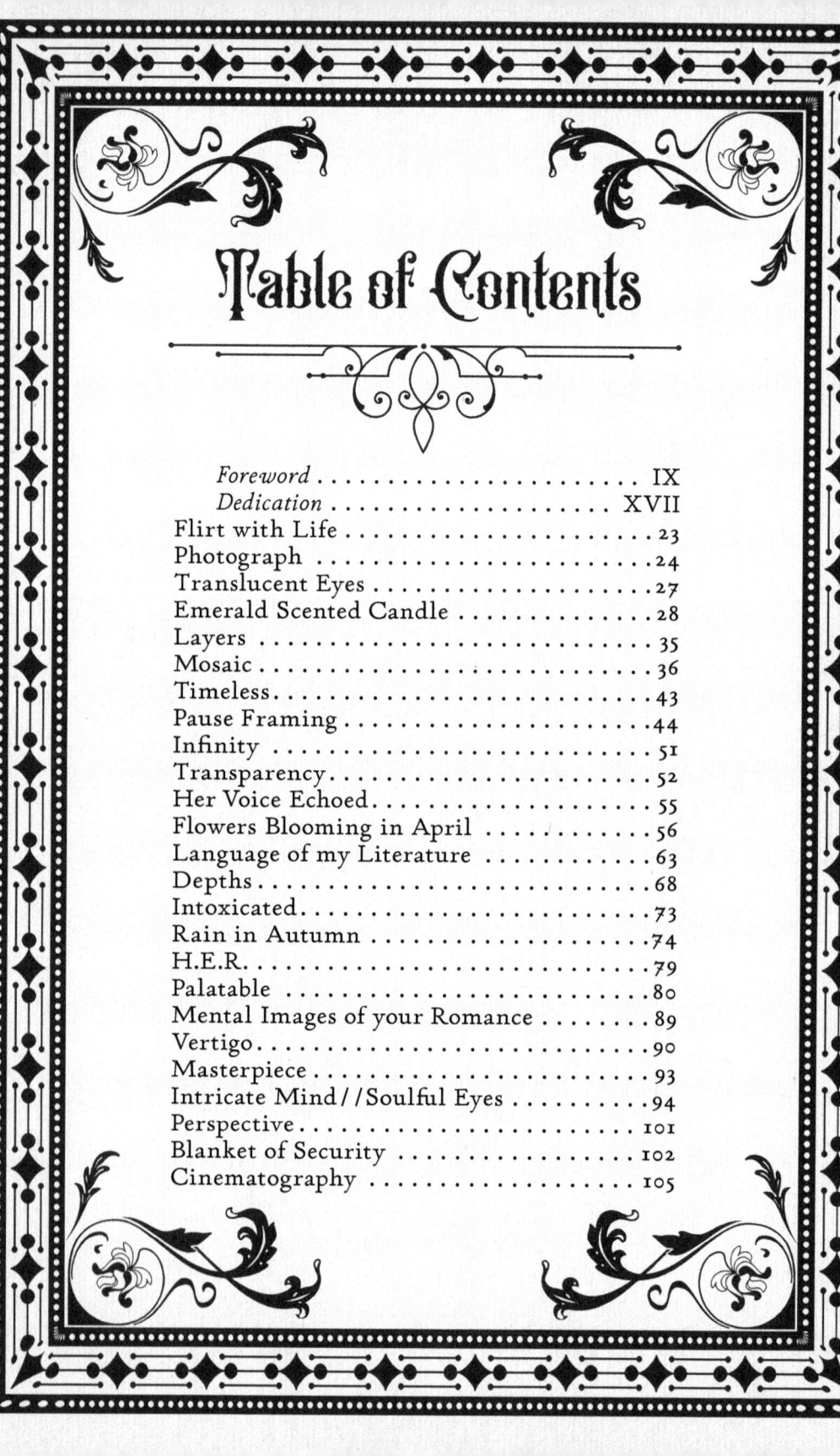

Foreword IX
Dedication XVII
Flirt with Life 23
Photograph 24
Translucent Eyes 27
Emerald Scented Candle 28
Layers 35
Mosaic 36
Timeless 43
Pause Framing 44
Infinity 51
Transparency 52
Her Voice Echoed 55
Flowers Blooming in April 56
Language of my Literature 63
Depths 68
Intoxicated 73
Rain in Autumn 74
H.E.R. 79
Palatable 80
Mental Images of your Romance 89
Vertigo 90
Masterpiece 93
Intricate Mind//Soulful Eyes 94
Perspective 101
Blanket of Security 102
Cinematography 105

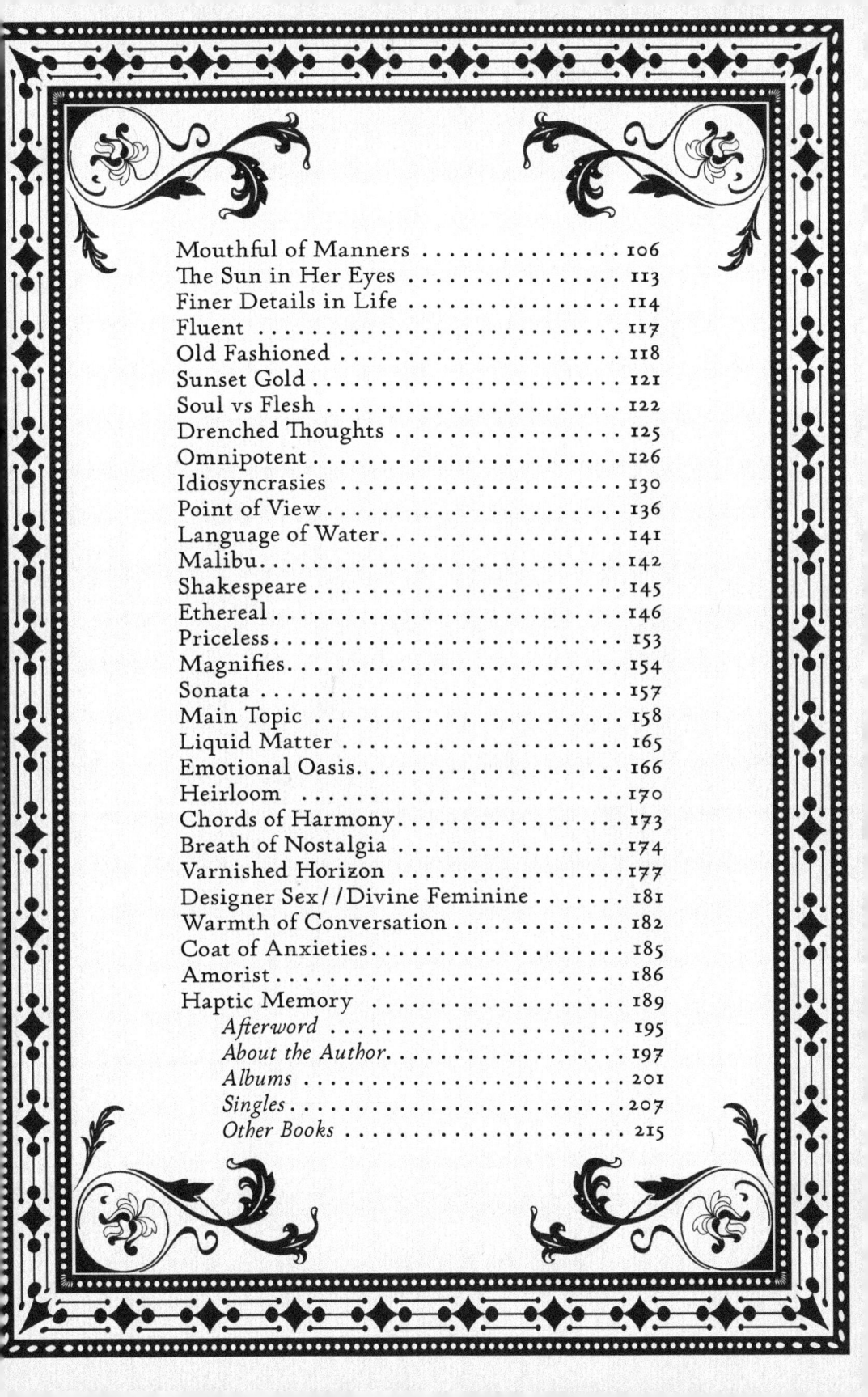

Mouthful of Manners 106
The Sun in Her Eyes 113
Finer Details in Life 114
Fluent 117
Old Fashioned 118
Sunset Gold 121
Soul vs Flesh 122
Drenched Thoughts 125
Omnipotent 126
Idiosyncrasies 130
Point of View 136
Language of Water 141
Malibu 142
Shakespeare 145
Ethereal 146
Priceless 153
Magnifies 154
Sonata 157
Main Topic 158
Liquid Matter 165
Emotional Oasis 166
Heirloom 170
Chords of Harmony 173
Breath of Nostalgia 174
Varnished Horizon 177
Designer Sex//Divine Feminine 181
Warmth of Conversation 182
Coat of Anxieties 185
Amorist 186
Haptic Memory 189
   Afterword 195
   About the Author 197
   Albums 201
   Singles 207
   Other Books 215

Poems

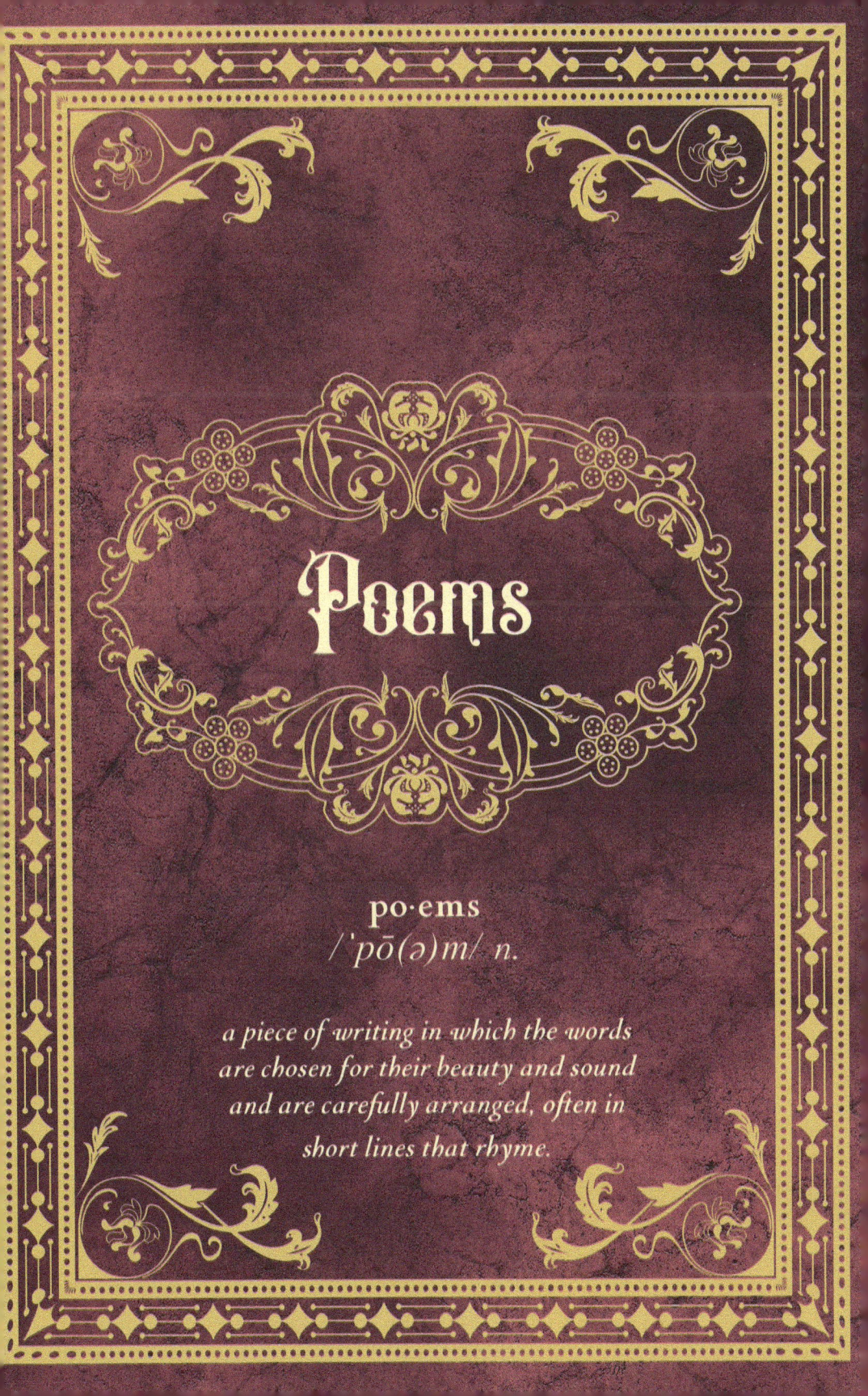

po·ems
/ˈpō(ə)m/ n.

a piece of writing in which the words are chosen for their beauty and sound and are carefully arranged, often in short lines that rhyme.

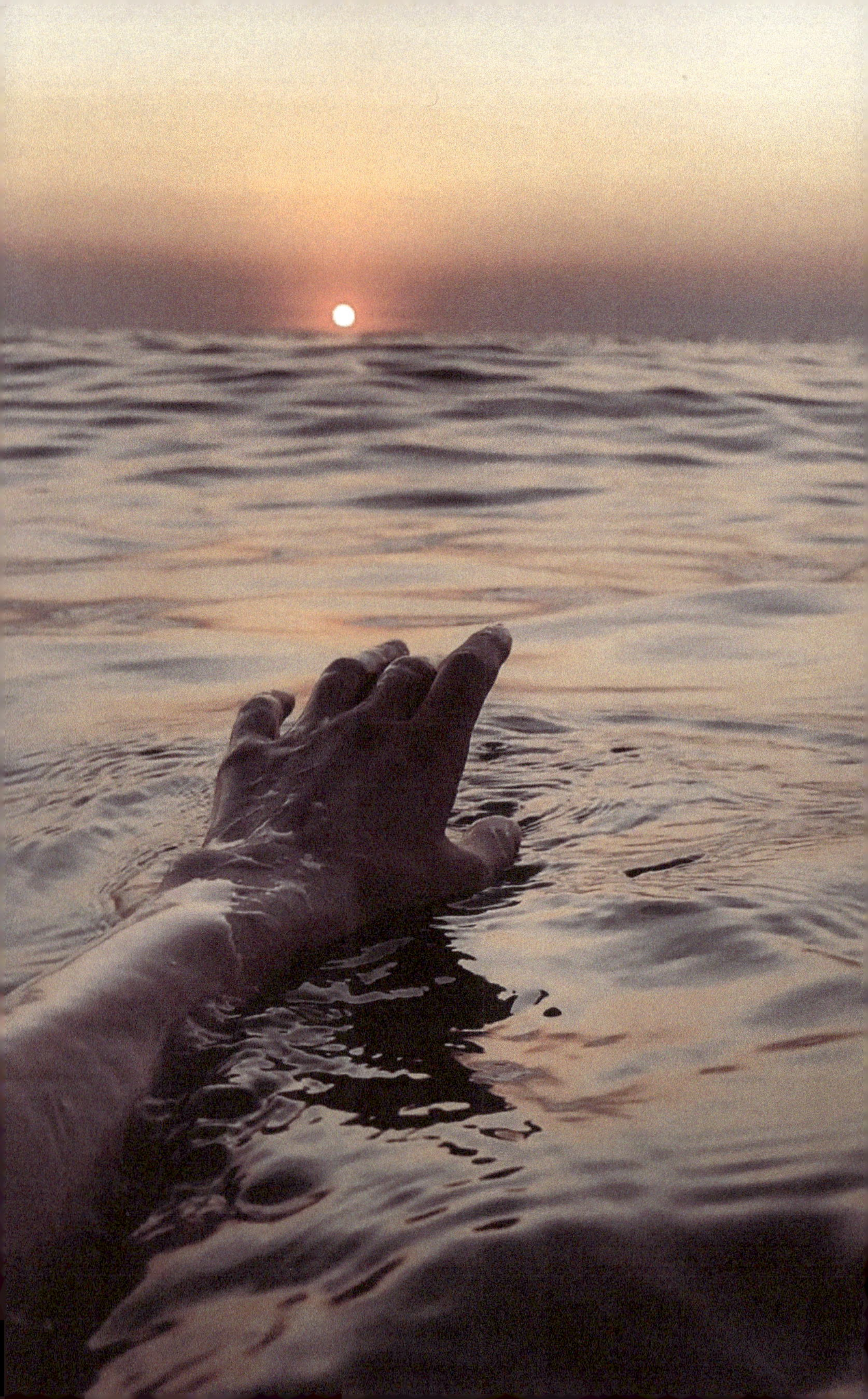

Flirt with Life

I fell in love with you the moment
I found out
how reckless and unapologetic
you *flirt with life* -
Straight in its eyes.

The way your feet
touch fallen leaves
from the trees,
or how your body smiles
the moment your framework
becomes engulfed in your leaf pile.

The moment the oceans current
kisses your toes and grabs ahold
of your soul
and how your body can never say no
no matter how cold
her temperature may be.

The way you've effortlessly resisted
every single straight line in sight
in order to simply

flirt with life.

Photograph

You make sitting
in front of your backyard tree
look so effortless - free.
The way your arms
are outstretched for God's reach -
Palms opened wide only for his eyes
to see.

Nothing beats this,
feeling the gravitating motion
of your artistry within the stillness
of a photograph that is you,
which is now in my hands.

Nothing beats this,
watching you sit in your element -

Earth's heartbeat.

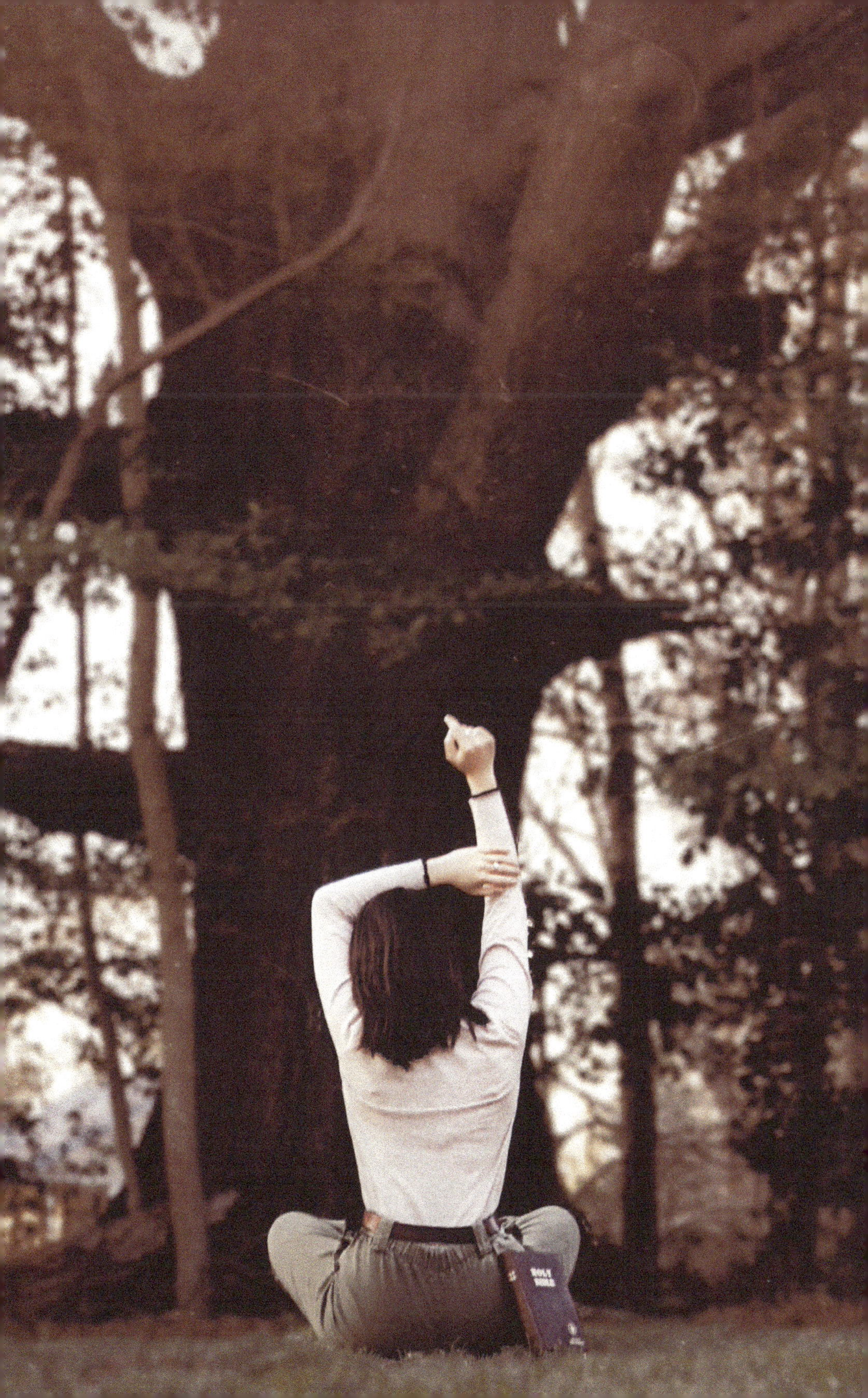

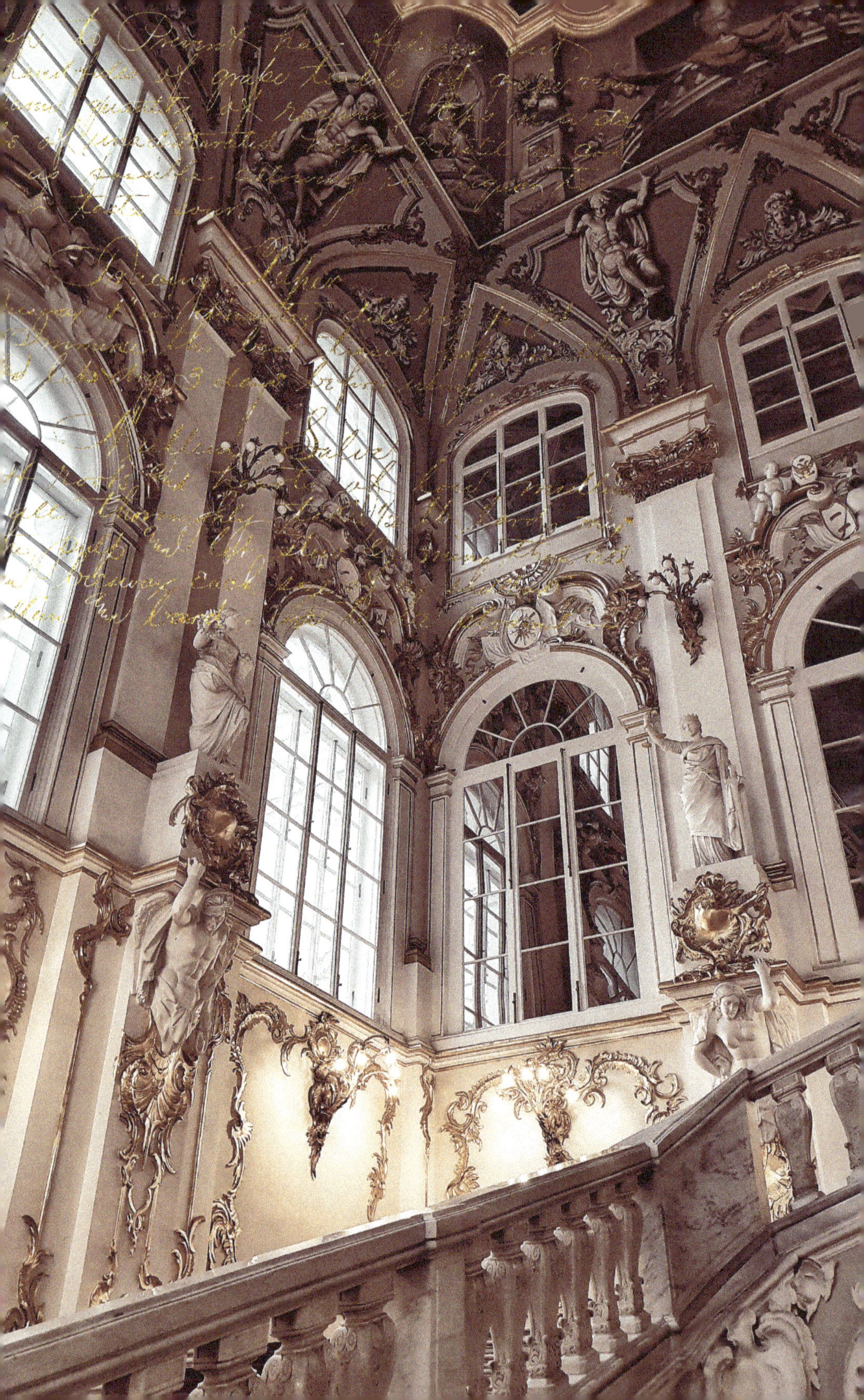

Translucent Eyes

You feel like a poem I've know by heart
and have memorized
line by line.

All my mind and translucent eyes
ever wants to do is merely
attempt to recite
your masterpiece of a being
through my unfiltered sight
with unlocked window blinds.

You remind me of a place and road
I've always known
but have never been shown
until now.

You feel like home.

Emerald Scented Candle

Our *Emerald Cedar* scented
candle is flickering,
and my unguarded heart is fluttering
in the most intense, yet, delicate way
that it has ever known how to
as I'm taking in
each individual feeling
of every single one of your comfort rubs
in our water-filled bathtub.

Stillness fills my soul
as I'm holding your body against mine
with your head on my bare chest
alongside our most stripped
and naked emotions —
Bare and honest.

I can't help but feel pure and utter bliss
between the sensation
of our synchronized lips
serenading the many unsaid,
yet familiar conversations
that we no longer need to resist.

My love, where have you been?

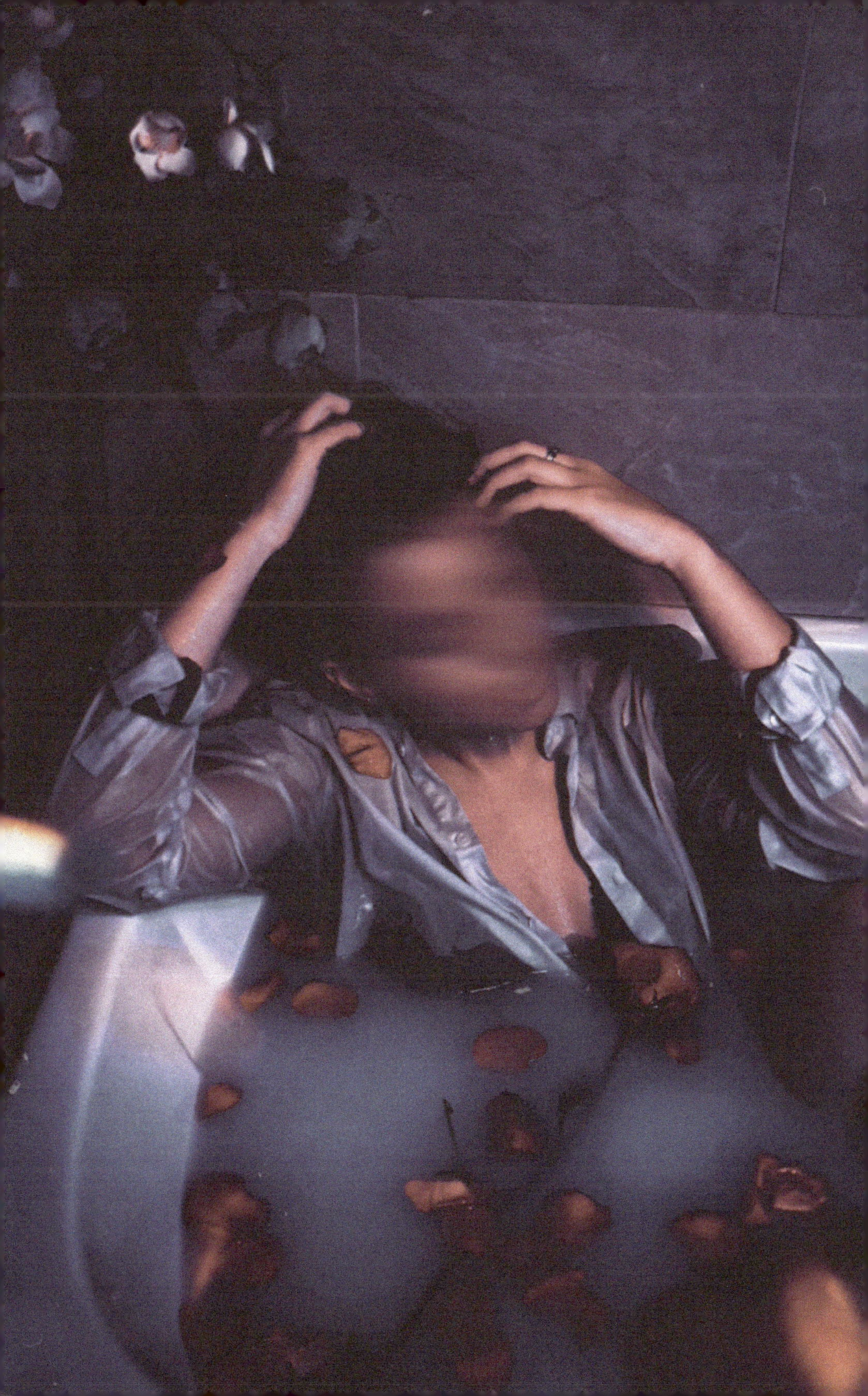

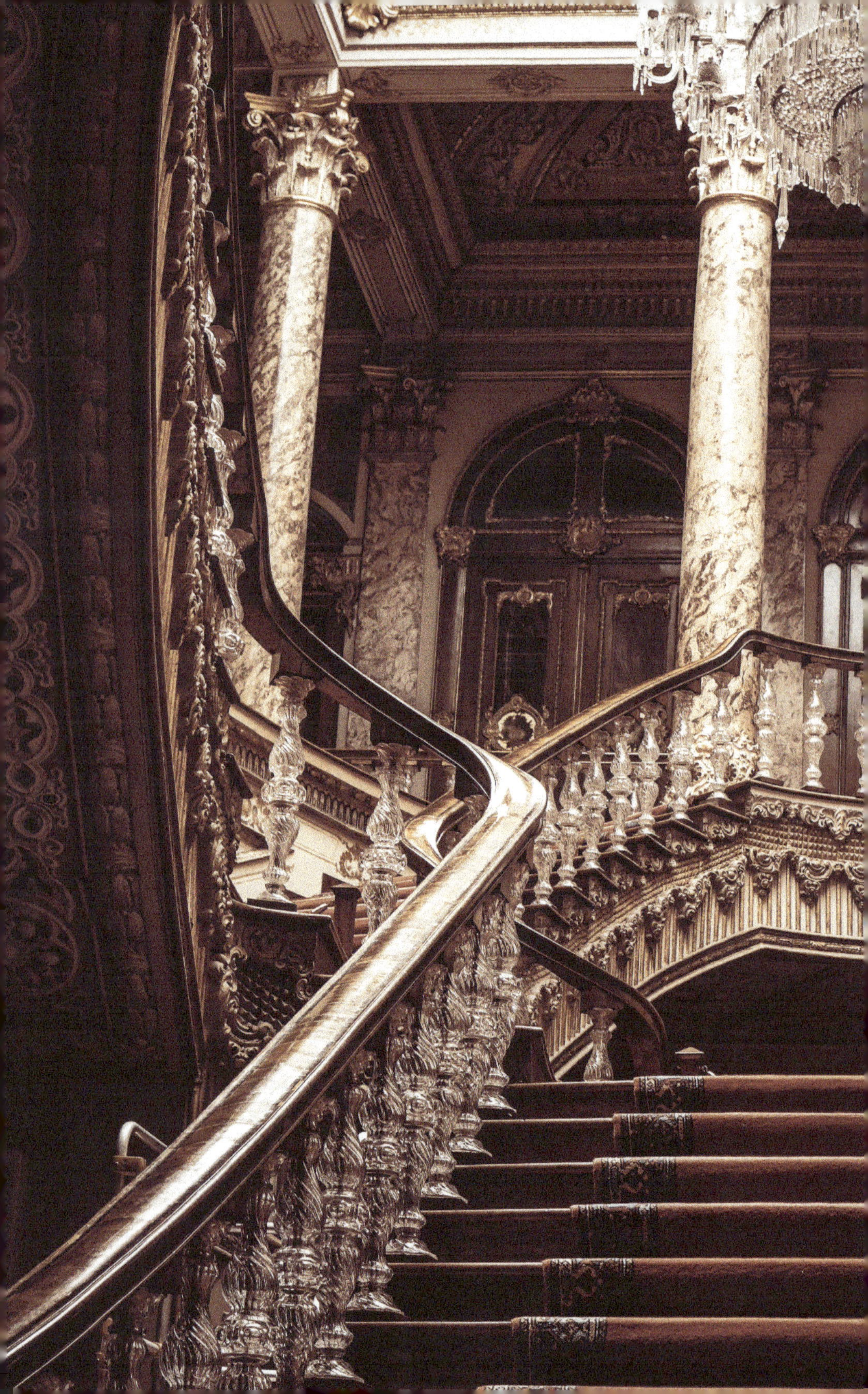

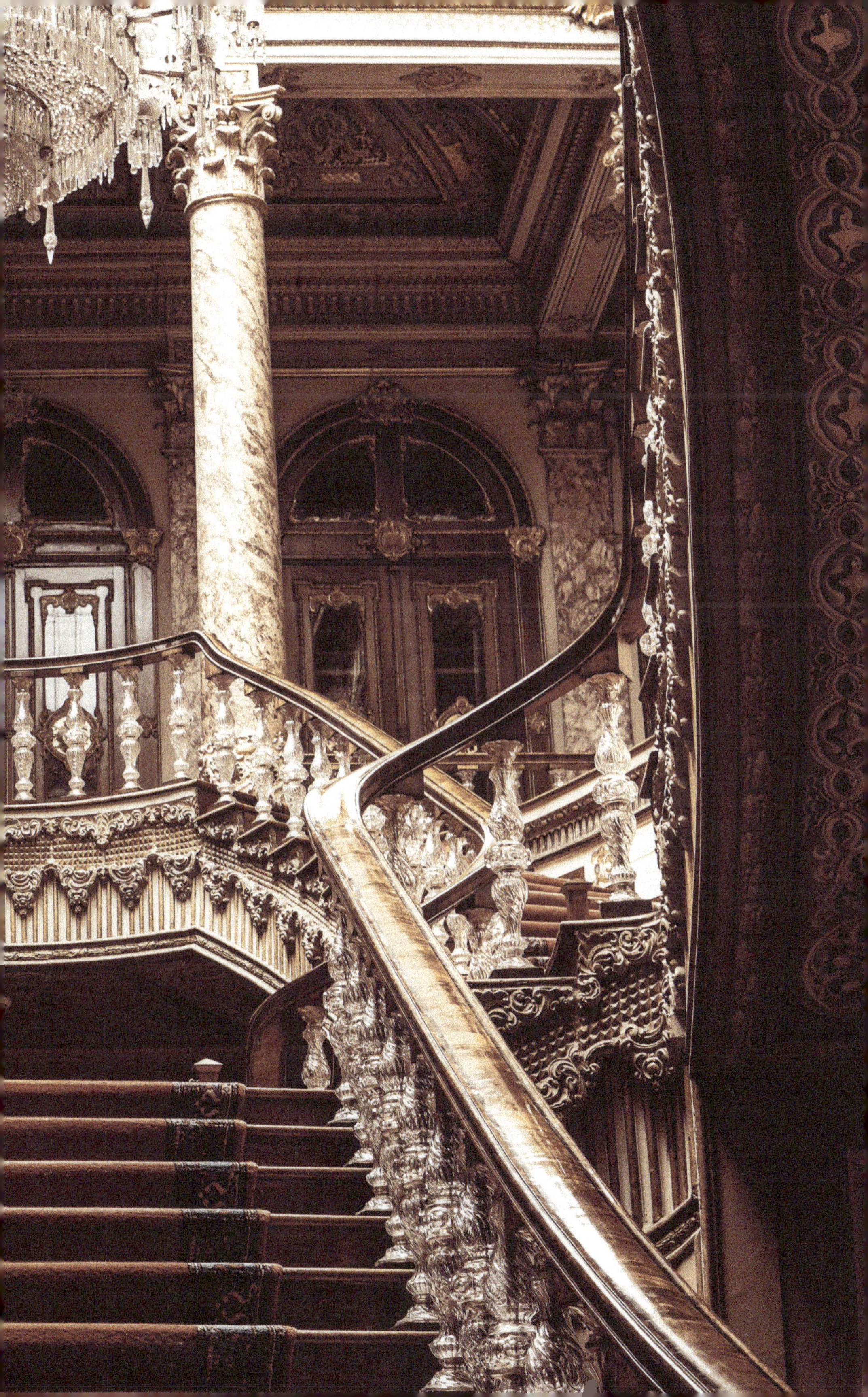

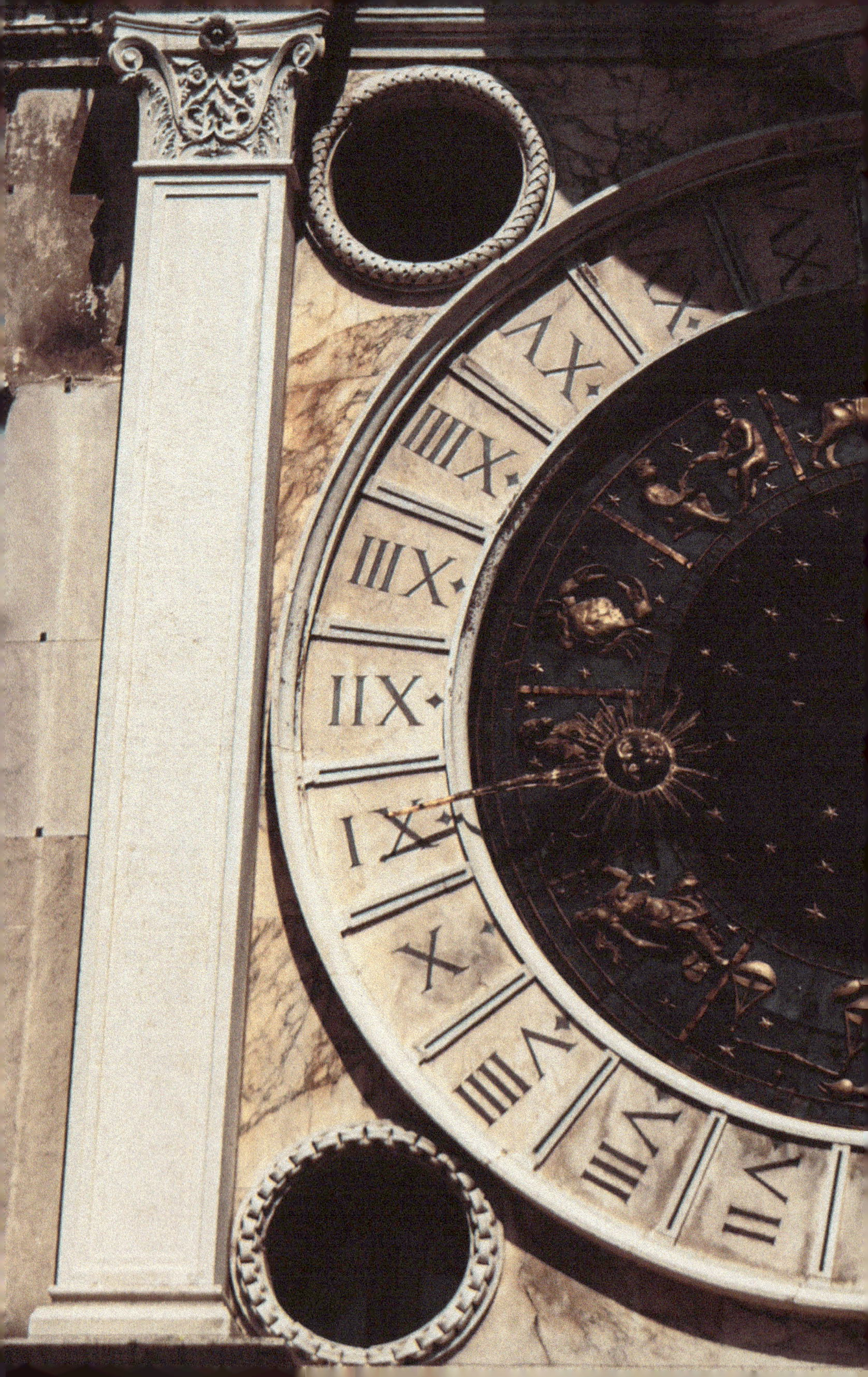

XV
XIIII
XIII
XII
XI
X
VIIII
VIII
VII

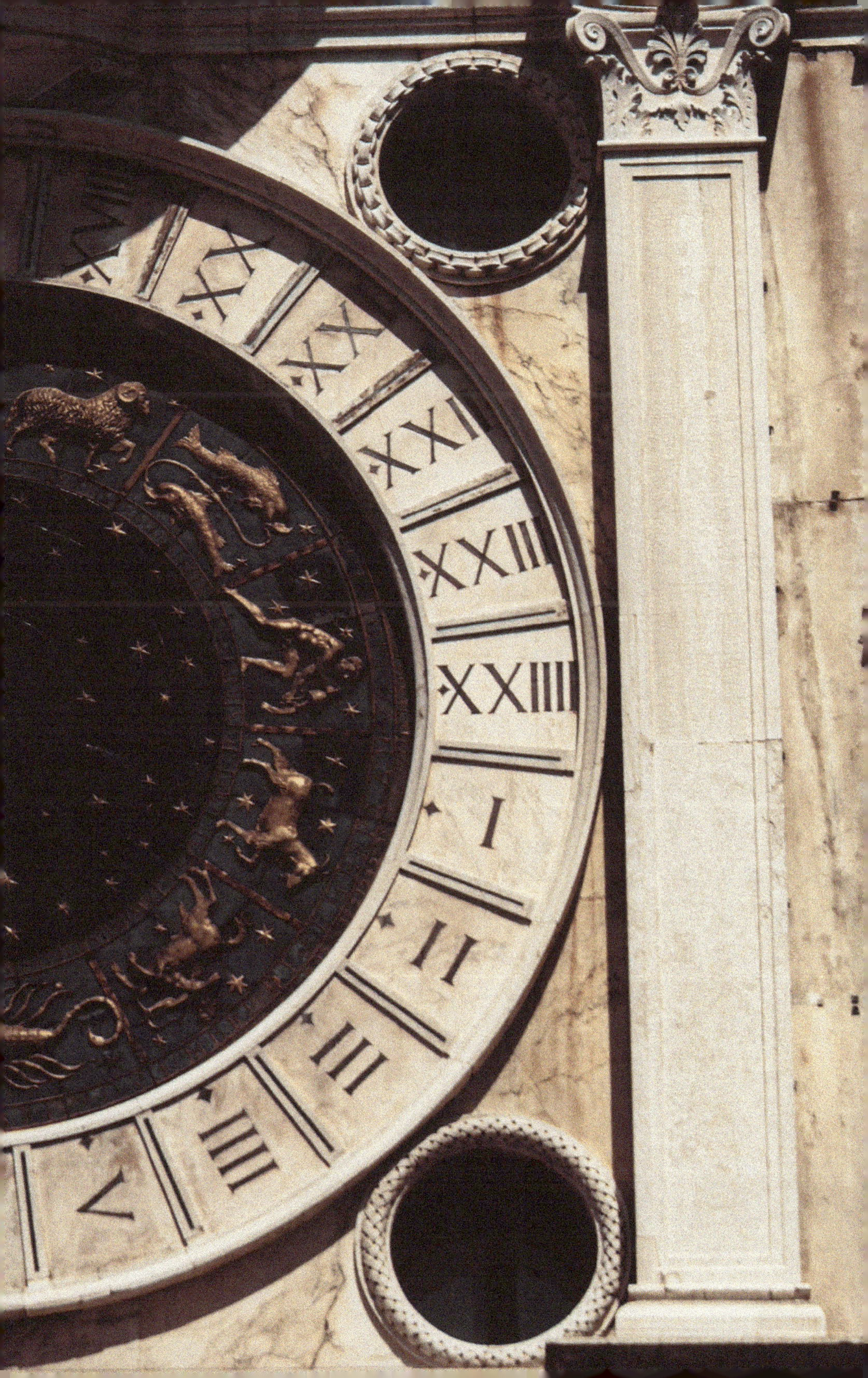
XXI
I
II
III
IIII
V

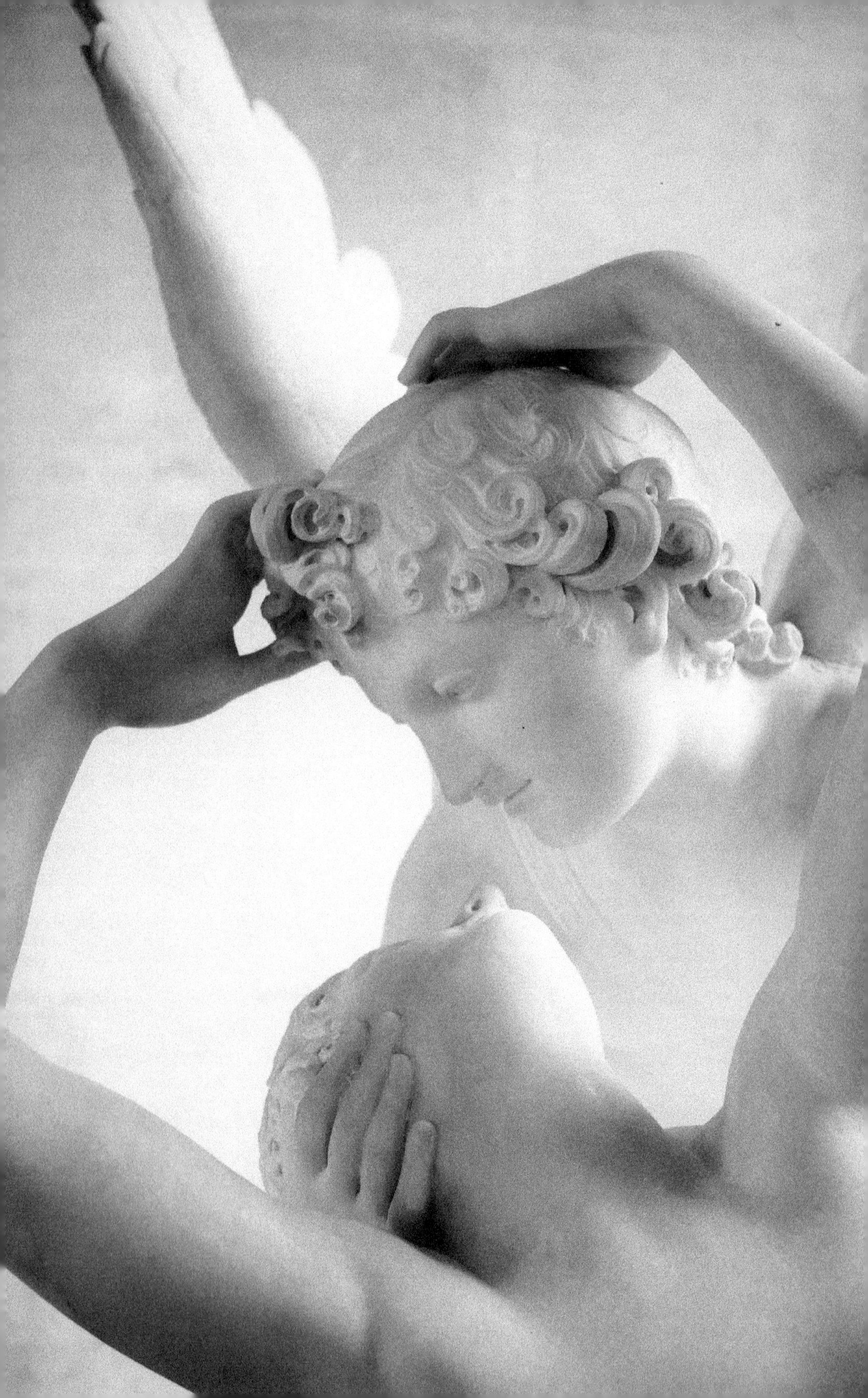

Layers

There are so many layers to you,
I could never choose
which one I love the most
even if I had to.

It would be a crime
to malnourish you from such compliments
with all of this unpromised time.
I refuse to fall victim to complacency
and give you anything less than consistency.

I'll do my best at loving every single one of your depths.
You deserve nothing less than the type of love
that's pure and honest.

Mosaic

You are a mosaic
of everyone
you have ever loved.

Your *fine lines,*
scattered sight,
distorted color assortment
and *uneven mixtures*
in your *pallete*
are all aspects of you that are spread
throughout your portrait.

Your canvas
is a made up mosaic
of everyone
you've ever loved
enough to hand and trust
with your brush.

And after all this time, I can still never get enough.

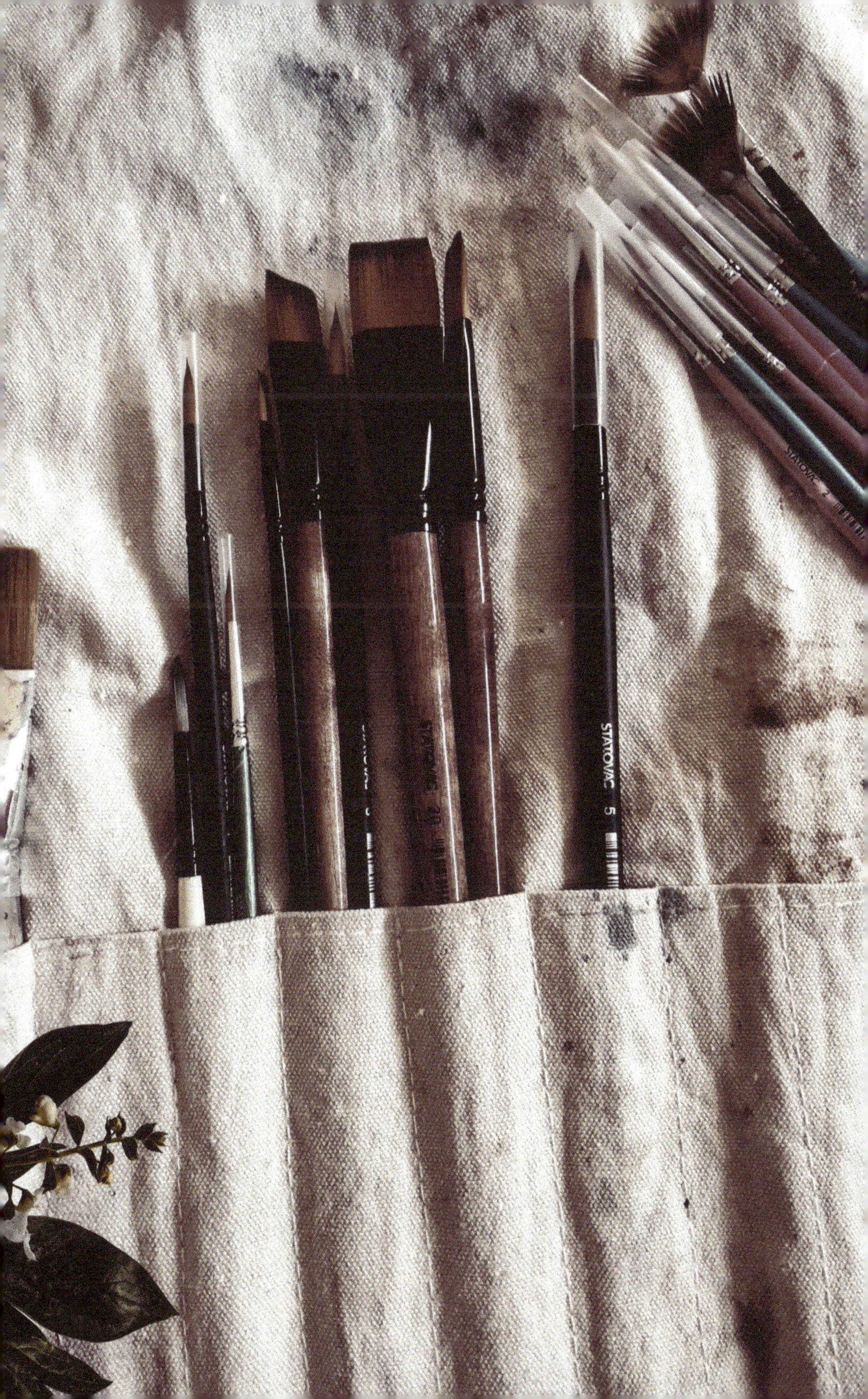
STATOVAC 5

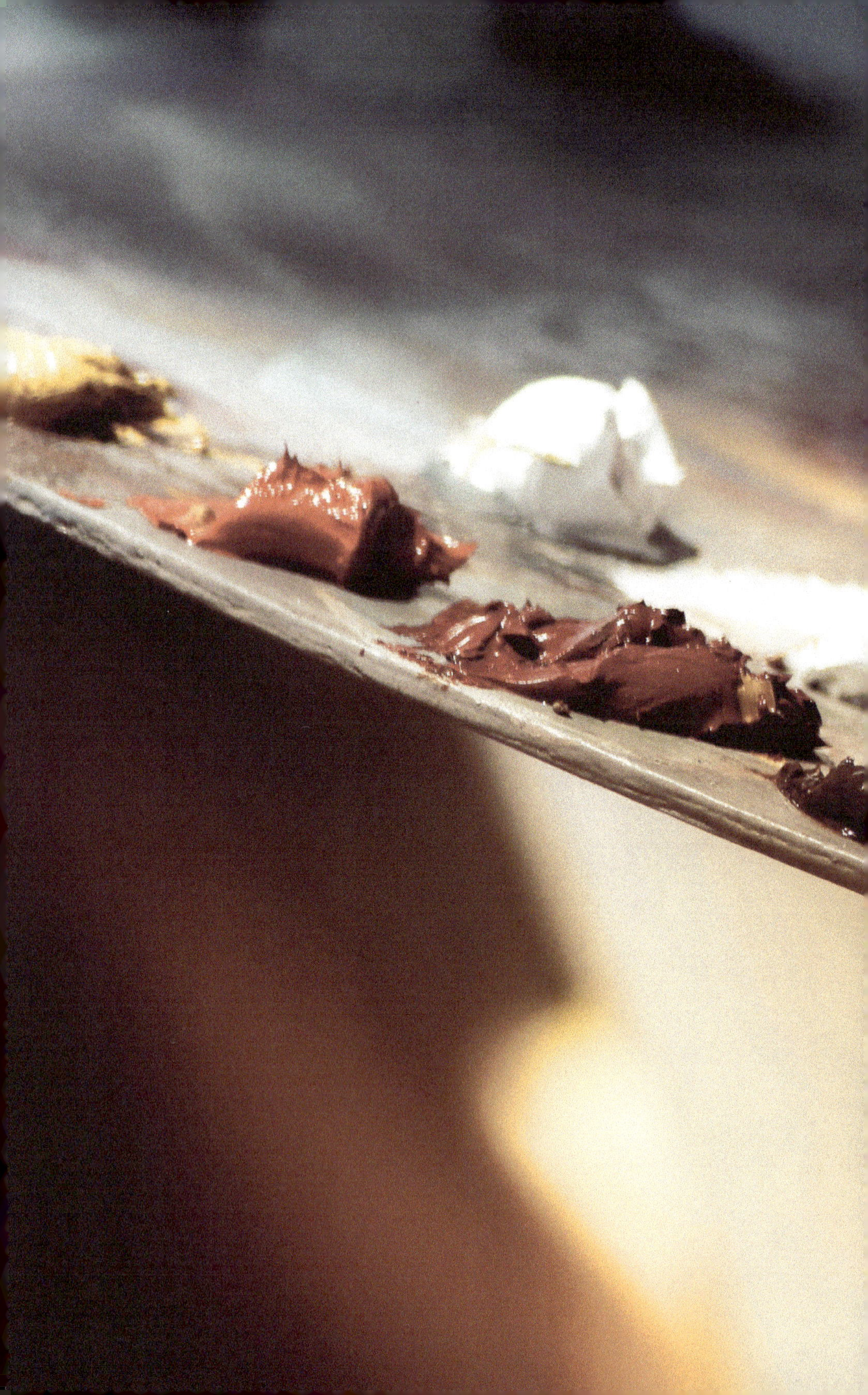

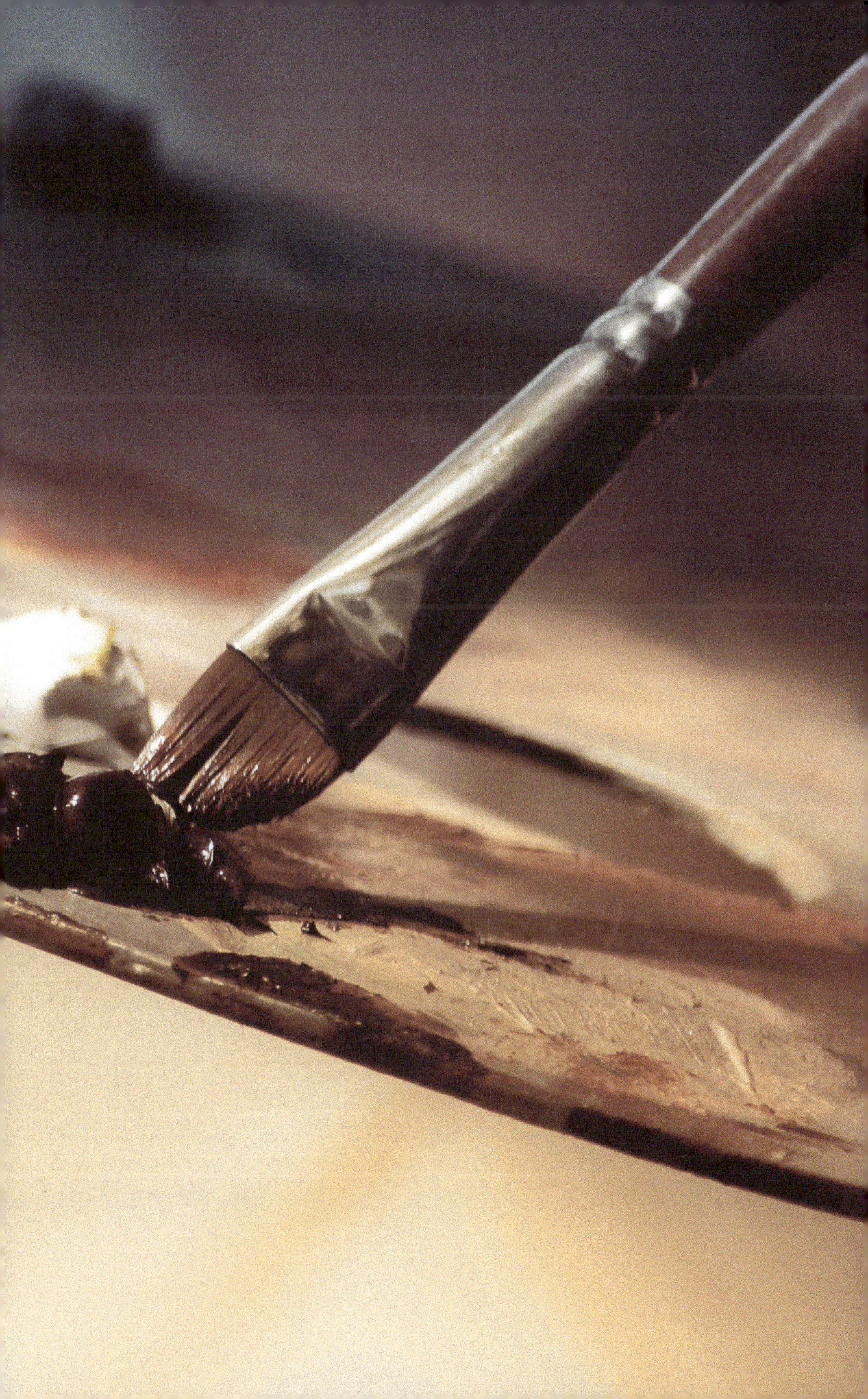

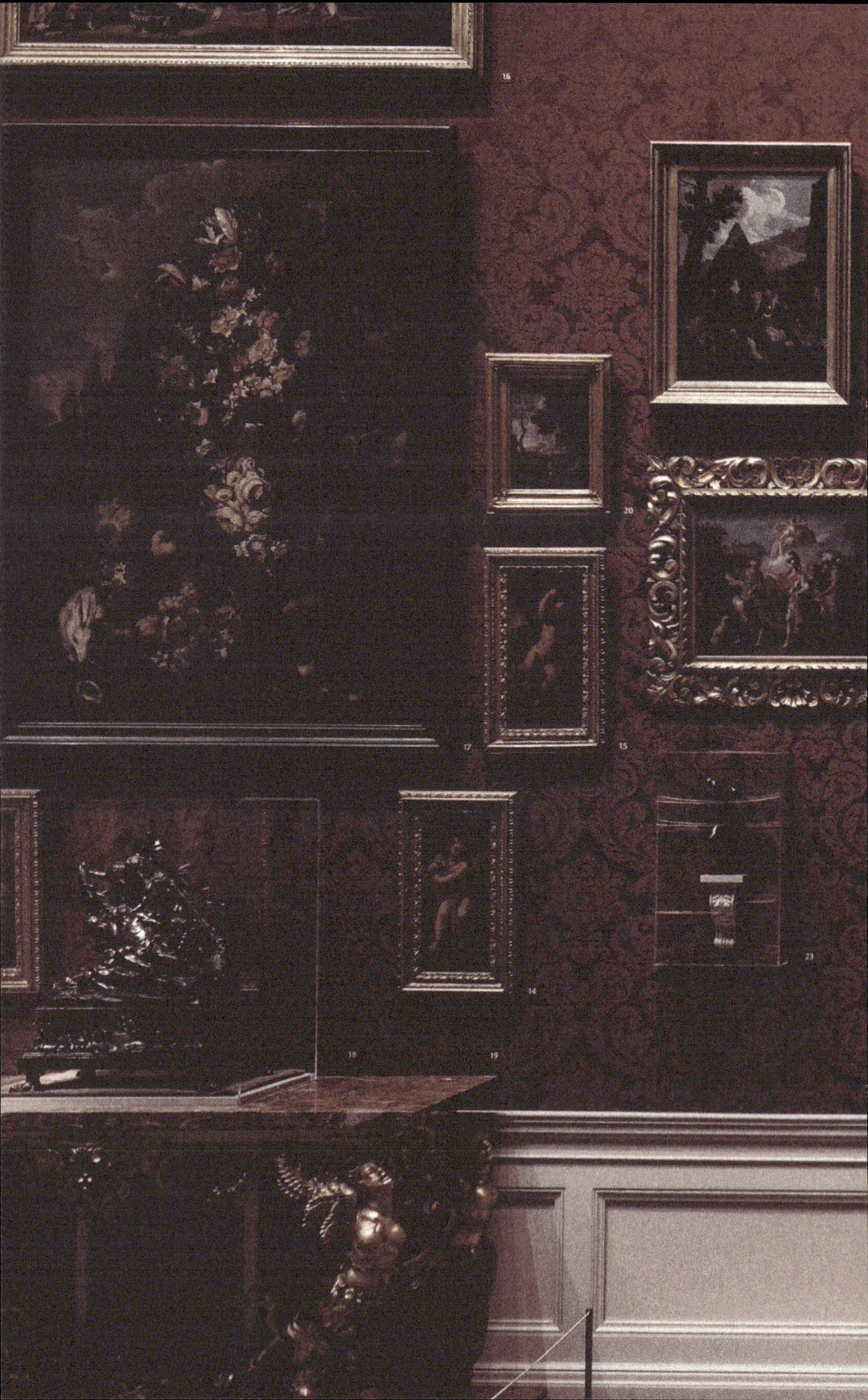

24

25 28

26 29

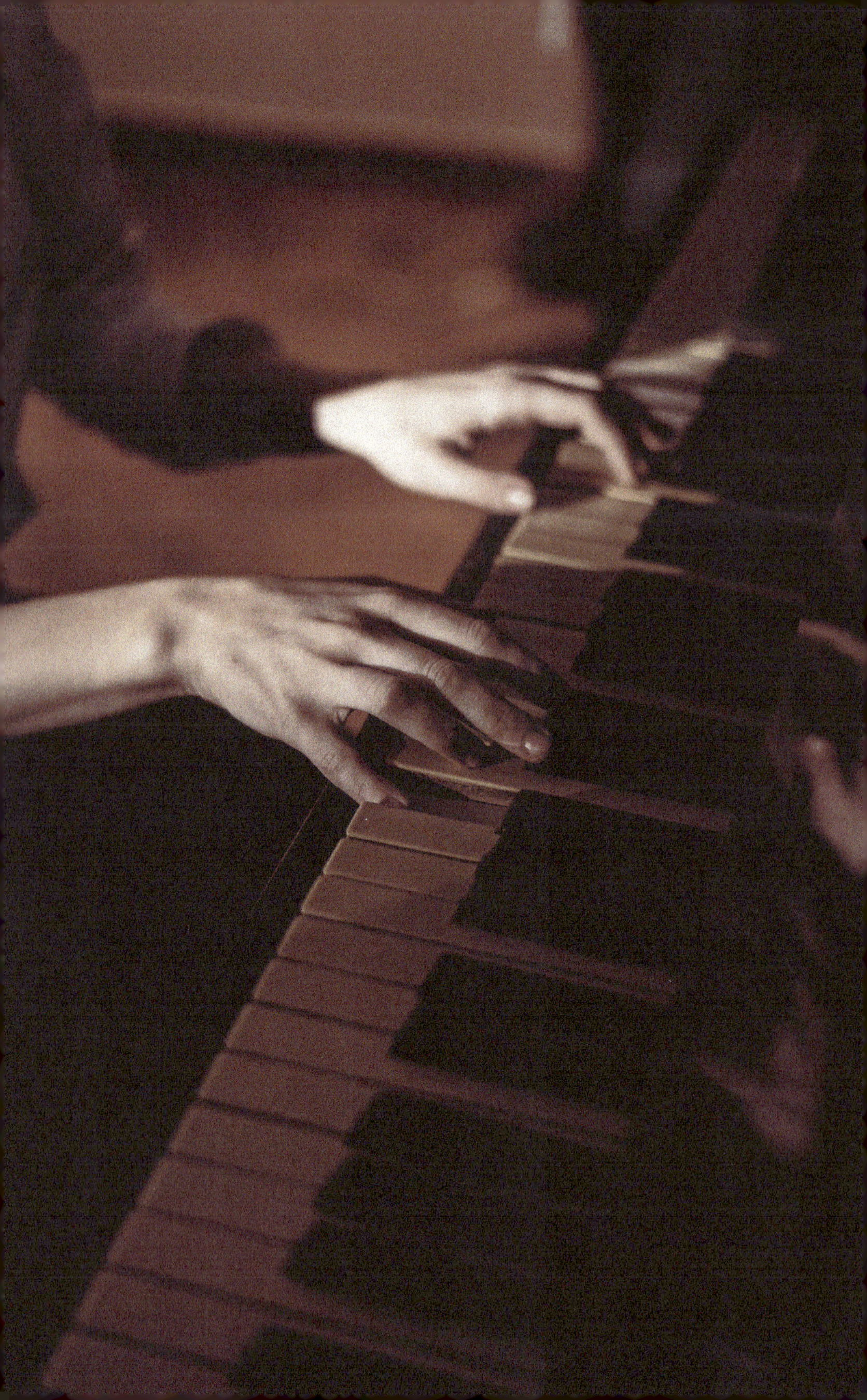

Timeless

It feels as if your hands
know every single *string and key*
to my *body*.

Every inch of my *structure sings*
unique melodies
whenever you get yourself in tune
with what you want to do.

You've become the composer —
Grabbing a hold of distinct volumes; high or low,
controlling every tone; *crescendo*.
Adjusting my pitch; *falsetto*.

You're the *writer to my symphony* —
Handling each one of my lines
with thoughtful insight and ease.
Effortlessly regulating both our notes
into *perfect harmony*.
Cautiously handling my sheets
with delicacy,
aiming to find the build and have me finish; bridge.

Your touch,
your essence,
is just like music - timeless.

Pause Framing

As my eyes flash
like a *shutter camera*,
I catch myself
pause framing
lively moments
with you any second that I can
to capture the occasion
in an attempt to save us in time.

Being privileged with the gift
of vision is an understatement.
The fine line crease in your eyes
as you laugh
and grip tightly to my hand,
I can't help but take a step back
and appreciate a glance
of your framework.

I want to keep this exact second
engrained in fine print
within my recollections.

You're the type of lover that enhances life.

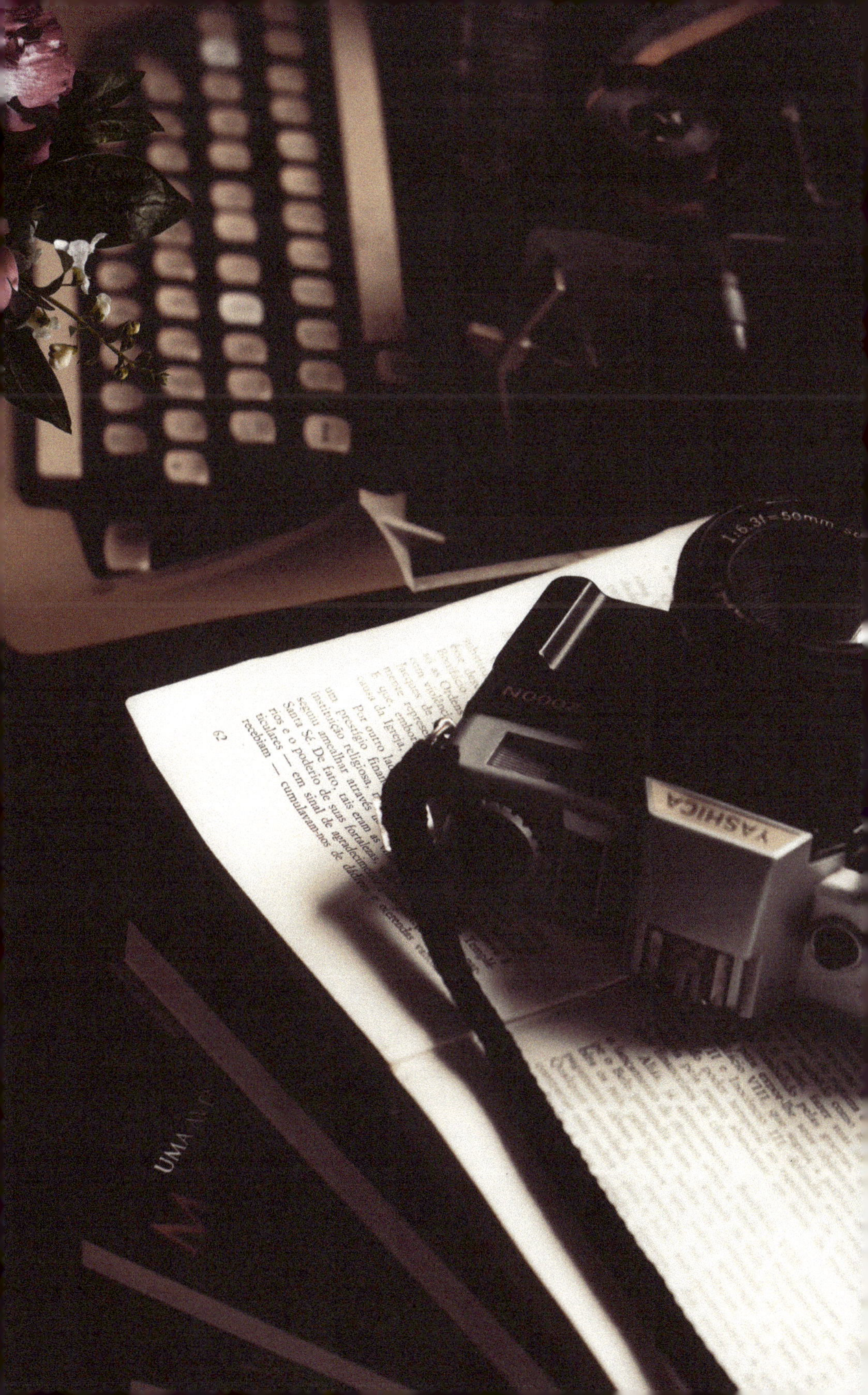
YASHICA

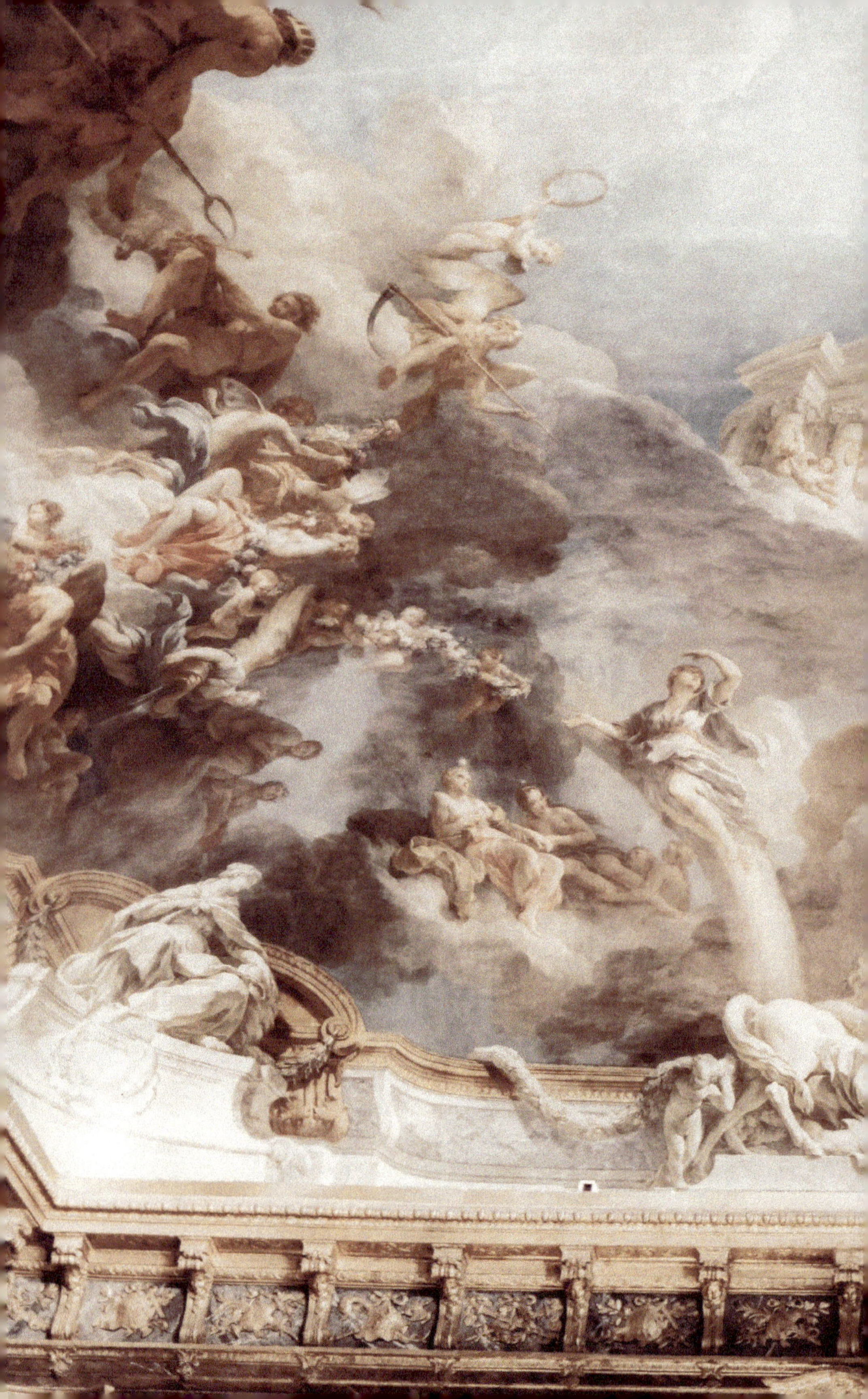

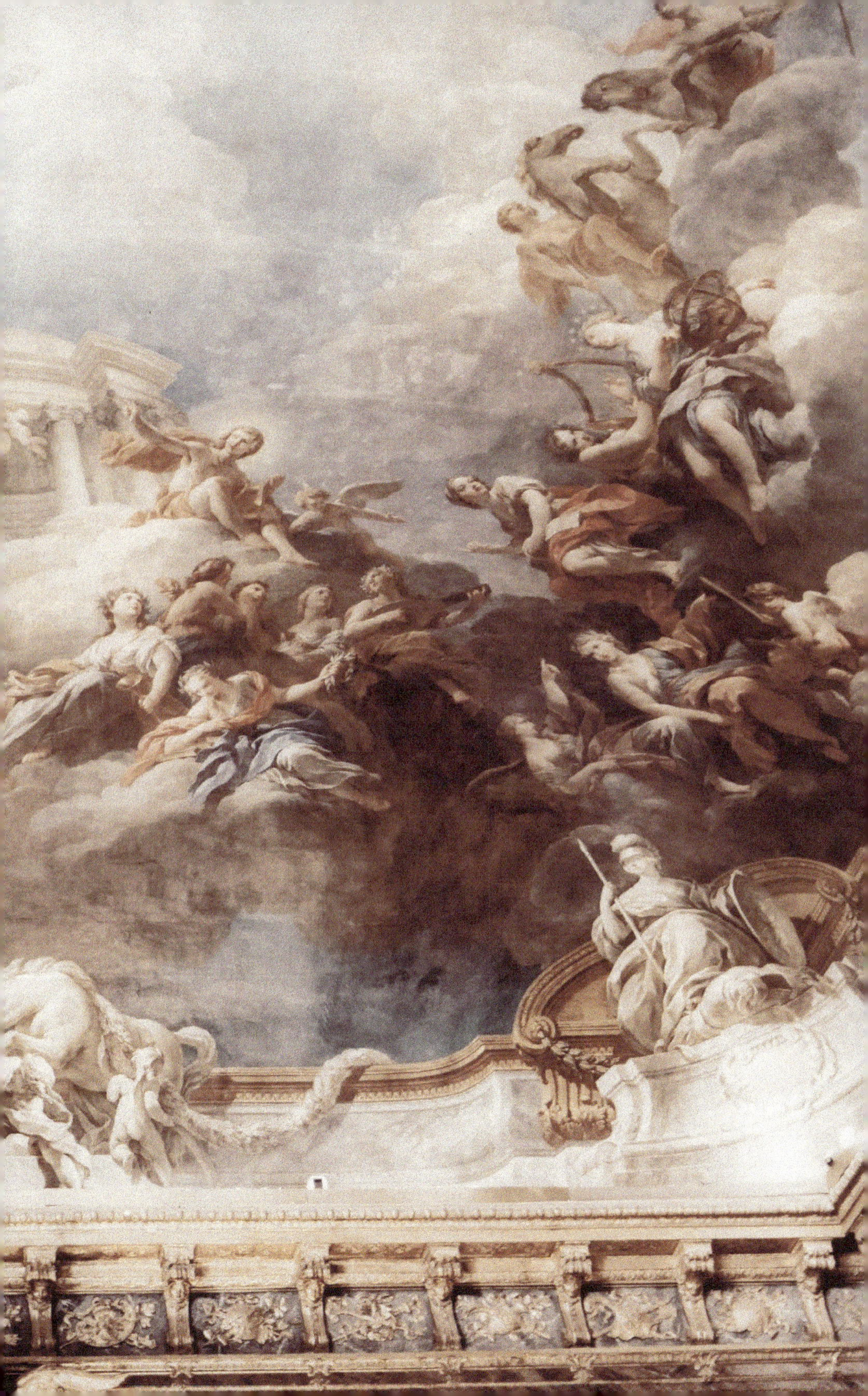

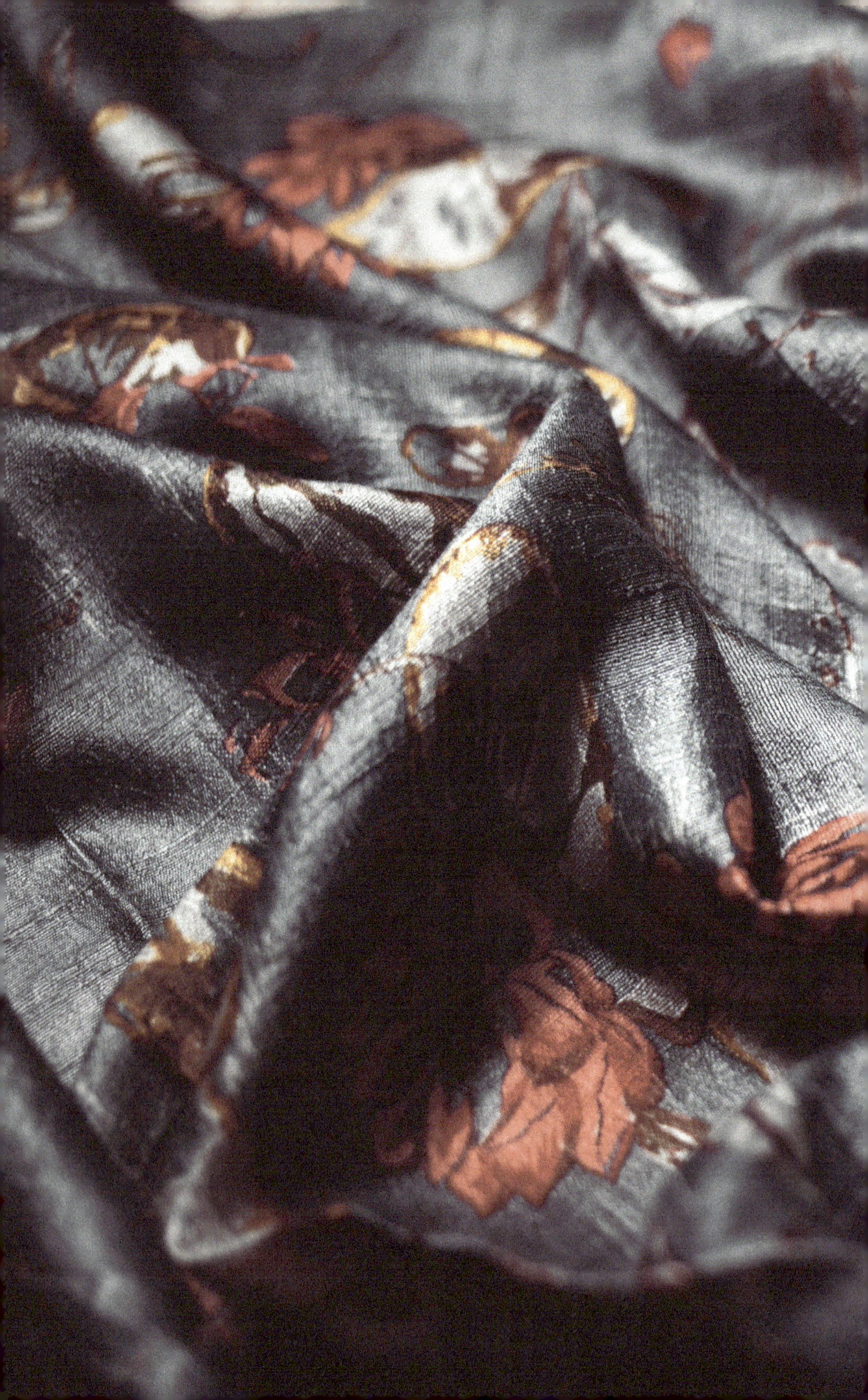

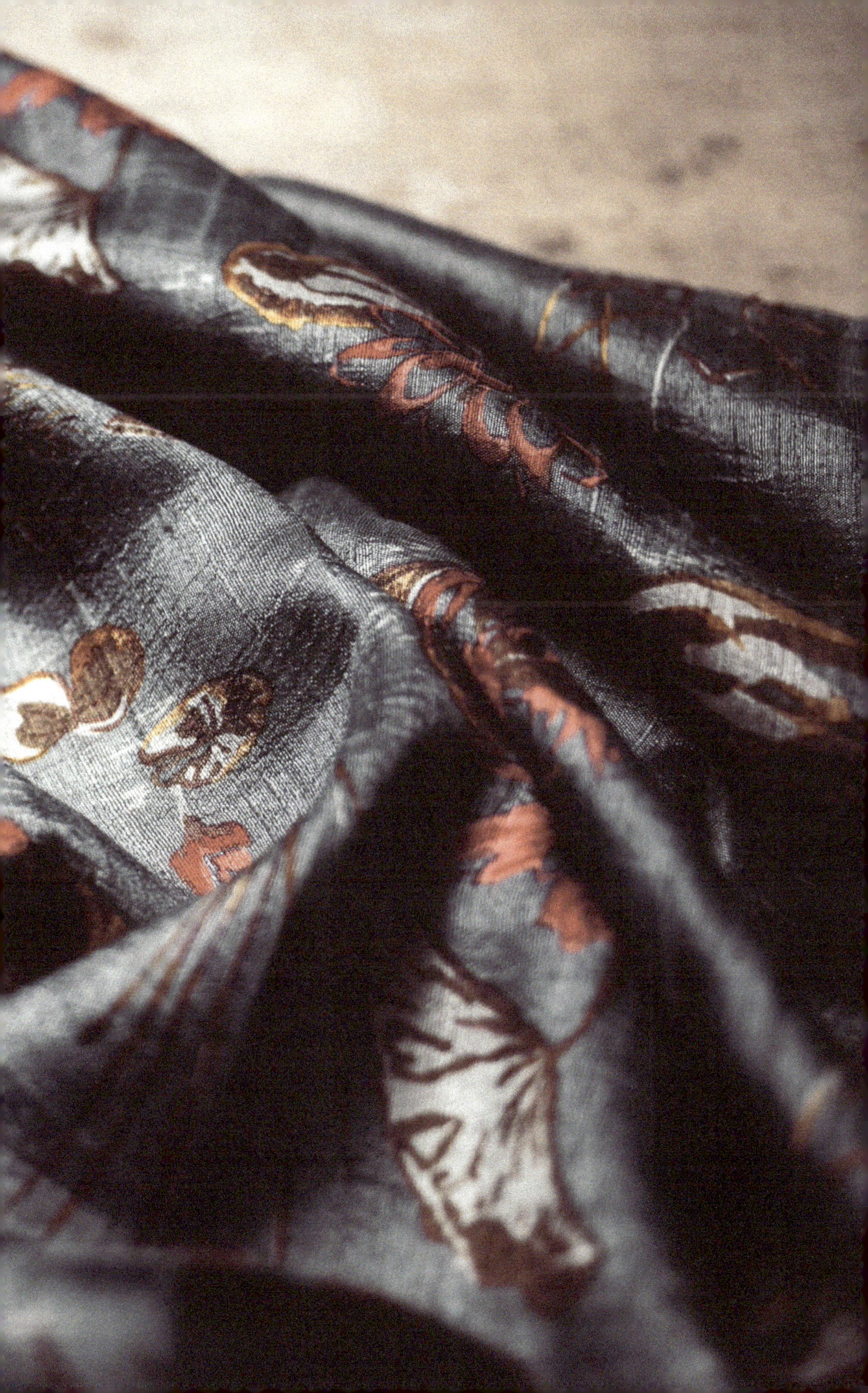

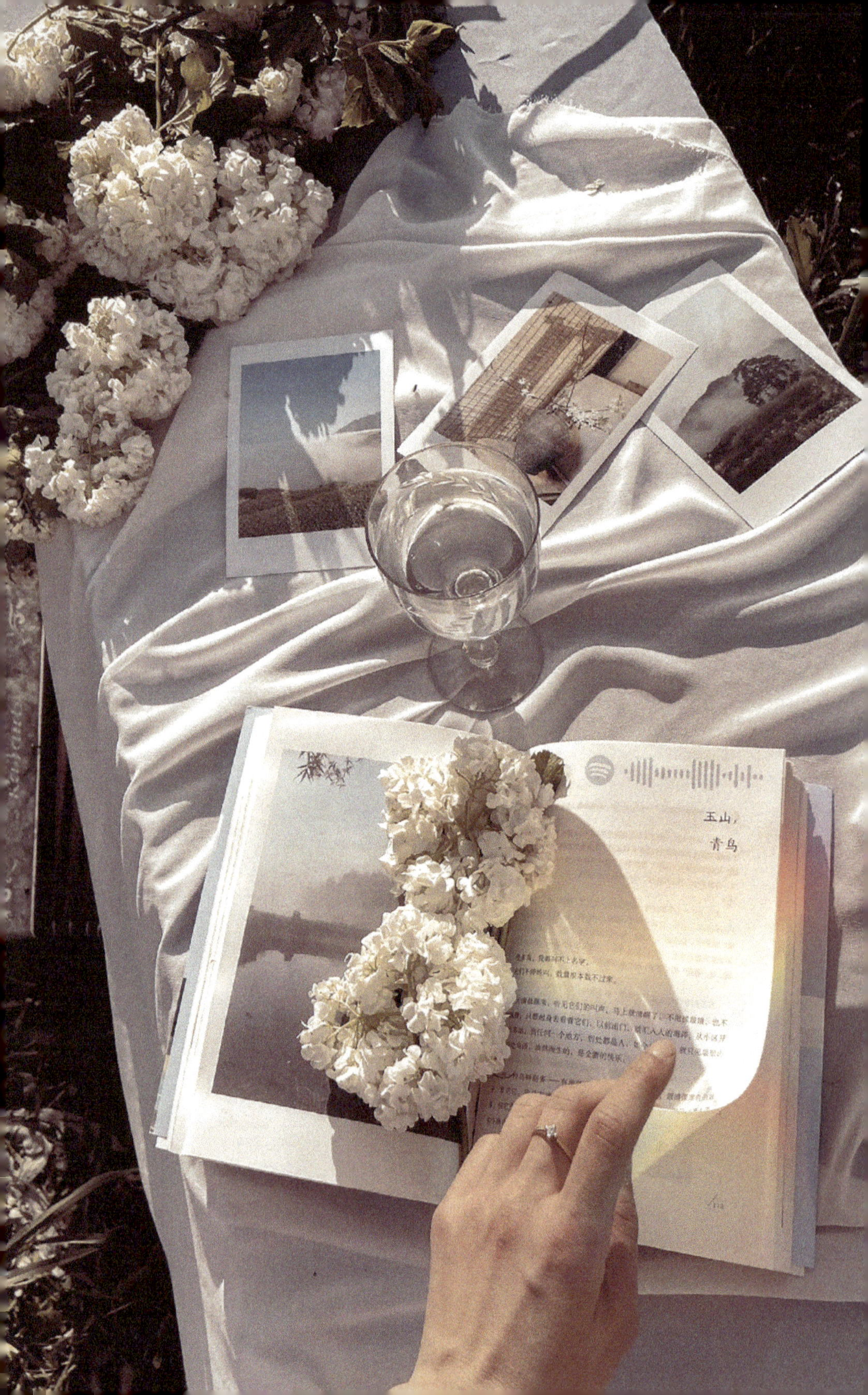
玉山，
青鸟

Infinity

Why would I ever want to love softly
when all I can ever guarantee
to you is intimacy with passion and intensity?
Everything else is foreign to me.

The last thing
that I ever want to do is cheat
you and me
out of expressing anything
that's less than pure, unapologetically.

I'll love you to infinity.

Transparency

I'll be honest,
it's pretty hard to comprehend
that this type of feeling
is something within my reality.

I used to believe that I was the only
one who can ever love myself at this level of capacity—
so deeply.
But, that was until you showed me differently.

You caught me blindly
with how attentive your soul could see; nonchalantly.
How you make me feel as if I'm made of glass
from the way you're able to see straight through me
with so much transparency; effortlessly.

You make me feel crystal clean,
despite the previous fingerprint streaks.

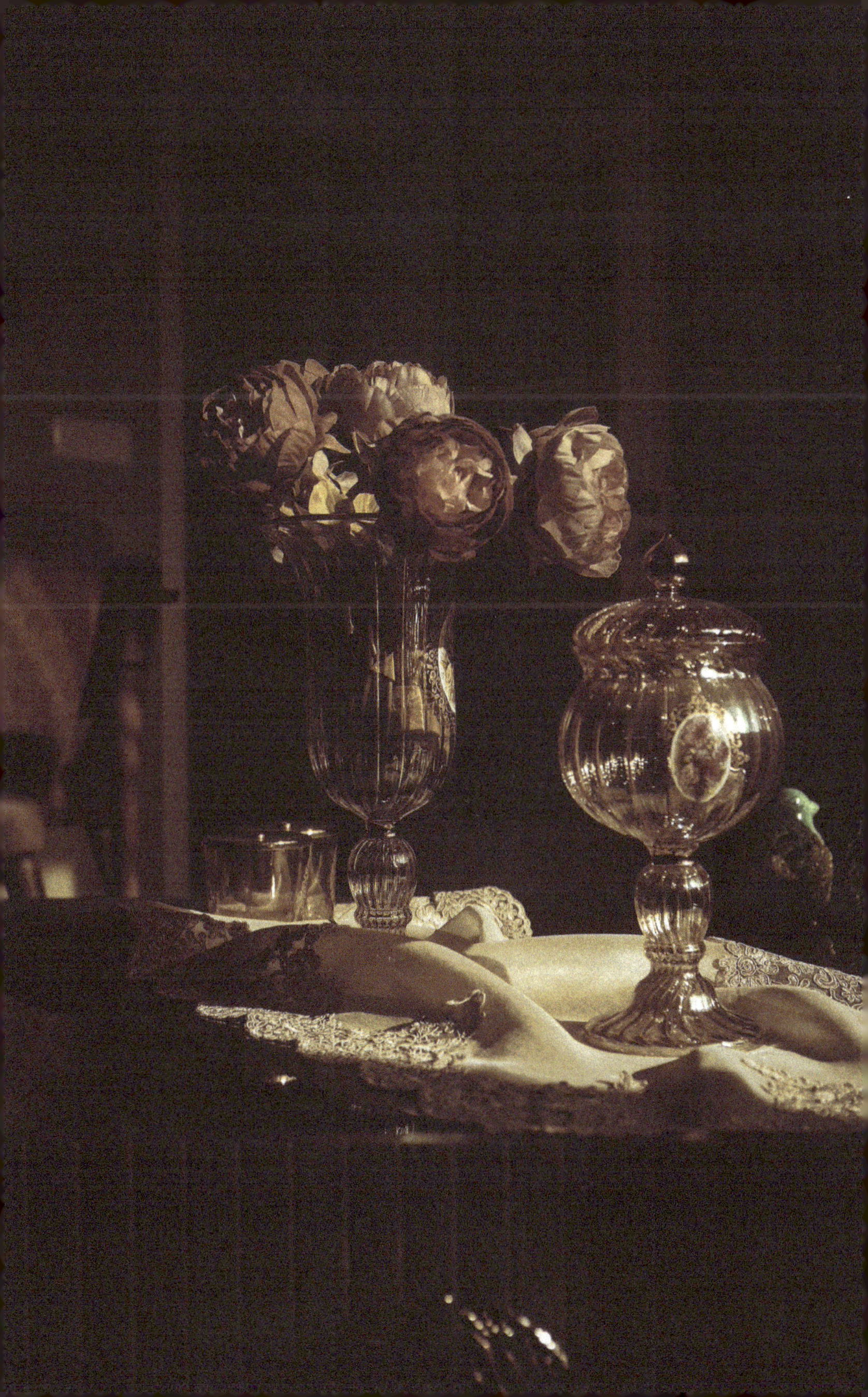

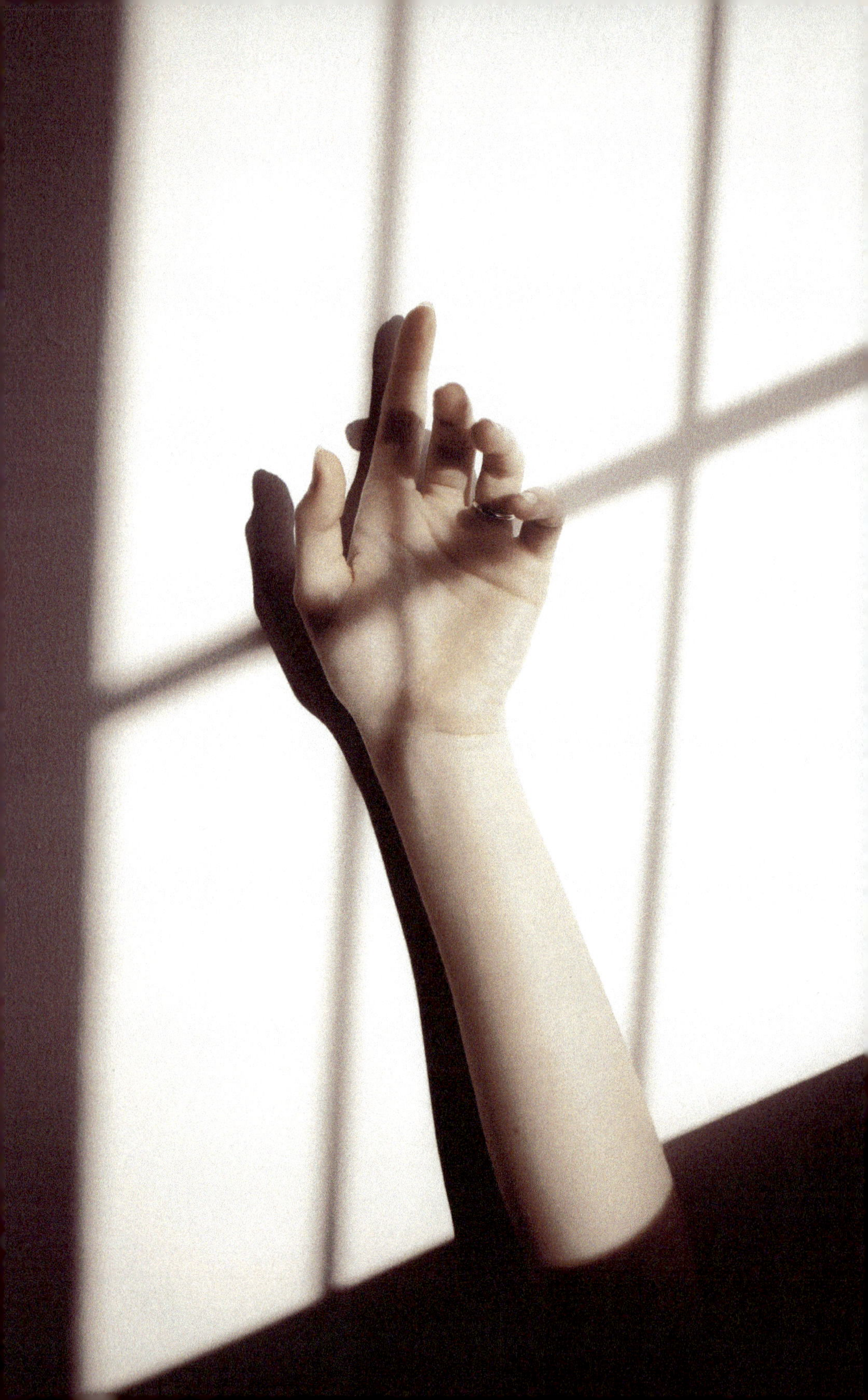

Her Voice Echoed

Her *voice* echoed
into my soul
as her throat shook
with so much concern,

*"Just don't go,
you mean so much to me."*

"I could never do such a thing",
is all I could think
as both of her hands affectionately pressed
against the sides of my cheeks.

Each palm holding
it's own *unspoken language*
exchanging nothing but immense
and intense tenderness.

I'm not leaving.

Flowers Blooming in April

You feel like *flowers blooming in April,*
and all I want to do is be able
to sneak peek a preview of you as I sit
in anticipation
with both hands under my chin
staring out the window
to see your color
come rushing through the pavement.

Don't mind me
as I soak in every ounce of your nourishment
from a distance - uninterrupted,
because you're blossoming
as you're meant to be - vibrantly.

I never intend to hasten this process.
Growth requires patience.

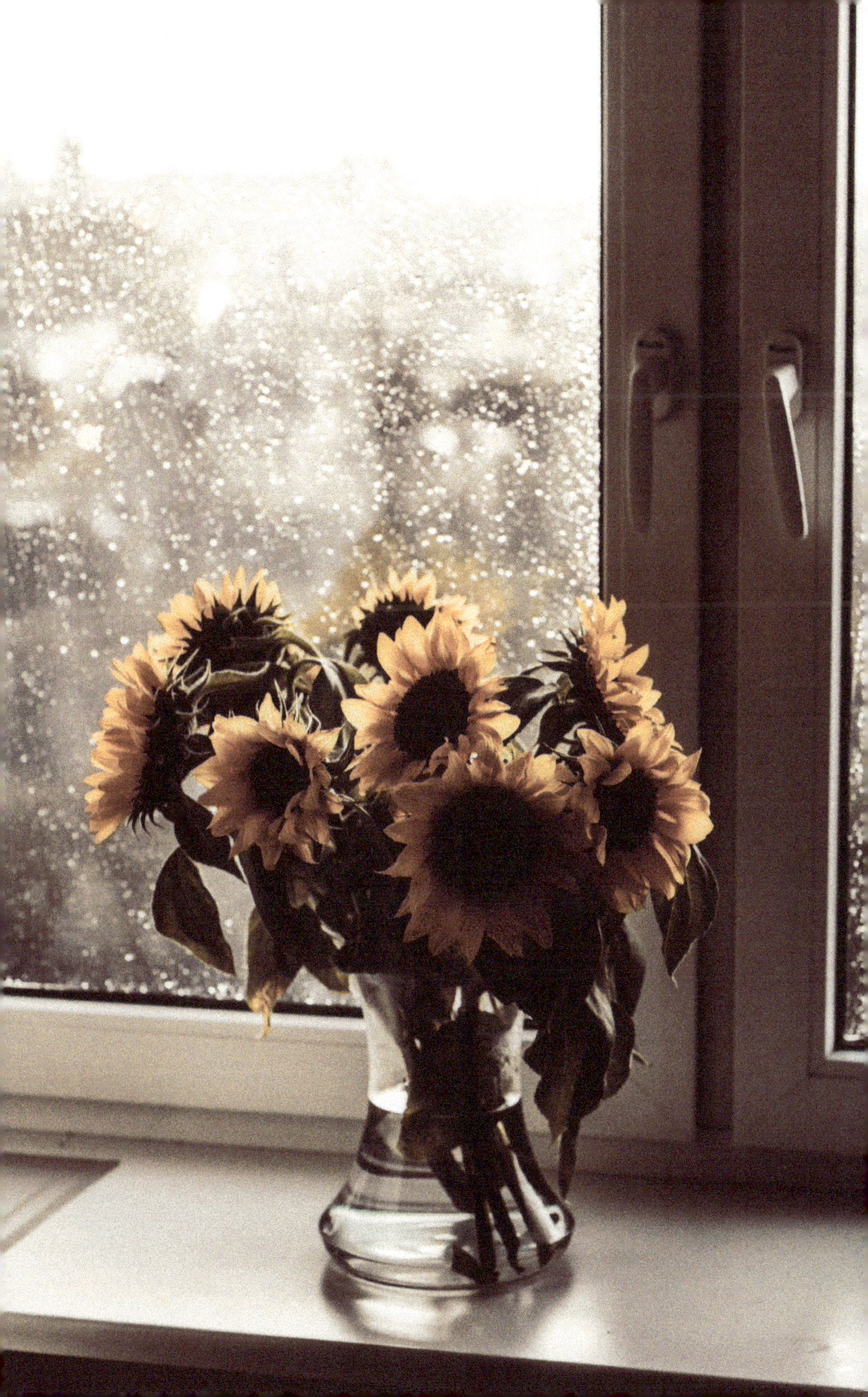

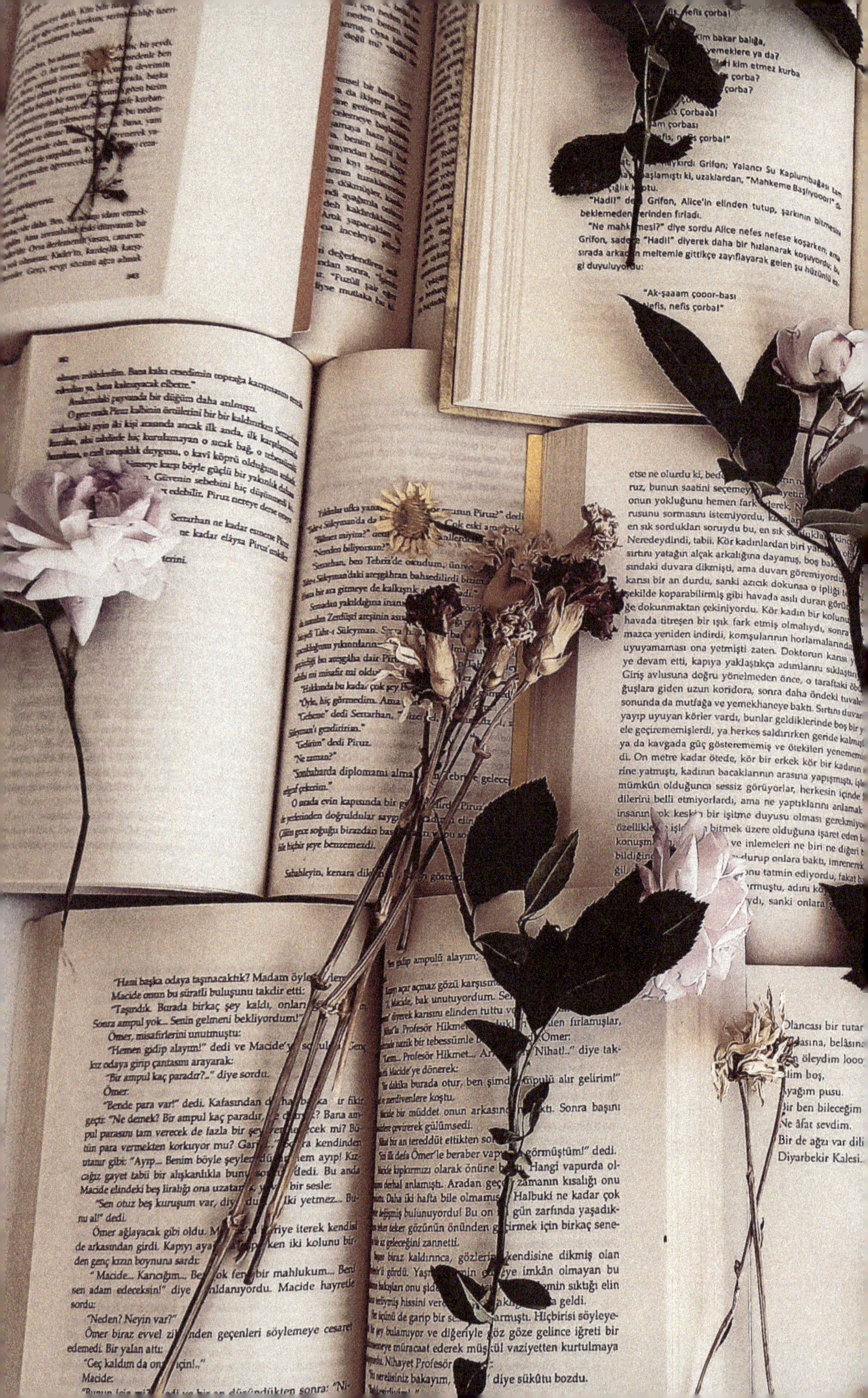

ON BİRİNCİ BÖLÜM
Kim Çaldı Tatlı Çörekleri
Momo
Michael Ende
136
137

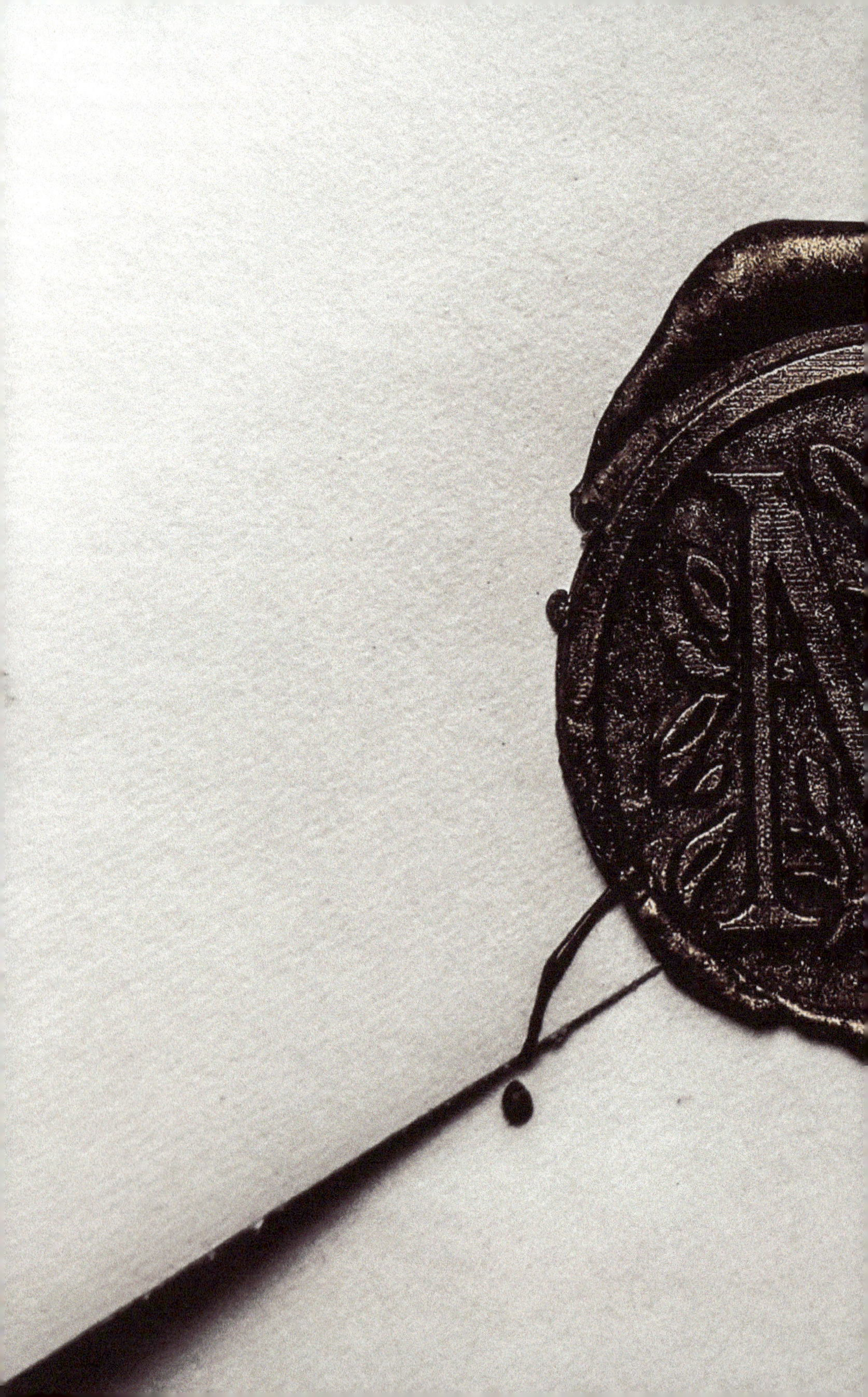

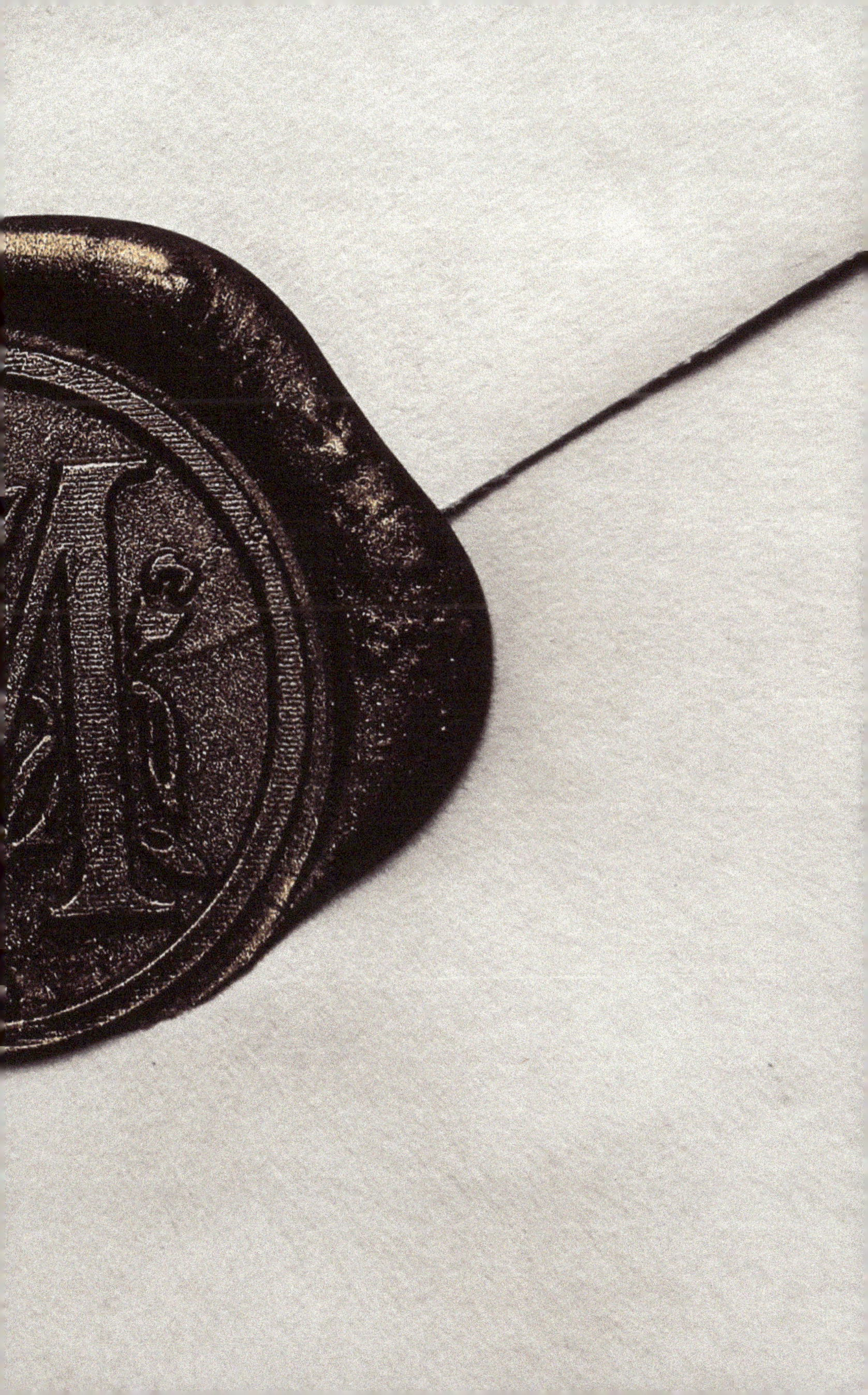

Arithmetik, einschließlich Algebra. 95

Jede der Gleichungen beginnt mit der Benennung, mit welcher die vorhergehende aufhört, es greift daher jede Gleichung, wie ein Glied einer Kette in das vorhergehende, daher nennt man einen solchen Ansatz einen Kettensatz. Eine Kette ist ... Glied, in das erste eingreift, und so sagt man auch, die Kette beim ... Benennung des letzten Gliedes die des Frageliedes ist, ...

Für den Ket... ...chte Benennung bei.

1. Wir b...
2. Jede ...

hat, da wi... ...htigen, doß bi... ...esen

...glied

Methode

Chr.) in

...gaben mit

...zusammen

e Regeldetri

Unterschied

Sätze handelt,

durch Ketten-

...erden. Bei

Elemente

eigentliche

in seinem

...ie wir

...päter viel

...hübsch

...hten

...lle

...h.

73...

...enlaß

...rieb

das

...indet

...er

...war, daß man

Language of my Literature

        I think of you
             in
        everything.

In the spaces in between the seconds
and in every pause in between the silence.
You are in each individual interval.

You are the *language of my literature*
when I'm lost for words —
Slowly gaining fluency in your dialect.

The muse to my canvas
when I aim to create something vibrant —
You are an unending colored palette.

        I think of you
          even in
        the unseen.

MOTHS
AND
BUTTERFLIES

NEW & RARE
BEAUTIFUL
LEAVED
PLANTS

DICTIONNAIRE
UNIVERSEL
D'HISTOIRE
NATURELLE

46
EN SOMMERSANG.
J. S. Welhaven.
Halfdan Kjerulf, Op.15.
Un poco lento.
Sang.
21.
Piano.
Recit.
Fag - re Dal,
p dolce
rit.
Moderato.
Sommer!
Her er Marken fuld af Blommer,
p legg.
her
Liv og Duft til Lun - den vin - ke, i hvis grøn - ne Hvælving
dolce
Straa - leglimt som Stjer - ners Hær.
poco lento
riten. col canto
dim. e rit.

Recit.
Blom - ster - duft,
gy - de
Læng - sel
49
min Sol og Stjer - ne, min
og Stjer - ne.
n Drøm, i min Drøm, i min Drøm kun
ner du.
riten.

Depths

If you have time tonight,
would you mind
dancing with my waves
under the moonlight,
and getting lost in my lullaby?

I want to pull you into me, like gravity,
and have you get lost in my tide.

I give you permission
to set foot into my ocean,
and to fall deeper
than what I show on the surface
without you having to worry
about an aggressive current,
despite my reputation,
because with you,
I'll be cognizant
enough to be delicate.

So, as I open up my emotions
and allow you to walk into the depths of my ocean,
just promise me that you won't take advantage.

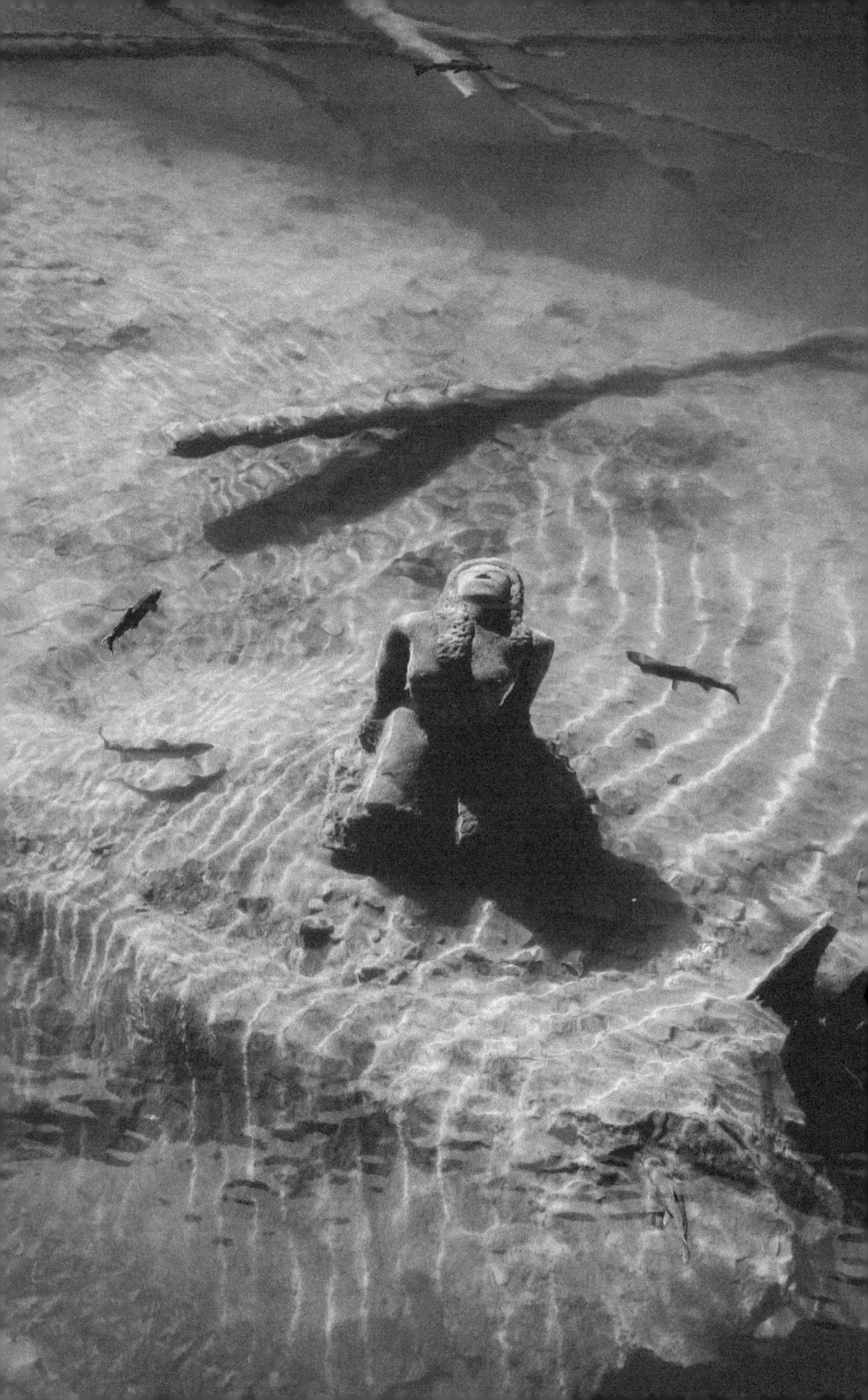

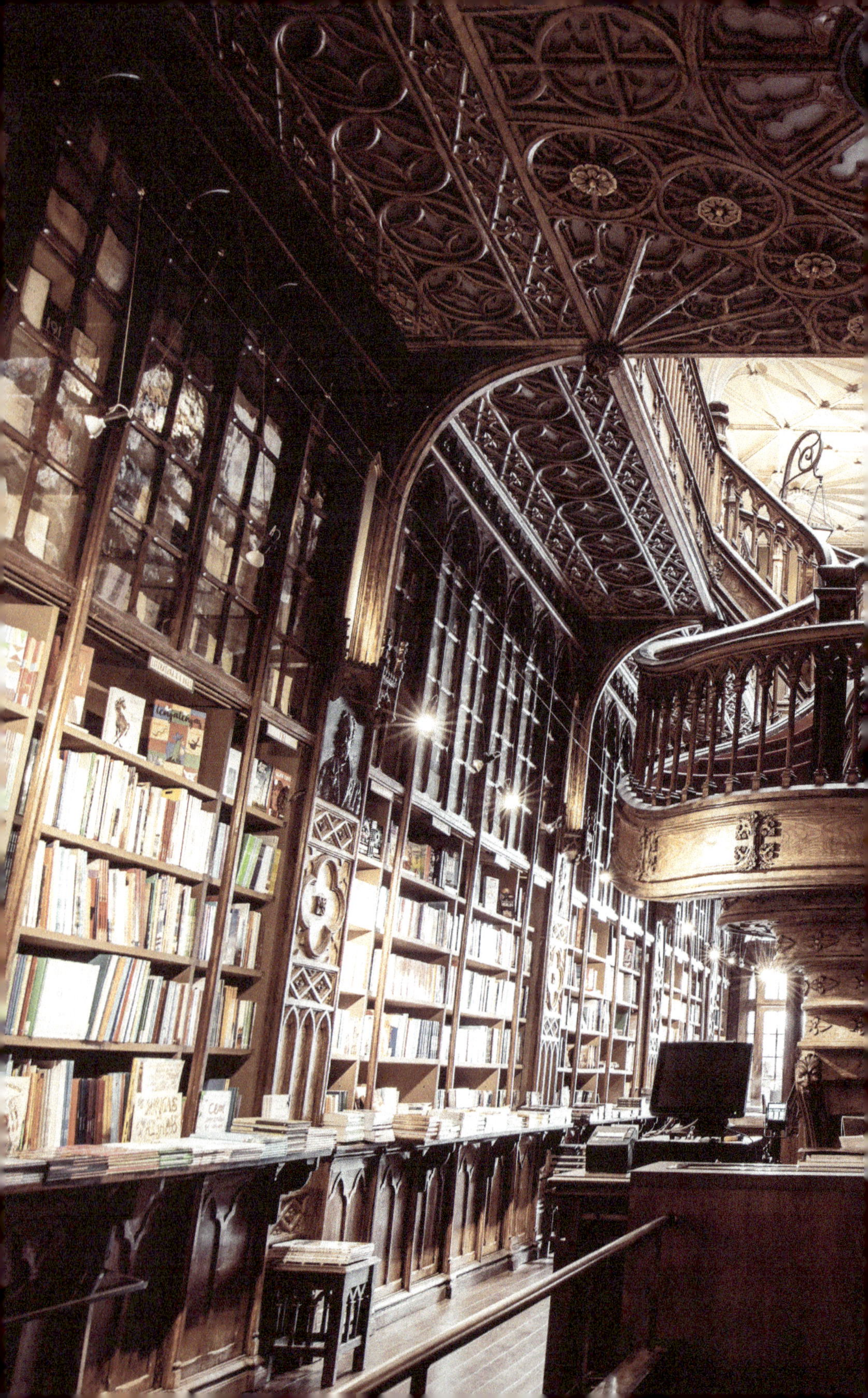

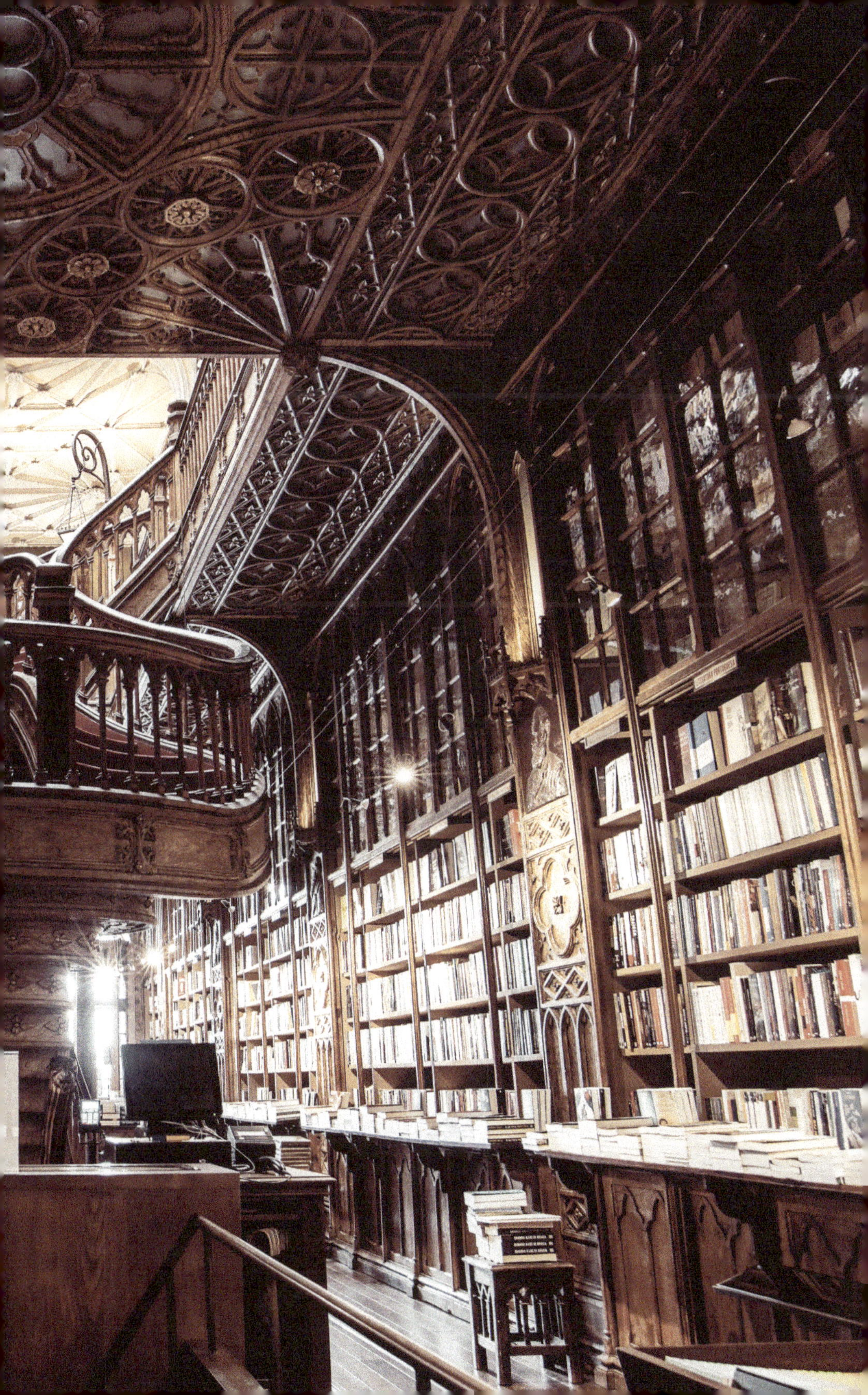

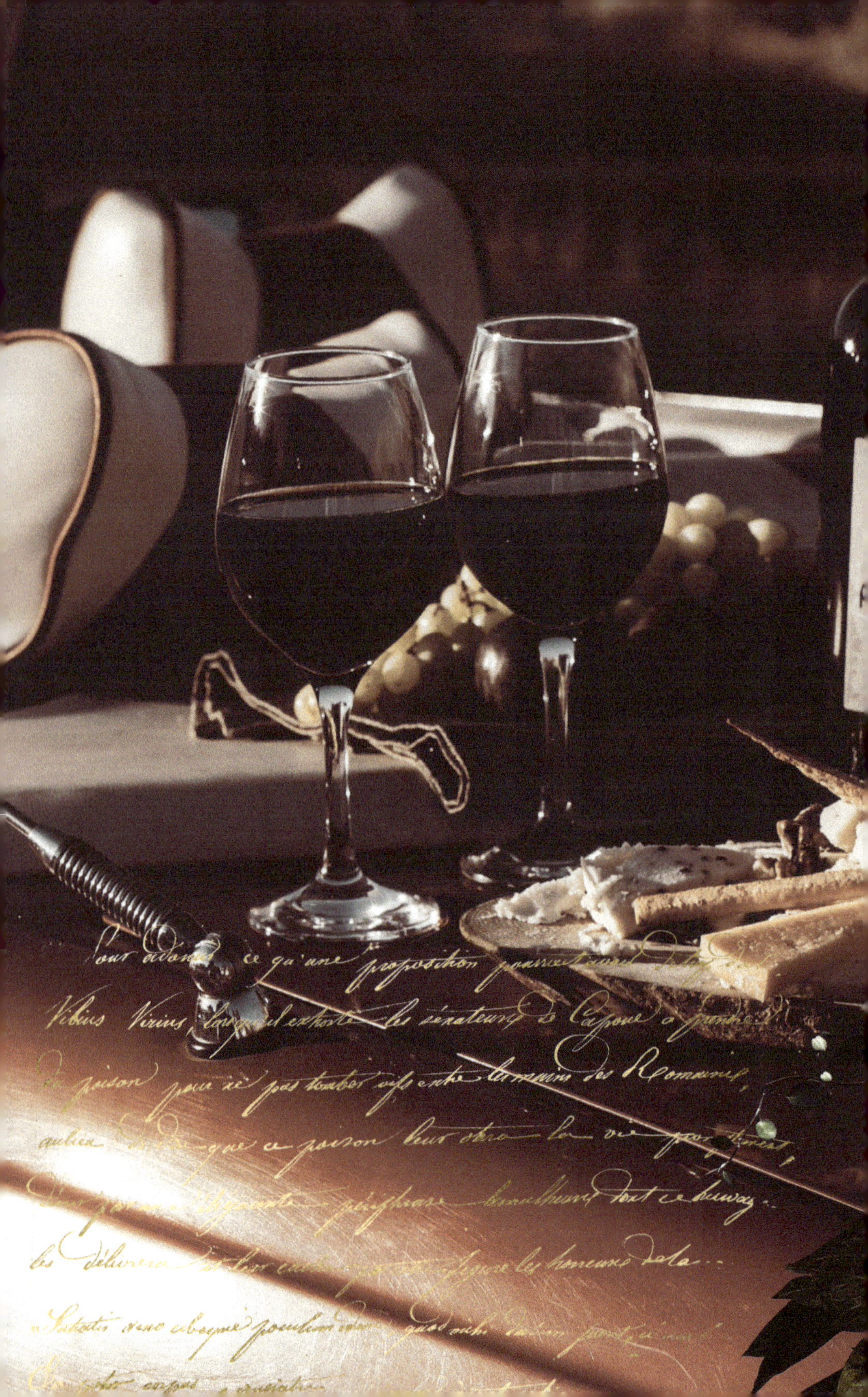

Intoxicated

There has always been something
about her *glance*
from the way that she *stares*
and how it leaves me *intoxicated*.

With intention.

Or how her *hands*
can easily keep me *grounded*
as her angel-like fingers
stroke through my curly *hair*.

I can breathe.

Rain in Autumn

She's *electric* and *deep rooted*
when she loves.
Honest and grounded
to her *nourishment*.

She feels like *rain in autumn,*
unpredictable and honest -
Yet expected,
and with every drop that has fallen
she sings a song
dedicated just for me - *my lullaby.*

The way she has harvested
parts of her soul into me
from planting her seeds
into my soil
left me just like the leaves -

F a l l i n g.

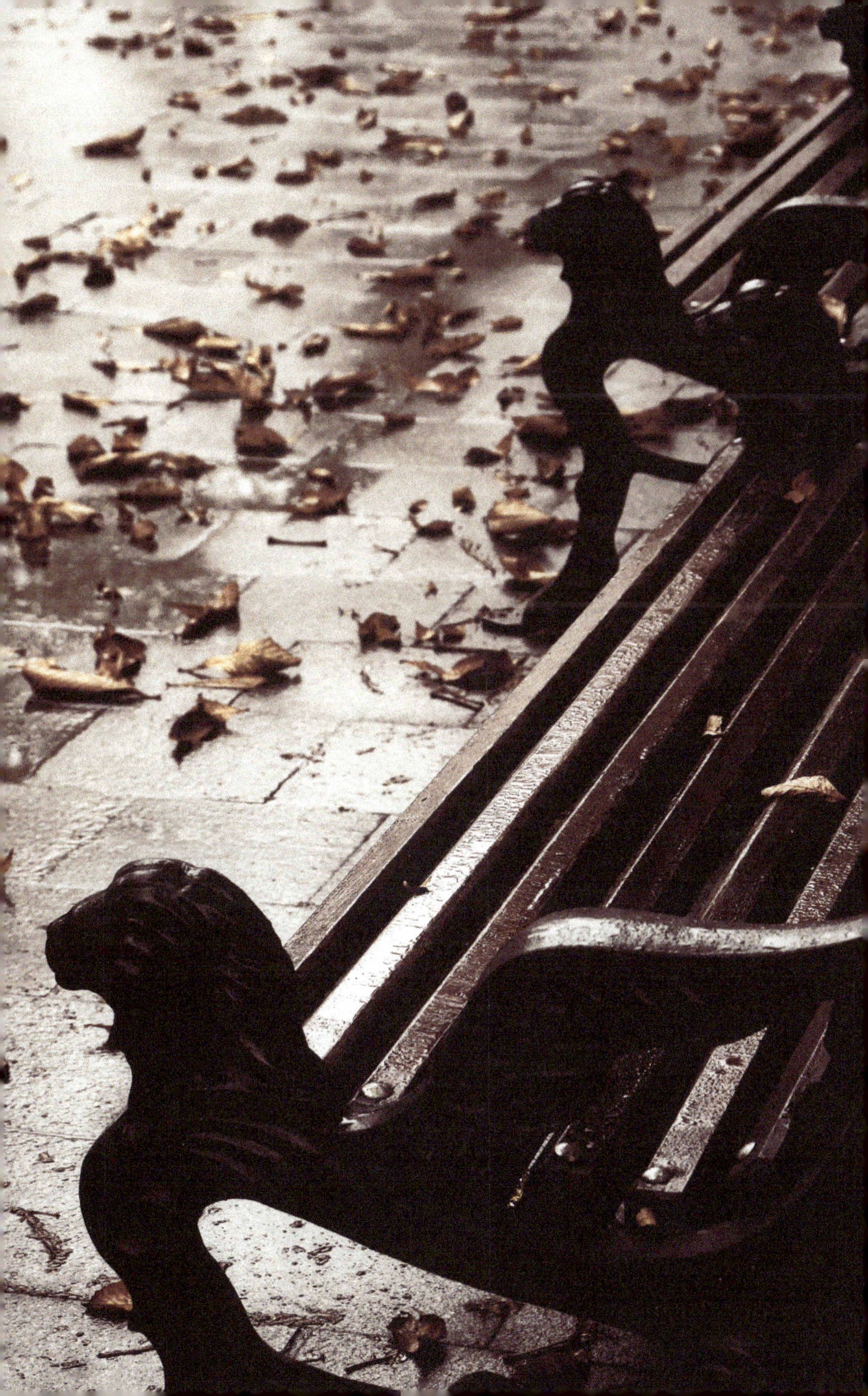

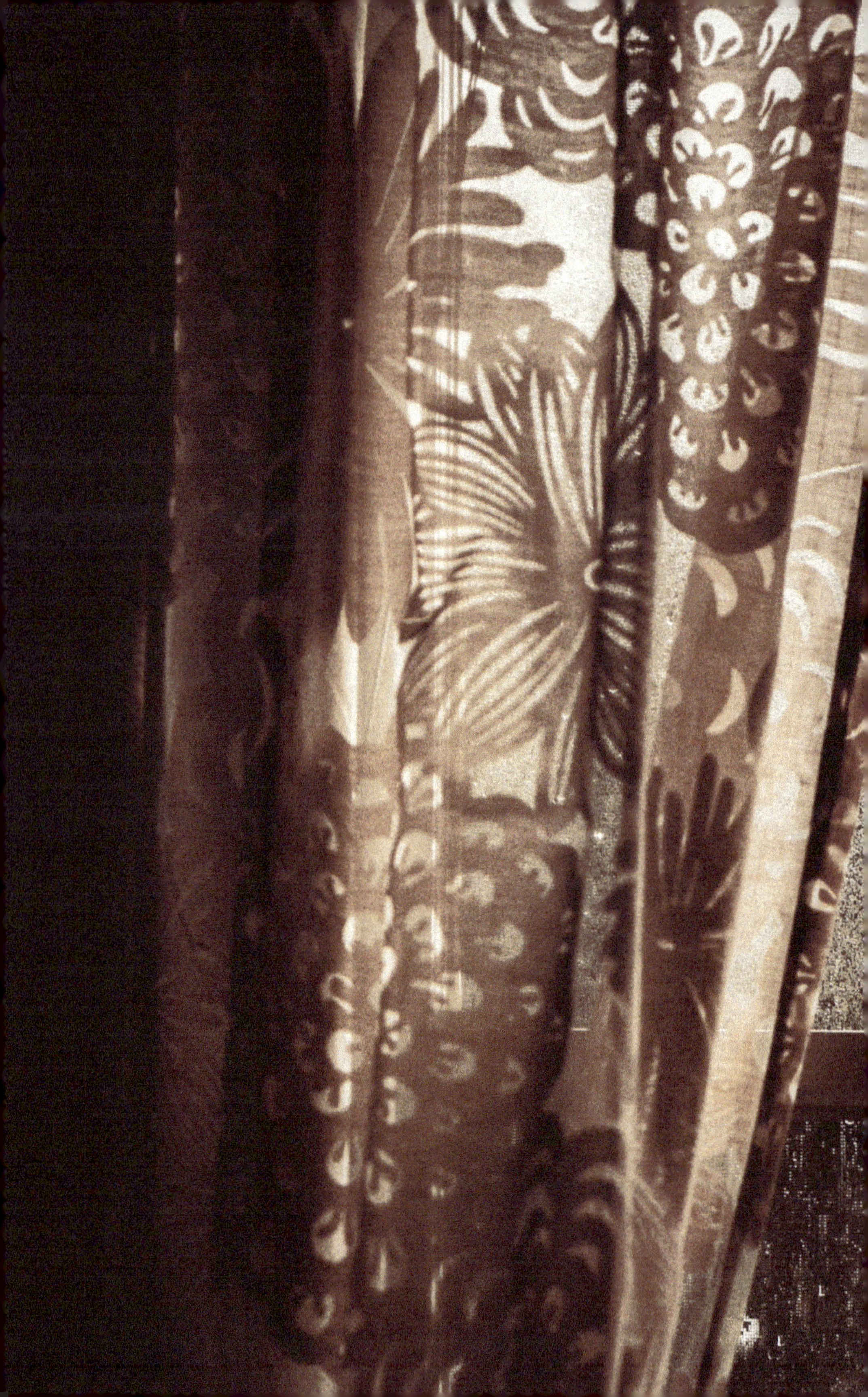

Your
voice sounds
how
love feels.

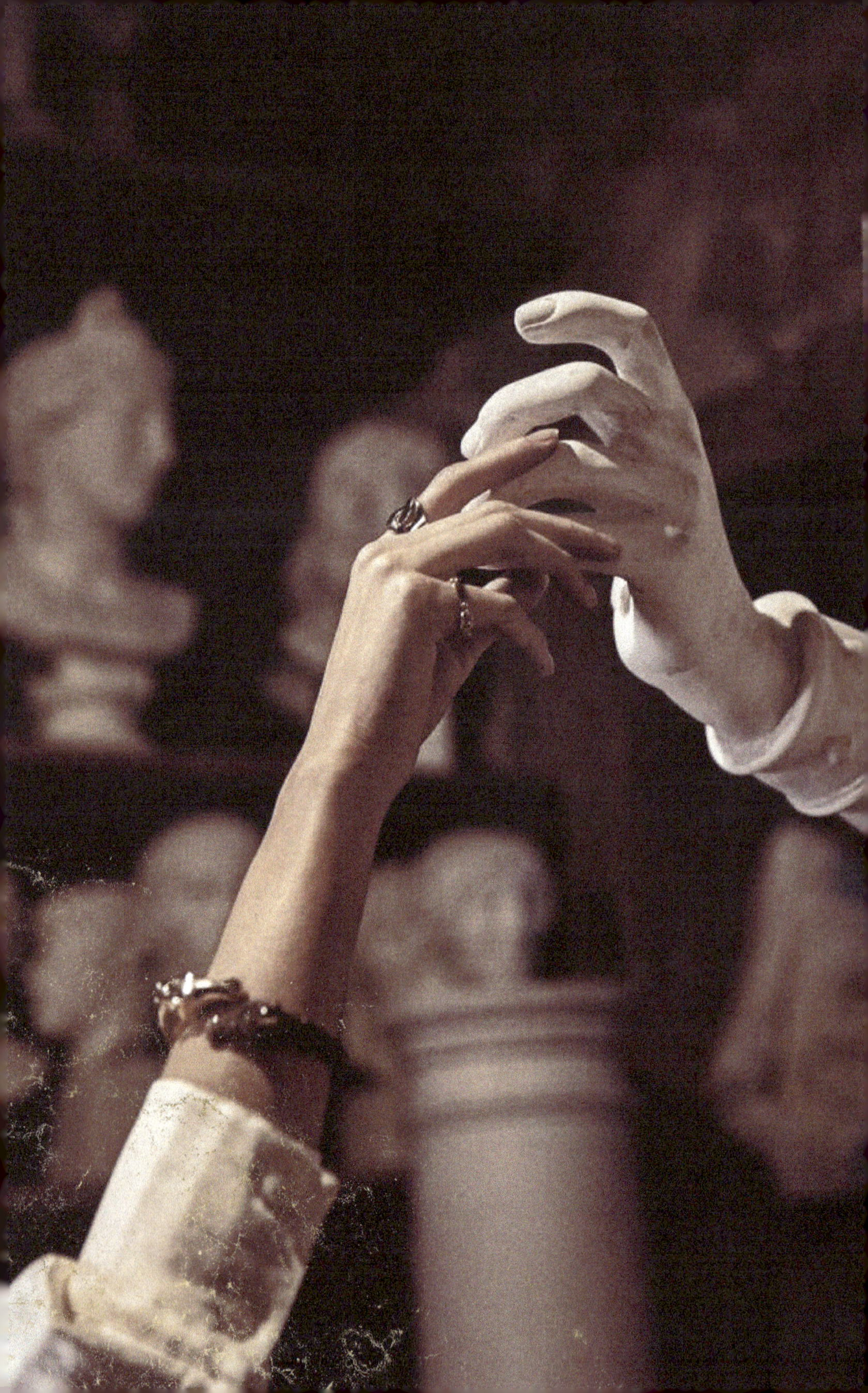

H.E.R

Her *smile*
shines just as bright and warm as golden hour
with a *voice*
that could grow flowers — *nourishing*.

Her *aura*
gives me familiar nostalgia
of a delicately vintage type of love — *old fashioned*.

In return, the least that I can ever offer her
with every possible option
available are my words.

Please, just *one more verse* -
Let me describe you with another verb.
My stories are about *H.E.R.*

Hand-writing everything remembered.

Palatable

You've made the cost of
vulnerability become affordable.

Handing over trust
inevitable.

The art of
conversations digestible.

Profound love palatable.

The story of us
sustainable.

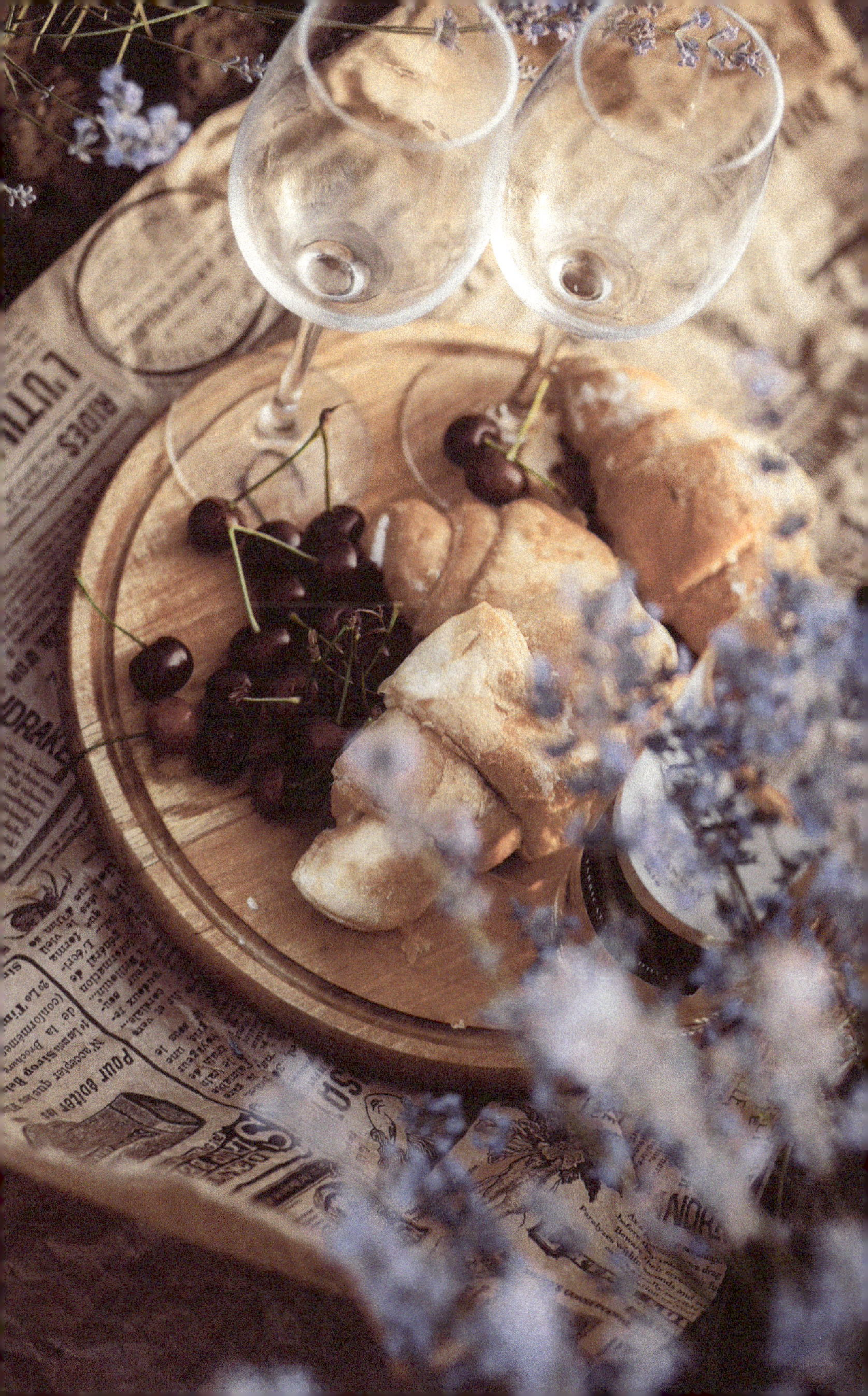

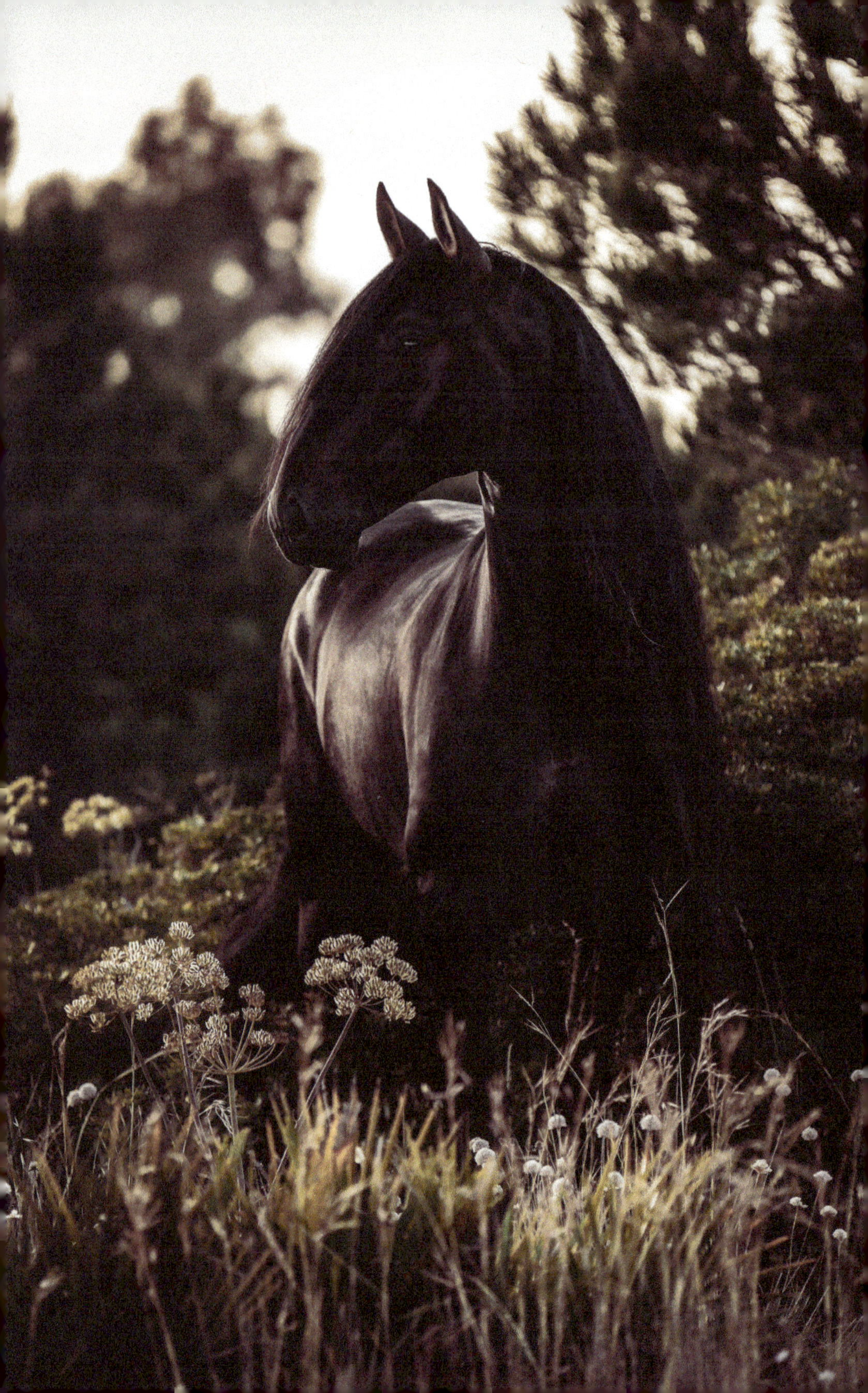

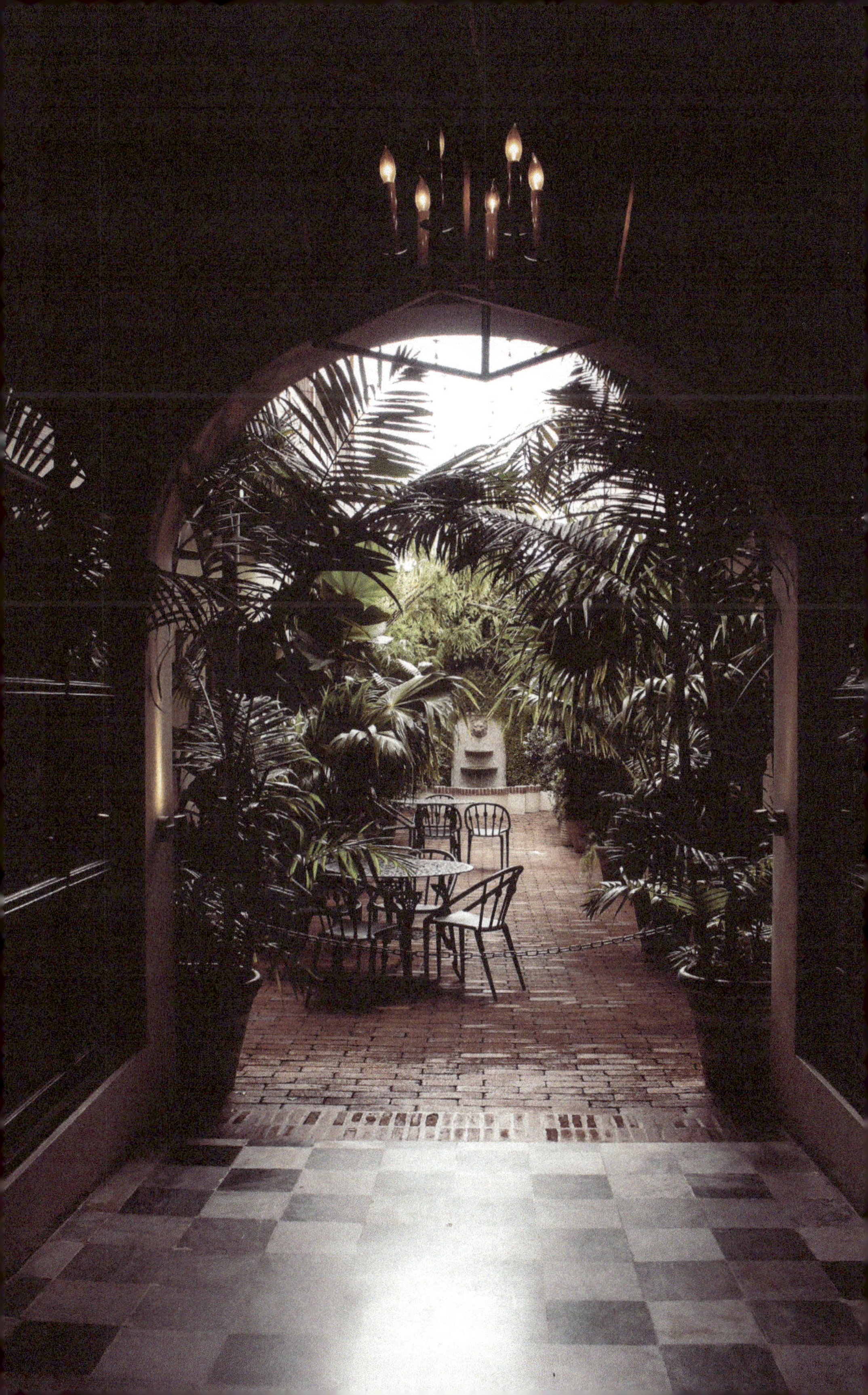

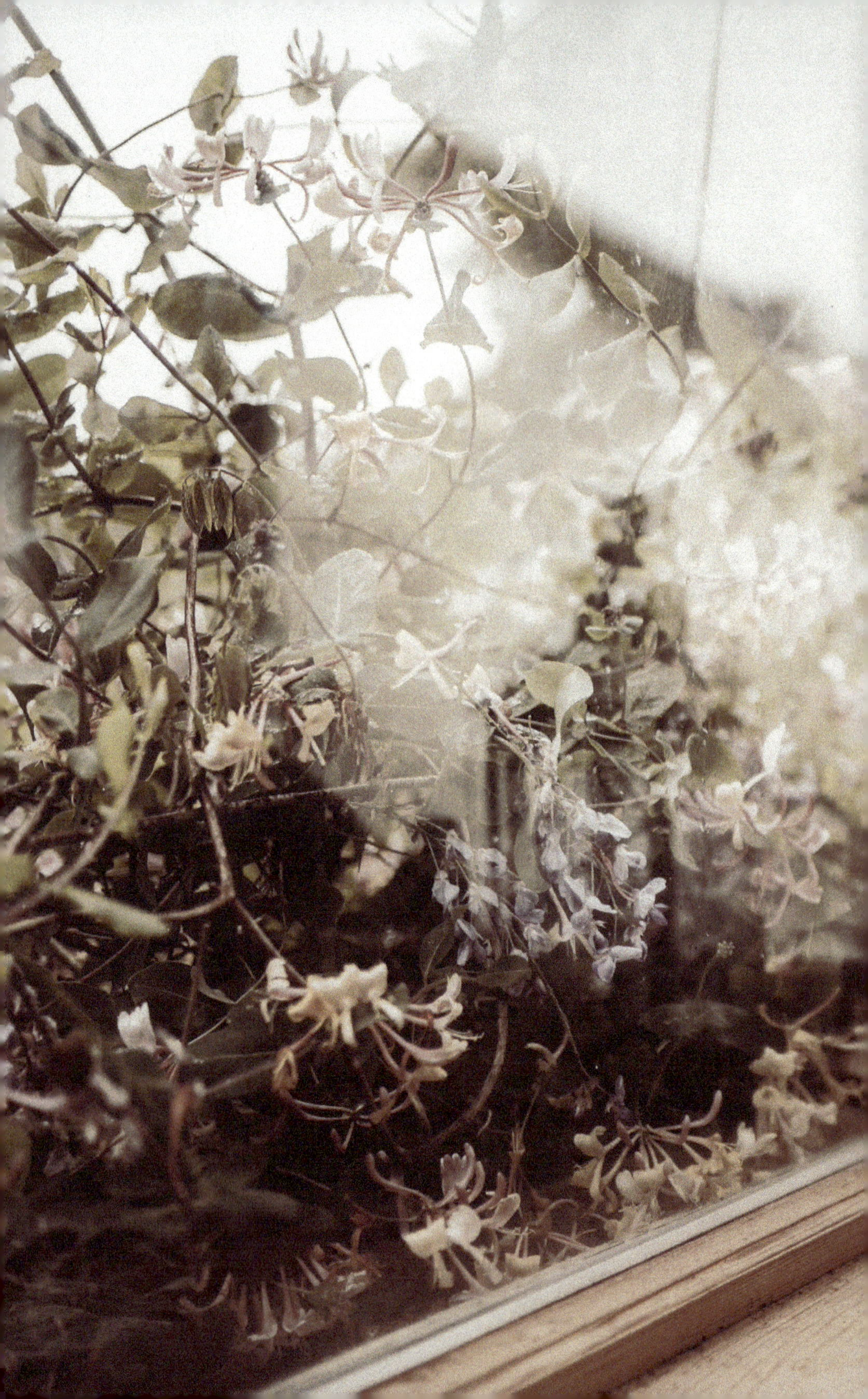

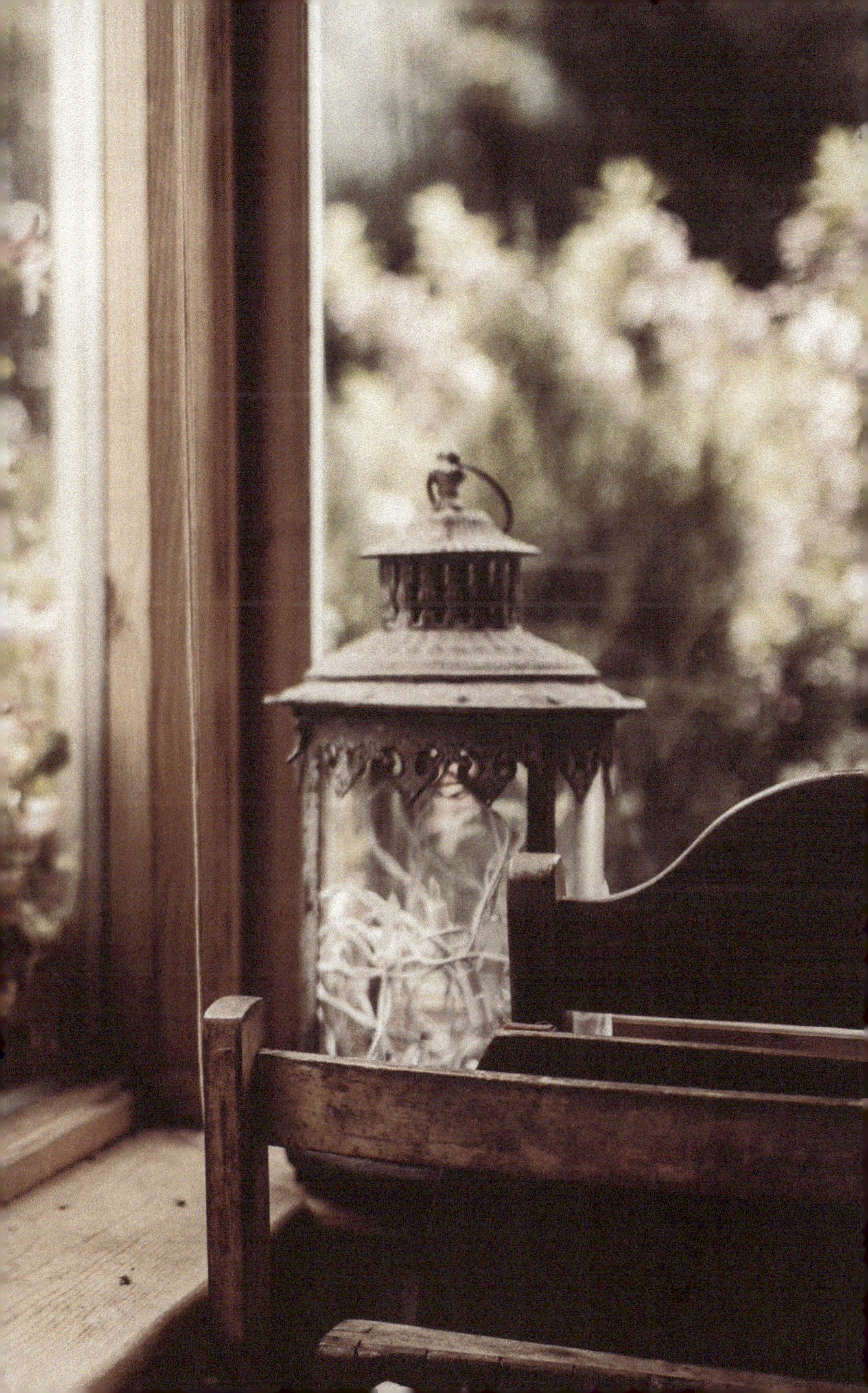

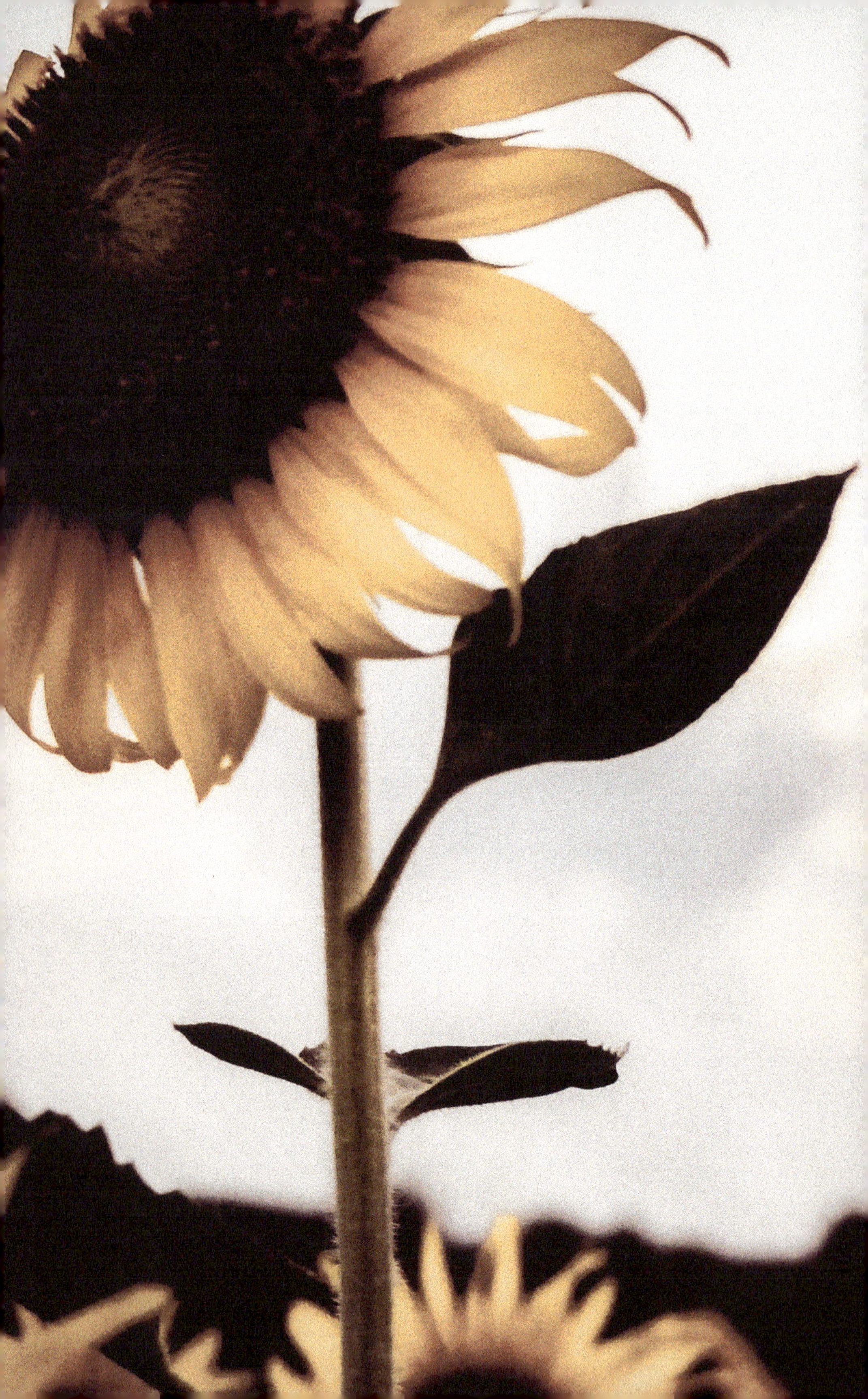

The morning came,
and so did she.

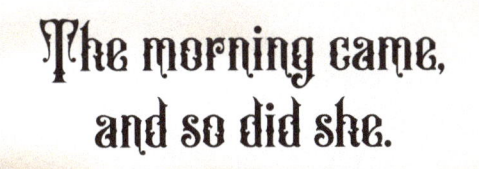

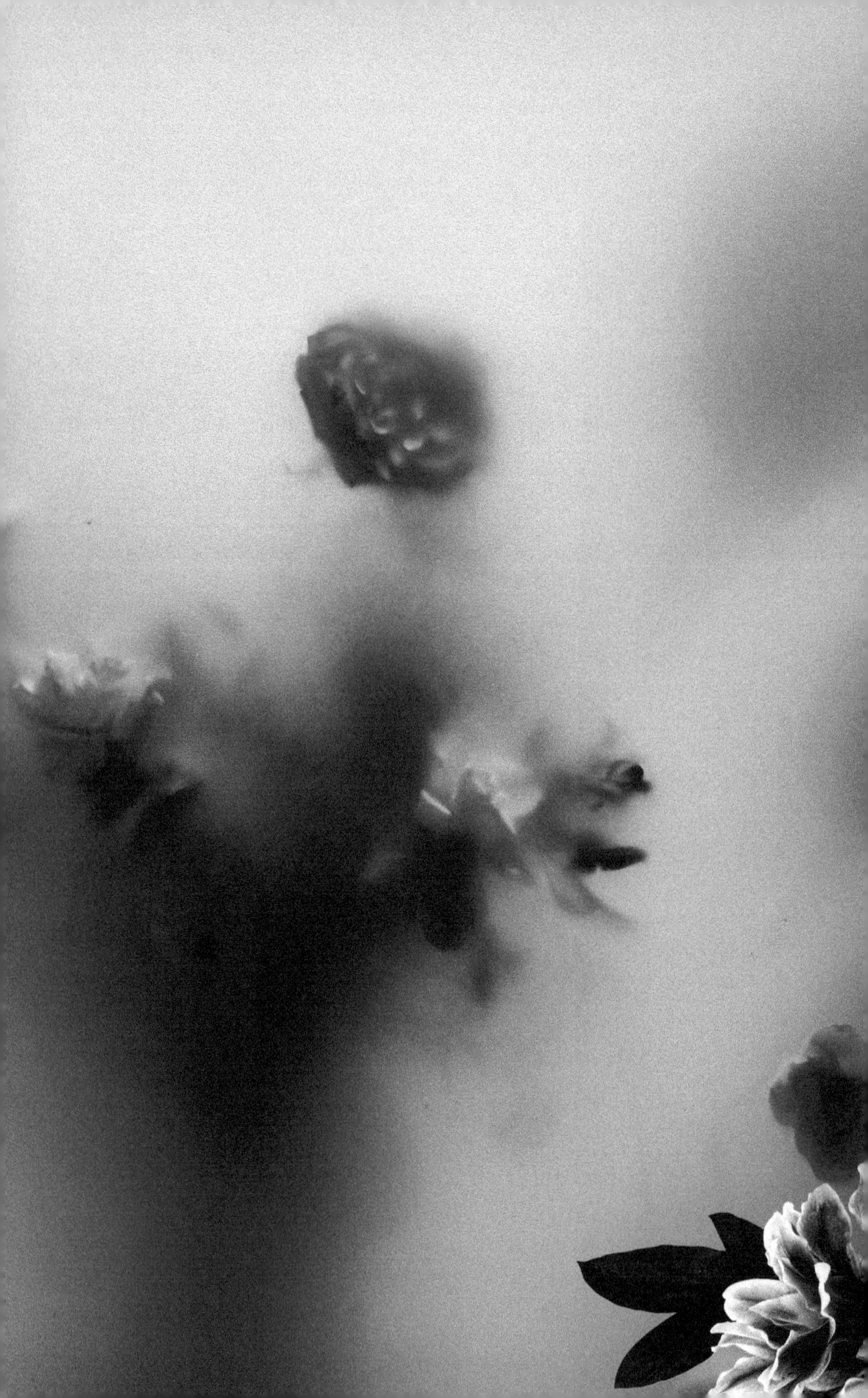

Mental Images of your Romance

It's six in the evening.

Our bodies are still tangled in between
these linen sheets with you fast asleep on me
as I slip into a deep daydream
that I can't help resisting.

I'm *overwhelmed* with the snippets
of your *lips* on my skin
touching every crevice.

Captivated, as I'm submerged in
the *mental images of your romance*
from your *hands* as they caress
the unseen details of my surface
from your delicacy - unmatched.

Paralyzed, beautifully confined
within your daze
from the way your *eyes*
see straight through my mind
as you memorize my body's shape
and the **prize** in between my thighs.

I'm daydreaming about you at six in the evening.

Vertigo

The thought of
ever letting you go
gives me
vertigo.

So, I hope you know,
you're mine.

To have
&
to hold.

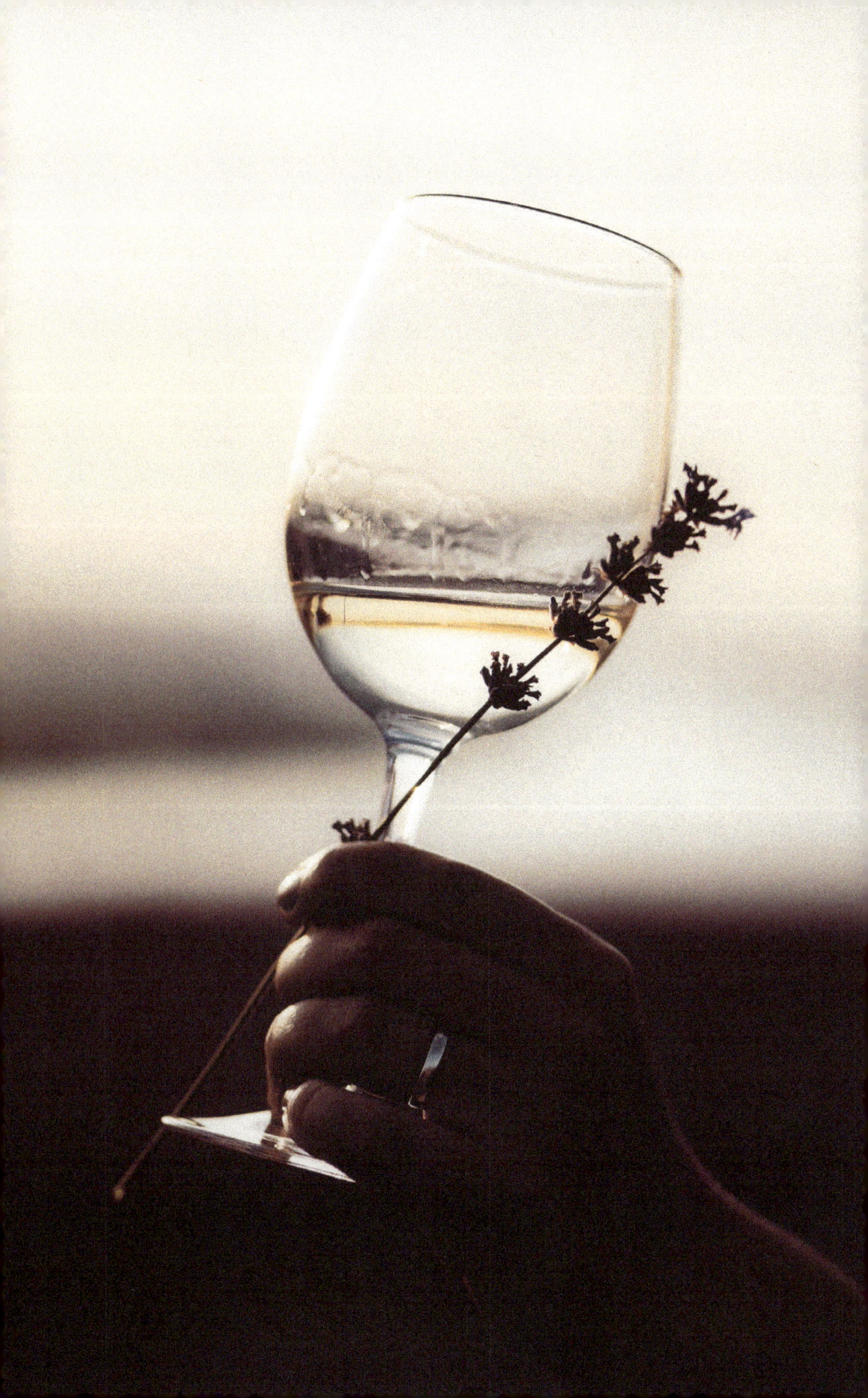

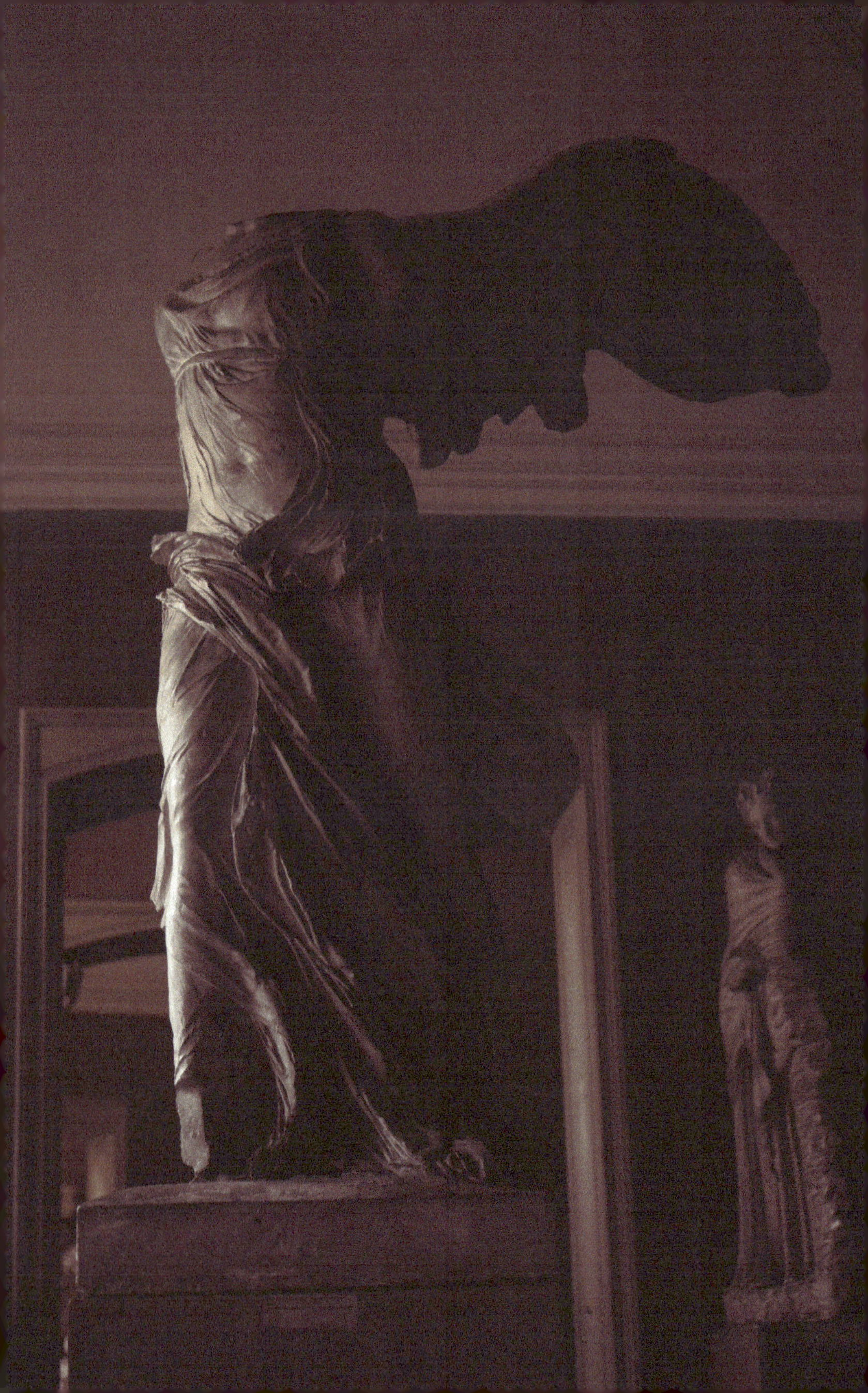

Masterpiece

I know a masterpiece
when I see one.
So, when I saw you,
my first instinct was to instantly
enclose you in a picture frame
and put you on display
so everyone can appreciate
you the same way.

But, then it hit me,
and I came to the realization that women,
women like you, cosmic,
don't deserve to be stuffed within
a box of limited inches
that would evidently keep your growth restricted.

You're boundless, you should be treated like it.

Intricate Mind//Soulful Eyes

Nobody ever catches my eyes
long enough to hold it
if I'm being honest.

I fall for intricate minds
and deep soulful eyes,
so when it came to you,
you caught me by surprise.

You still do, every time.

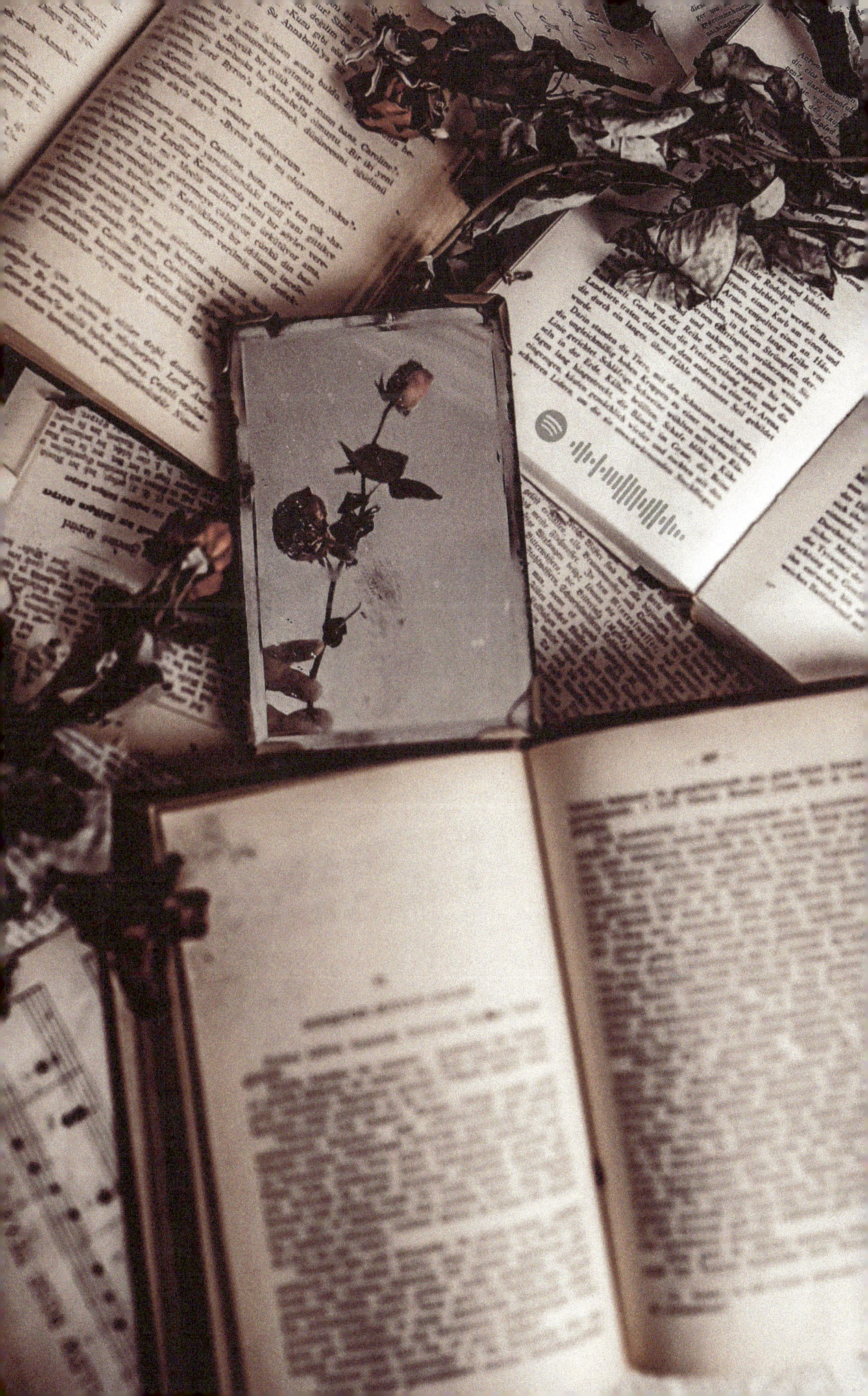

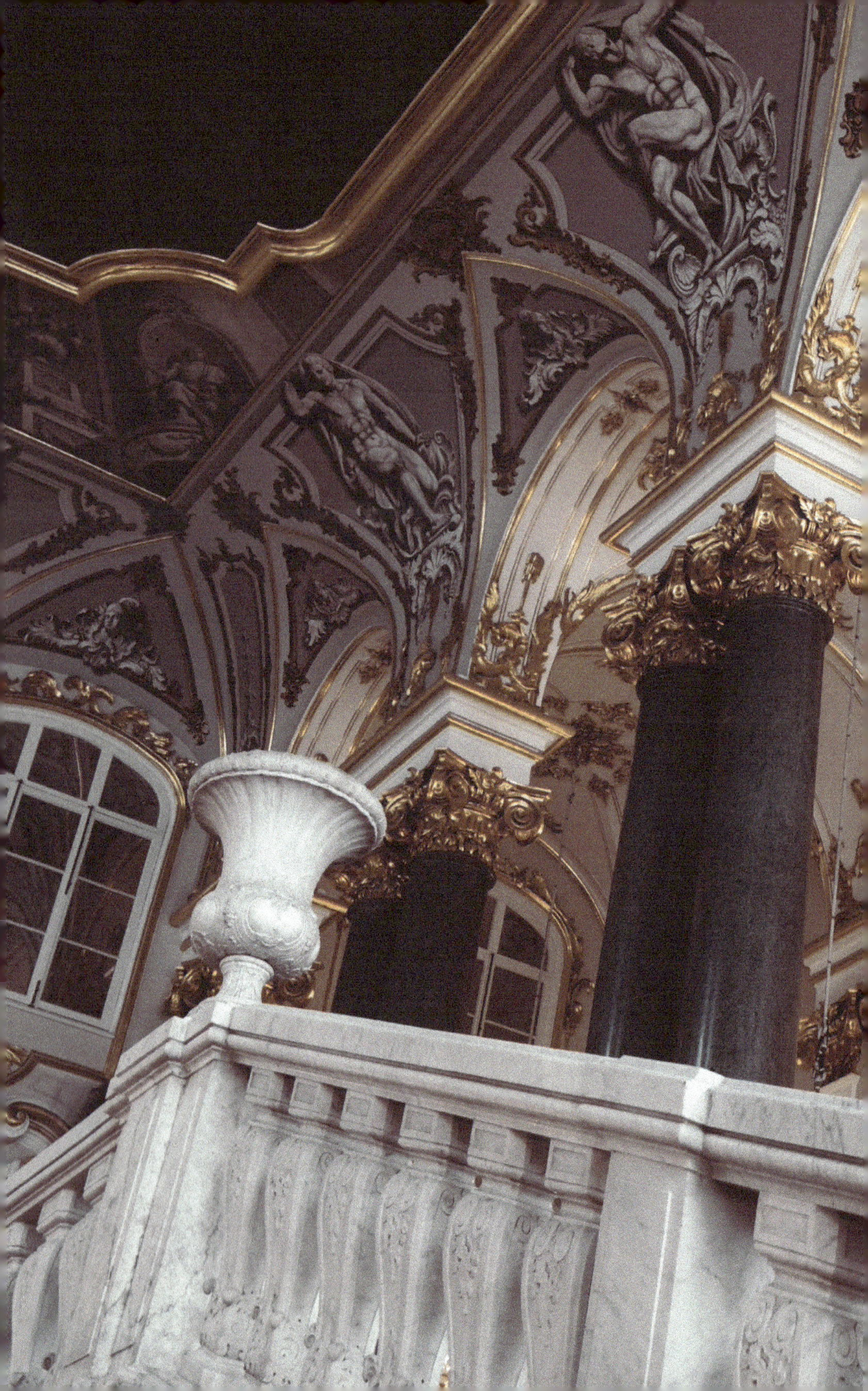

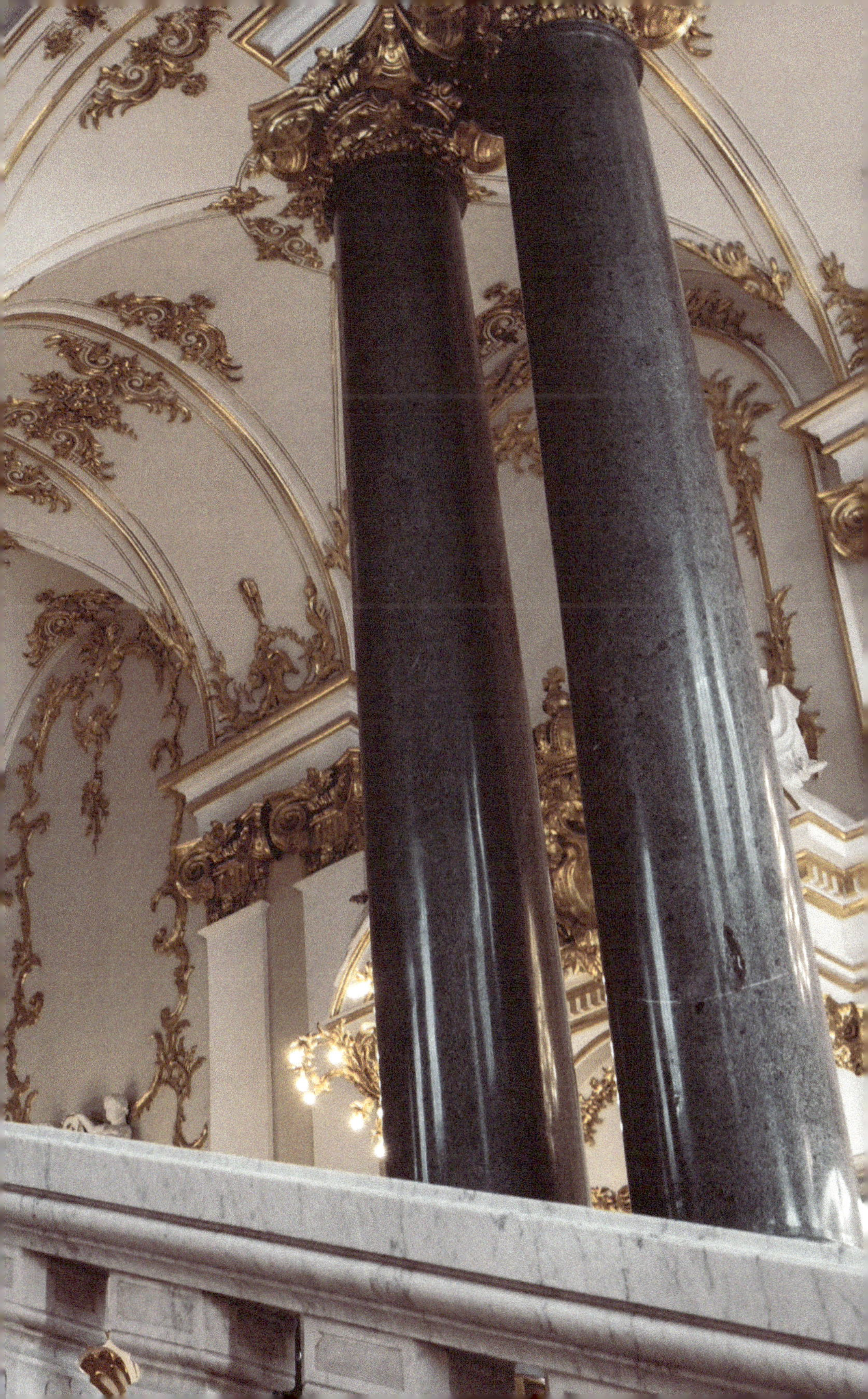

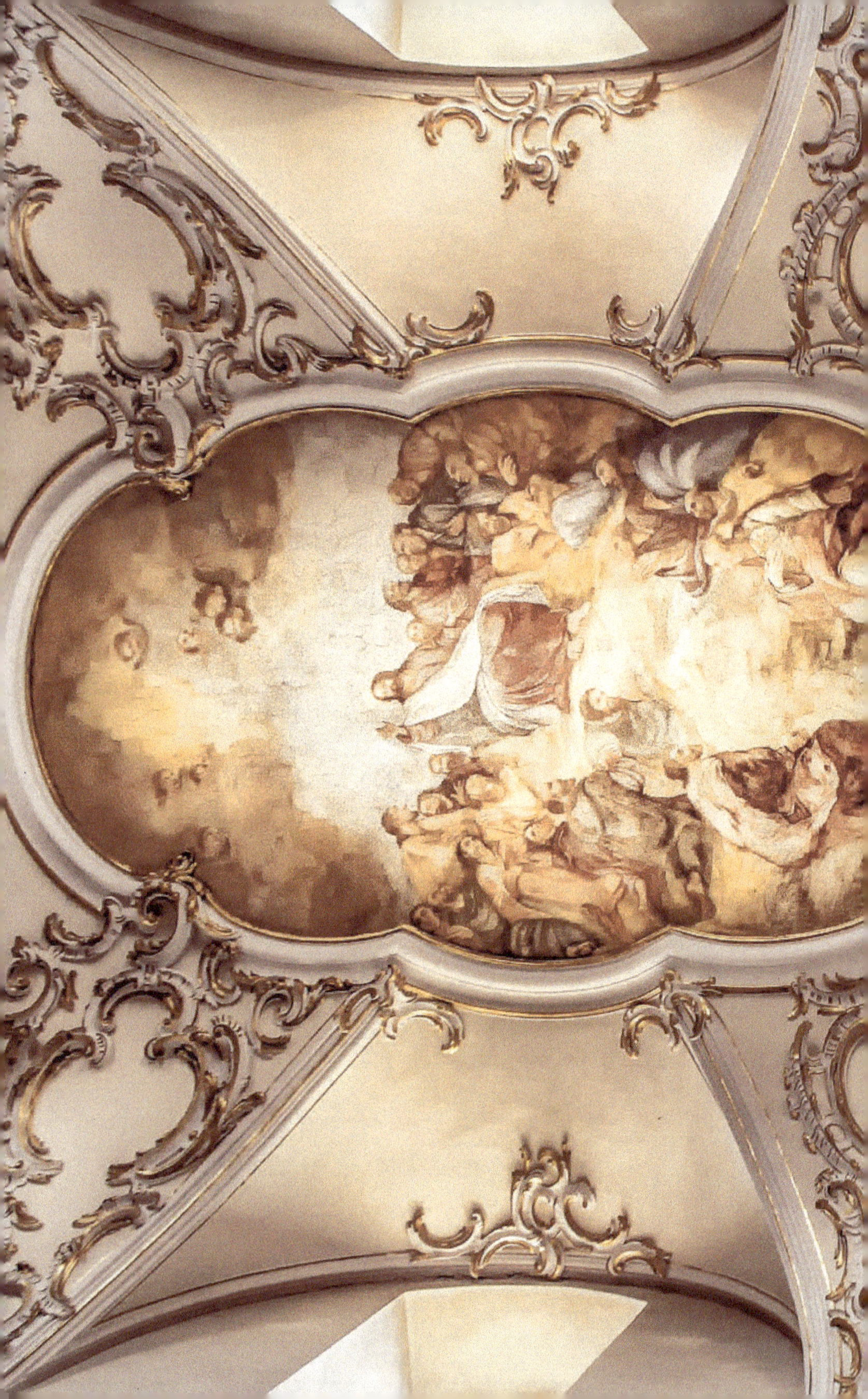

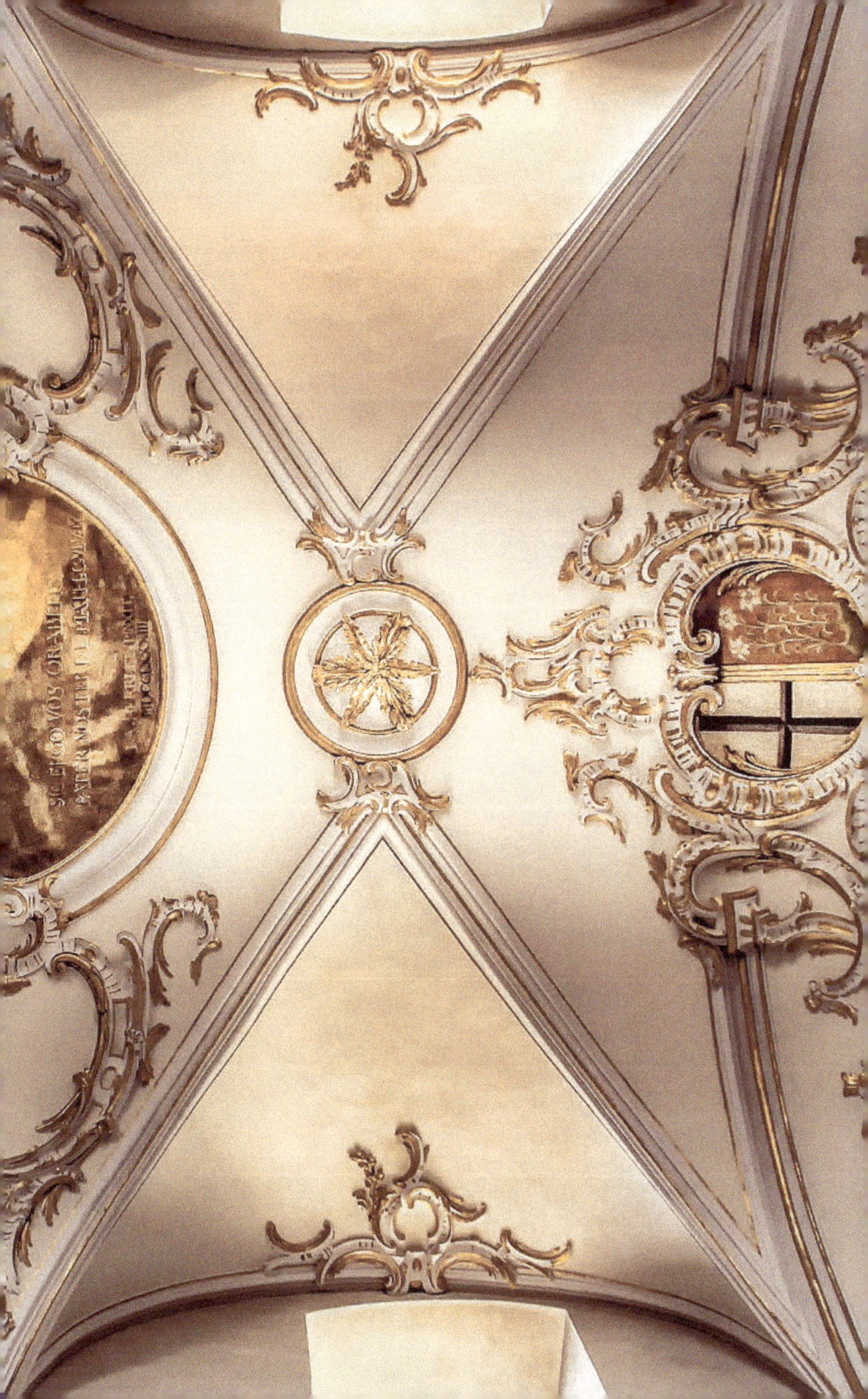
SIC ERGO VOS ORABITIS

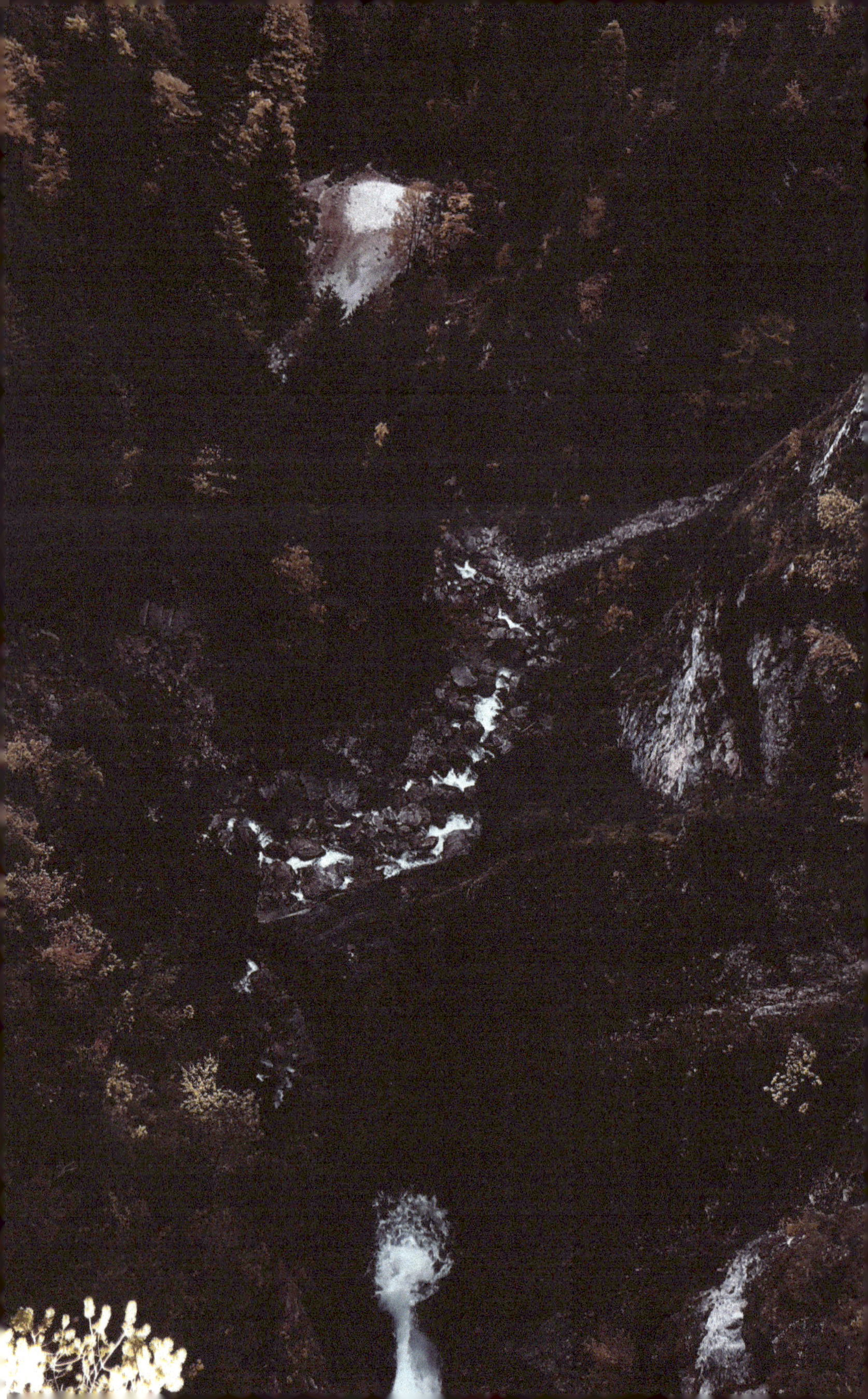

Perspective

You deserve a perspective
that isn't limited.
If you let me, I'll show you a life
that forces you to look through a different type of lens
and question every decision
you have ever had before this.

One that has no sense of set direction
for a particular destination,
but, to a place that is a safe space
for a mind to rest.

One so full of adrenaline that it lacks hesitation,
and the fear of being reckless becomes nonexistent.
You'll eventually become addicted
to the feeling of unrestricted existence.

A life that's no longer concerned with risks
or filled with all the generic, *"what ifs"*,
but engulfed in an endless curiosity
with everyday living where childhood dreams
and missed opportunities meet.

Come have a leap of faith with me,
let's both be unapologetically carefree.

Blanket of Security

Love is an indispensable currency,
yet, exchanging such thing is not an ubiquity.
That's where you and I have refused to conform
to such hypocrisy.
I'm confident in knowing
that you'd share it all with me.

Devouring me in certainty
within the beauty of your blessings.

Come with me, grab my hand
that's *drenched with tender nourishment*
as you write all your promises of reassurance
in the shape of a band.

Wrap me in a wedding ring
covered in your *blanket of security*
interlaced with *white purity*
with our last names becoming
a space of unity.

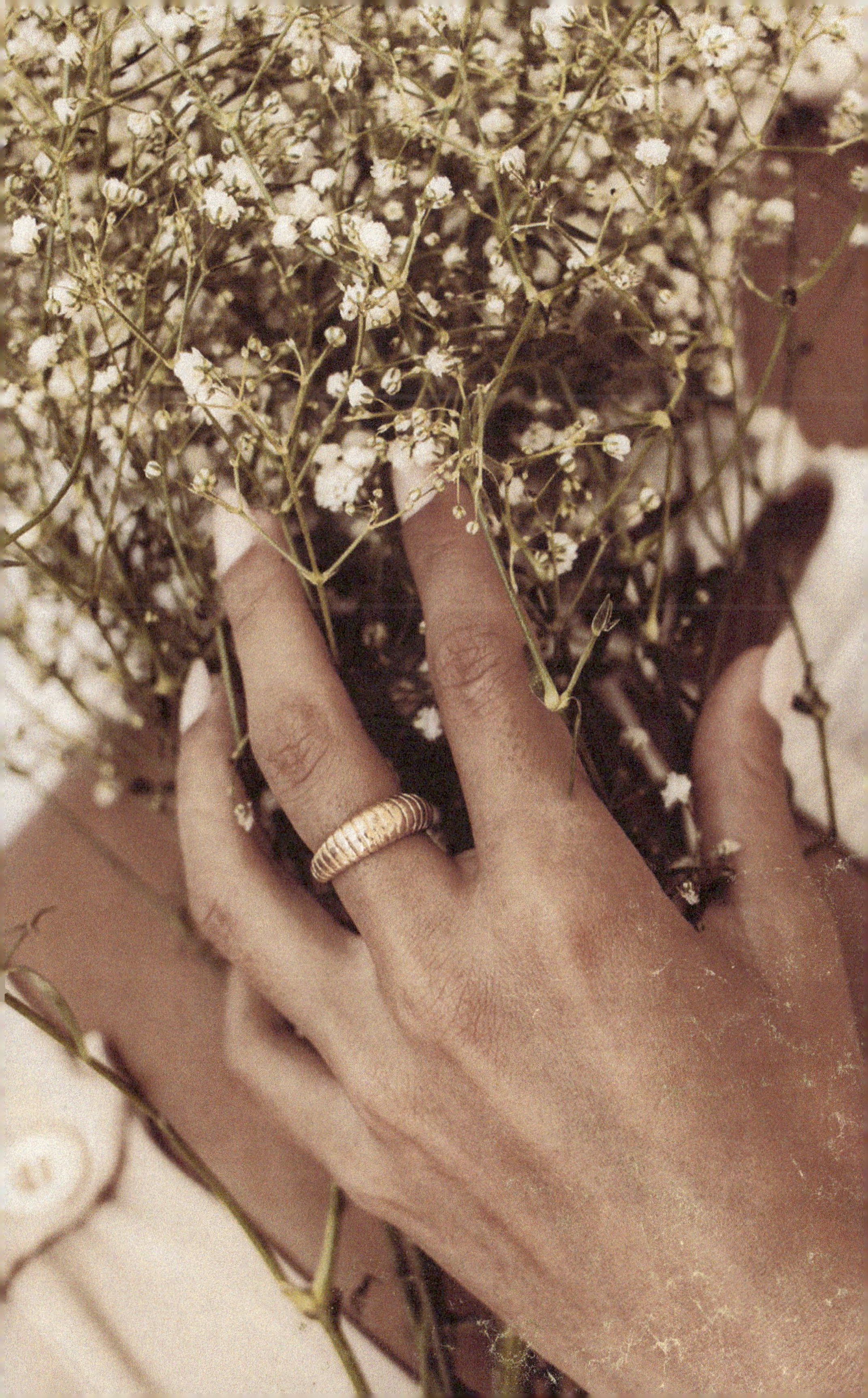

17

GALERIE LA VIGNE

Cinematography

*"If you were a movie
you'd be the opening scene."*

My *favorite actor* —
The most adored *picture to be in motion*
who can portray a *character*
and embody a *script*
writers could never finish.

Whose *dialogue*
can illuminate a packed theater
with not enough tickets
available for purchase.

I'd revisit you often
until the very last second of end credits —
My *Cinematography*.

Mouthful of Manners

The framework of your architecture
is imprinted as my alma mater.

Mouthful of manners
smothered in your nectar.

Bodies blending.

Stained sheets.

My favorite type of masterpiece.

The kind that unveils stretch marks in between
your *succulent thighs* only my eyes
have permission to see.
The type whose teeth
leave imprints in my skin,
and whose lips
leave hidden messages in hickies.

Explicit back arching,
leaving me wrapped in the warmth of your body heat.

Climactic ecstasy.

Pour adoucir ce qu'une proposition pourrait avoir de trop dur,
Vibius Virius, lorsqu'il exhorte les sénateurs de Capoue à prendre
du poison pour ne pas tomber vifs entre les mains des Romains,
au lieu de dire que ce poison leur ôtera la vie, périphrase
divin par une élégante périphrase le malheur dont ce breuvage
les délivrera et leur cache par cette figure les horreurs de la...

"Statuitis vero ubi que populum dona, quod nihil datum puerit, si non e
En fratio .... à contumeliis .
.... que manent.

With you

I'm home

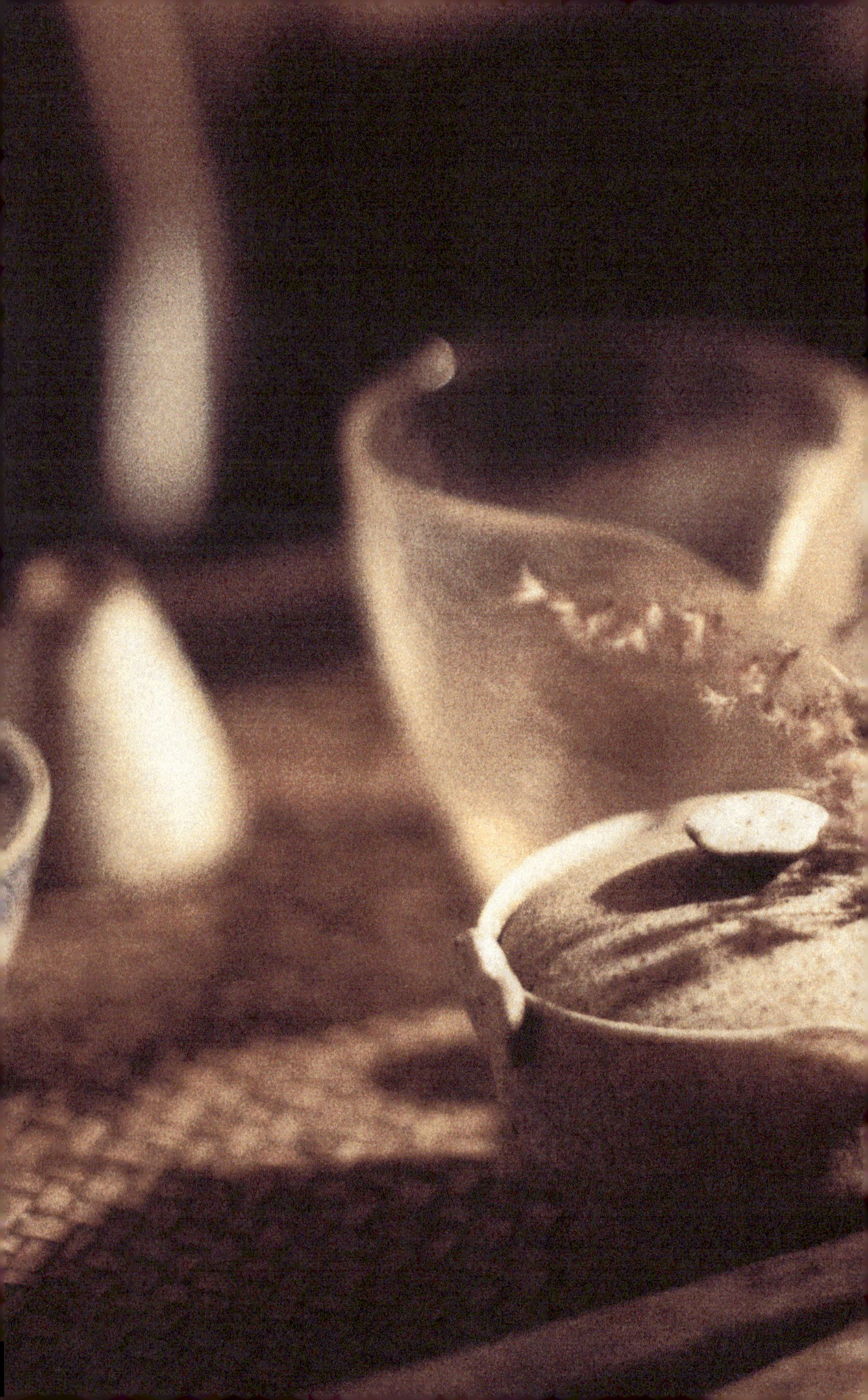

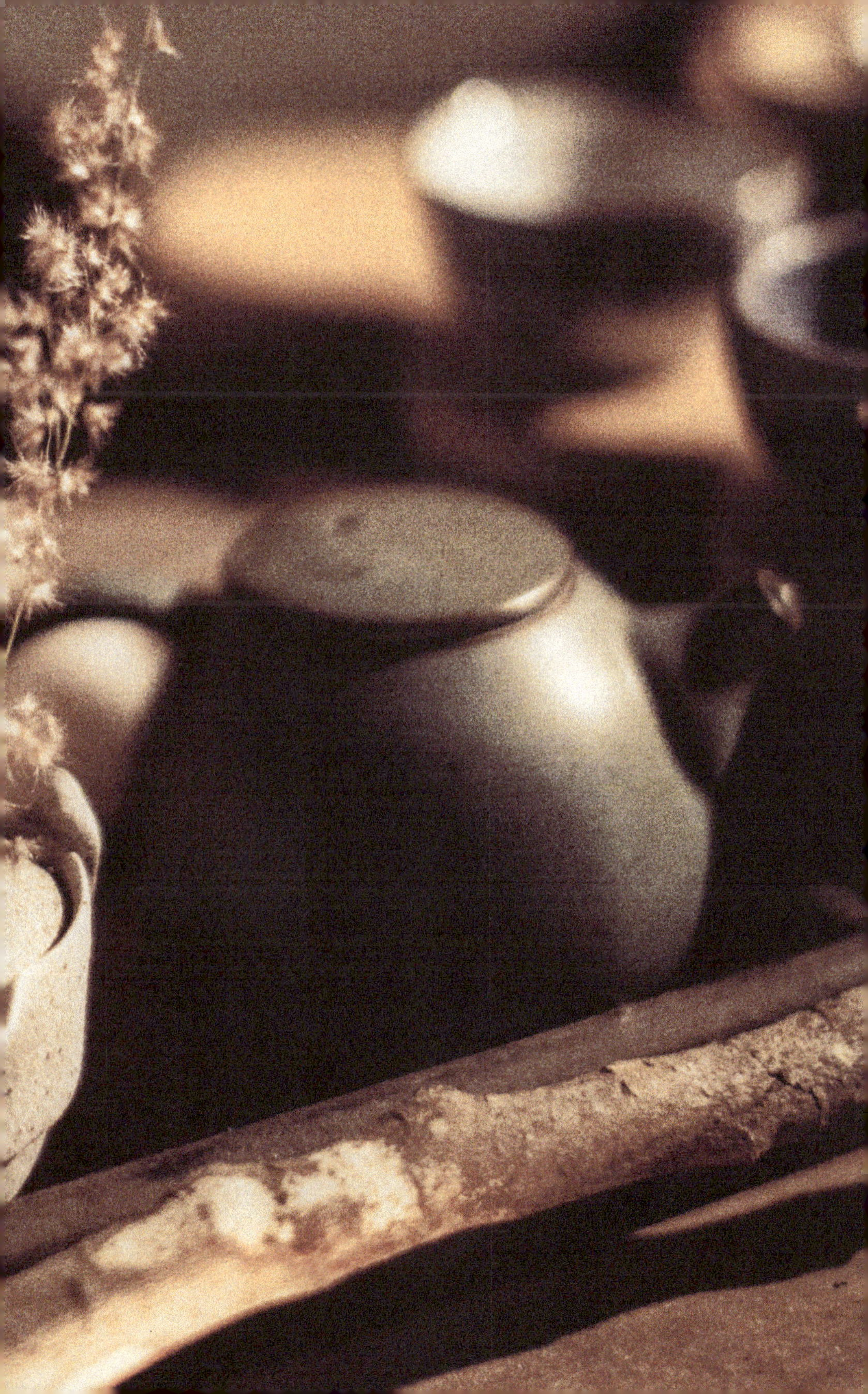

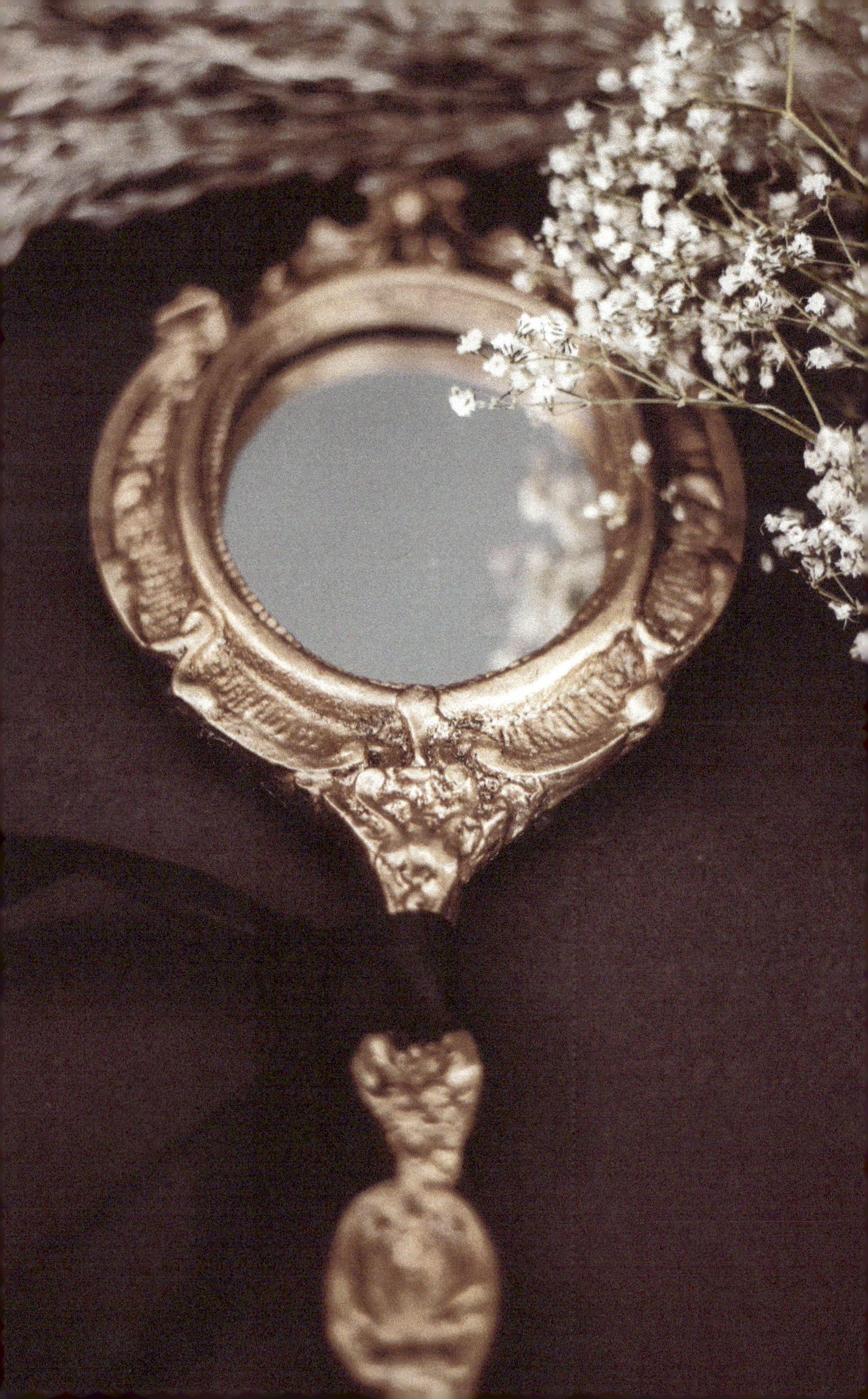

The Sun in Her Eyes

The sun in her eyes radiate a vibrancy
within each fine line eye crease.

Beautifully bridged
with a smile that ignites ablaze of warmth
with a "Welcome Home" message that you can't help but accept
the passion of an invitation.

Her presence eases the droplets of rain
and shows you the beauty within their reflection,
all at once.

The way she welcomes
what so many run away from.

I'm in awe.

I'm in love.

Finer Details in Life

She's the *finer details* in this life.

The *painter*
to my favorite lilac sky.

The *melodist*
of the roaring high tides.

The *conductor*
to my ears —
An everlasting symphony.

The *senescent sand*
that provides endless tranquility
with promised
footprints that follow me from behind,
guiding me back
so I don't lose track.

The *aged wine*
that kisses my eager lips,
leaving me tipsy at night.

And the perfectionist,
who brings the under-appreciated
details of this life to light.

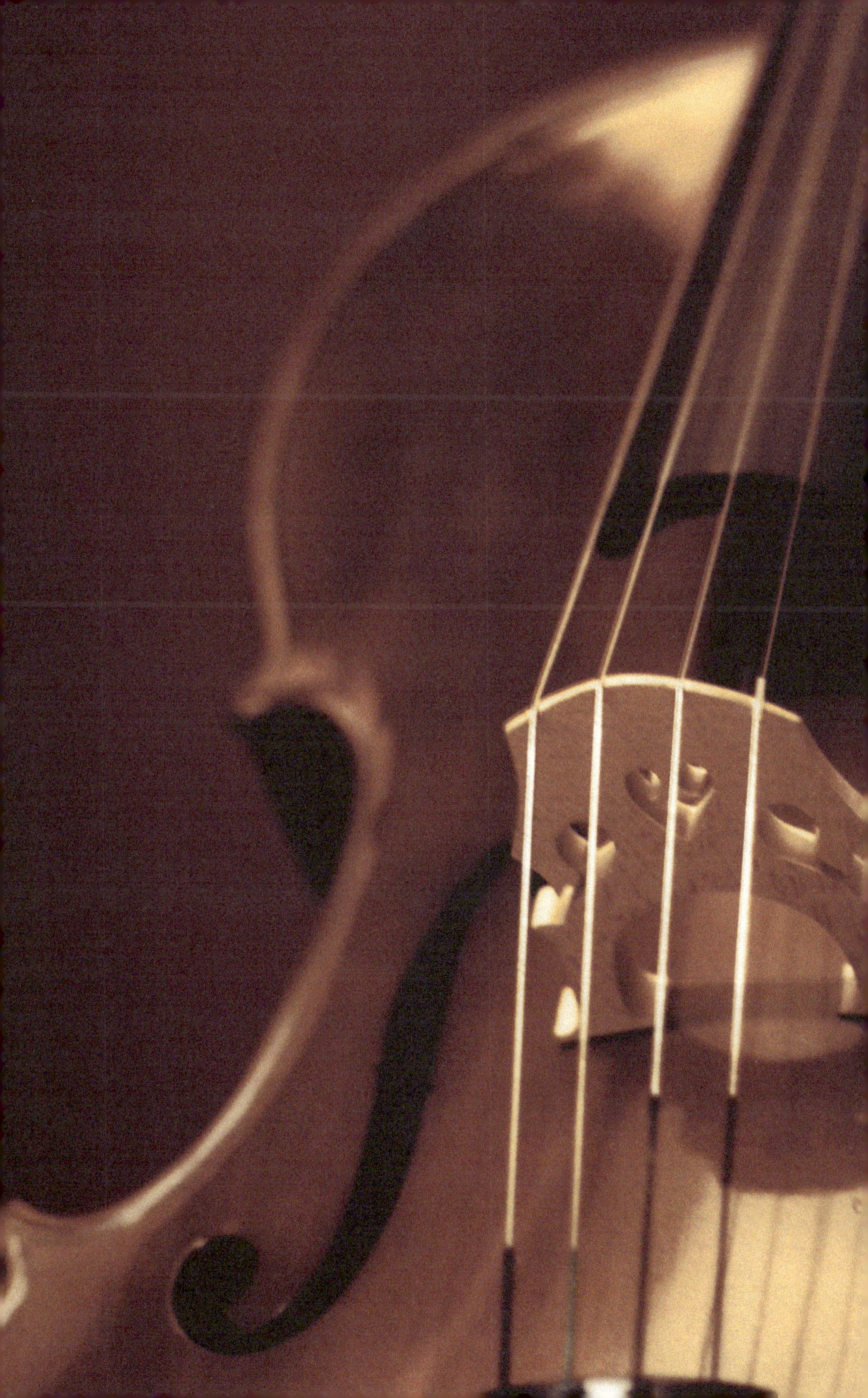

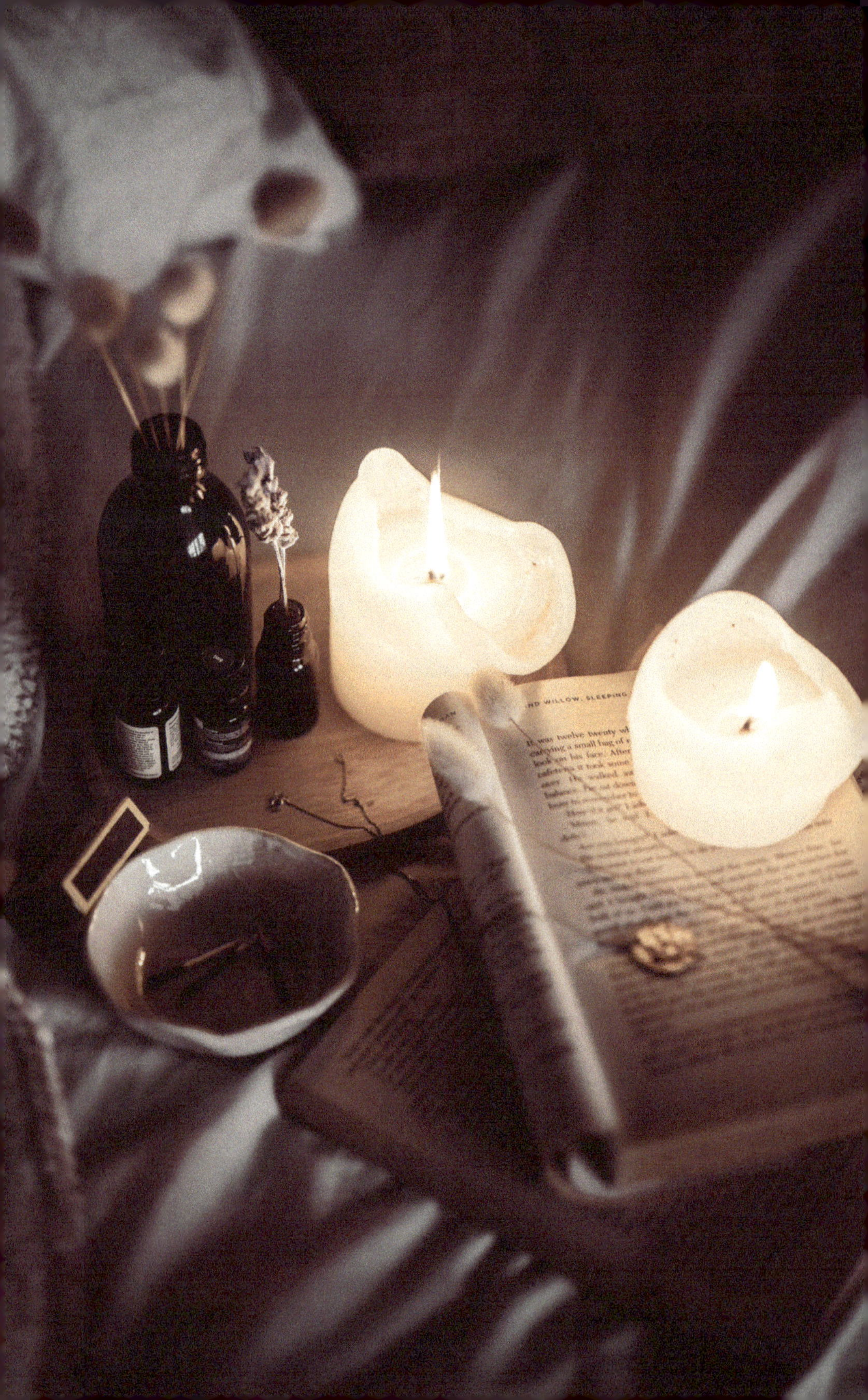
WILLOW, SLEEPING

Fluent

The voice of your eyes is deeper
than any language ever created.

Let me interpret every one of your messages
o n e   s e n t e n c e
at a time.

Line by line.

Just for you, I will become fluent.

Old Fashioned

The *taste* of you lingers
on my fingers
as you finish.

Without hesitation,
you fill me up to the brim,
and my *lips* sip you in
like an *old fashioned*.

How could my *thirst*
for you ever be modest and resist
going in for seconds?

Your taste leaves me intoxicated.

2. Scarlet Fever After-Effects
Put 5 drops of antidote dust in a pint of
...give a tablespoonful three times a day to
those that have been subject to the disease
This is something that has had....
effective and which never fails....

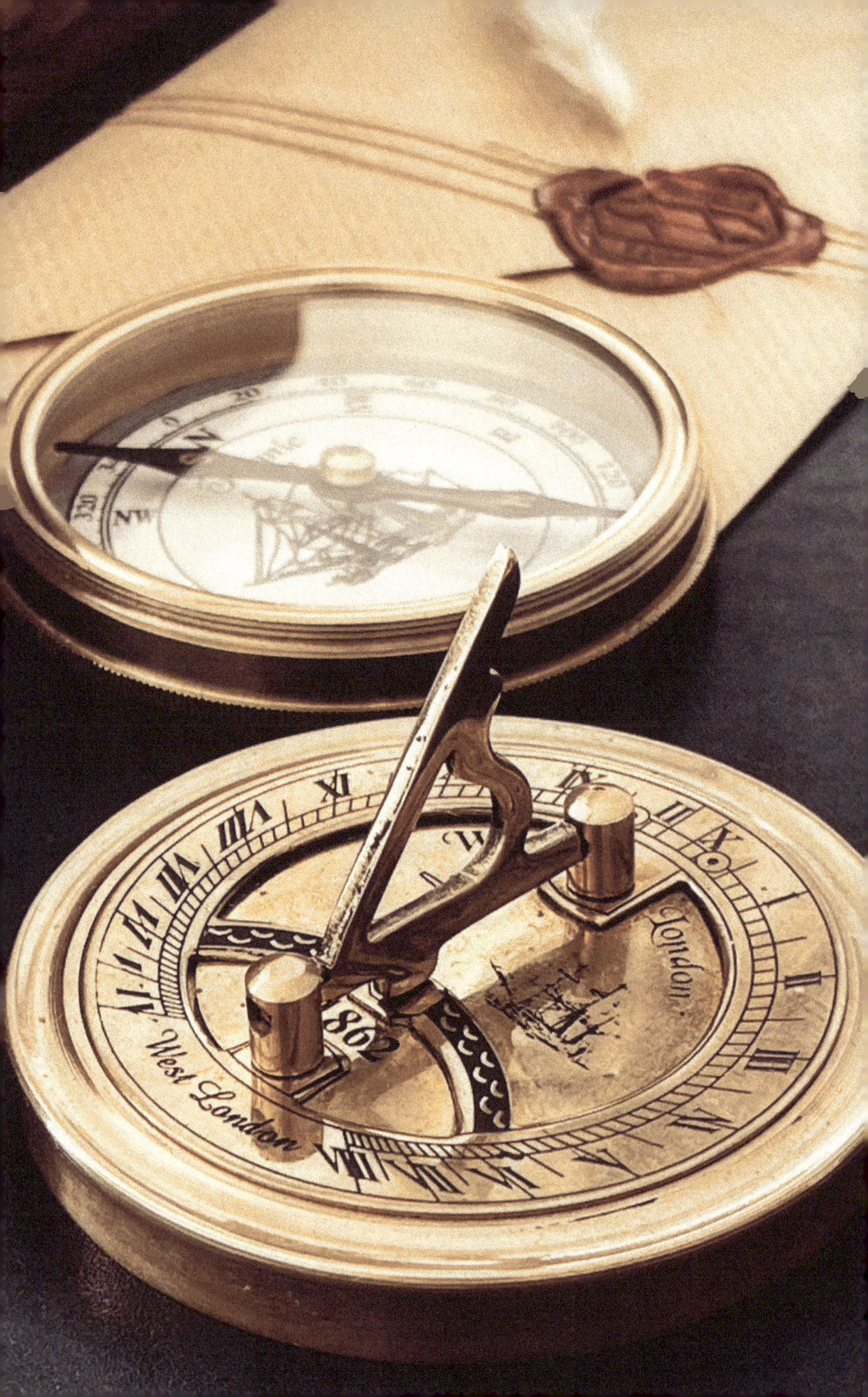
West London
London

Sunset Gold

Gentle salutations of *sunset gold*
pours down the avenue of her back.

Healing hands amidst purposeful communication
through confessional fingertips
leaves an imprint
of her signature blueprint.

Loving her out loud translates to a language
of gazing at the constellations casting on her skin,
counting the cadence within her breath -
tracing every ebb & crevice
of her curves & edges.

Forenoon sun rays awakens next to us
bleeding through the blinds,
committed to reach in for her warmth,
yearning for her touch,
eager to become enough.

Soul vs Flesh

Our souls
connected
before our flesh
ever did.

And
that made
all the difference.

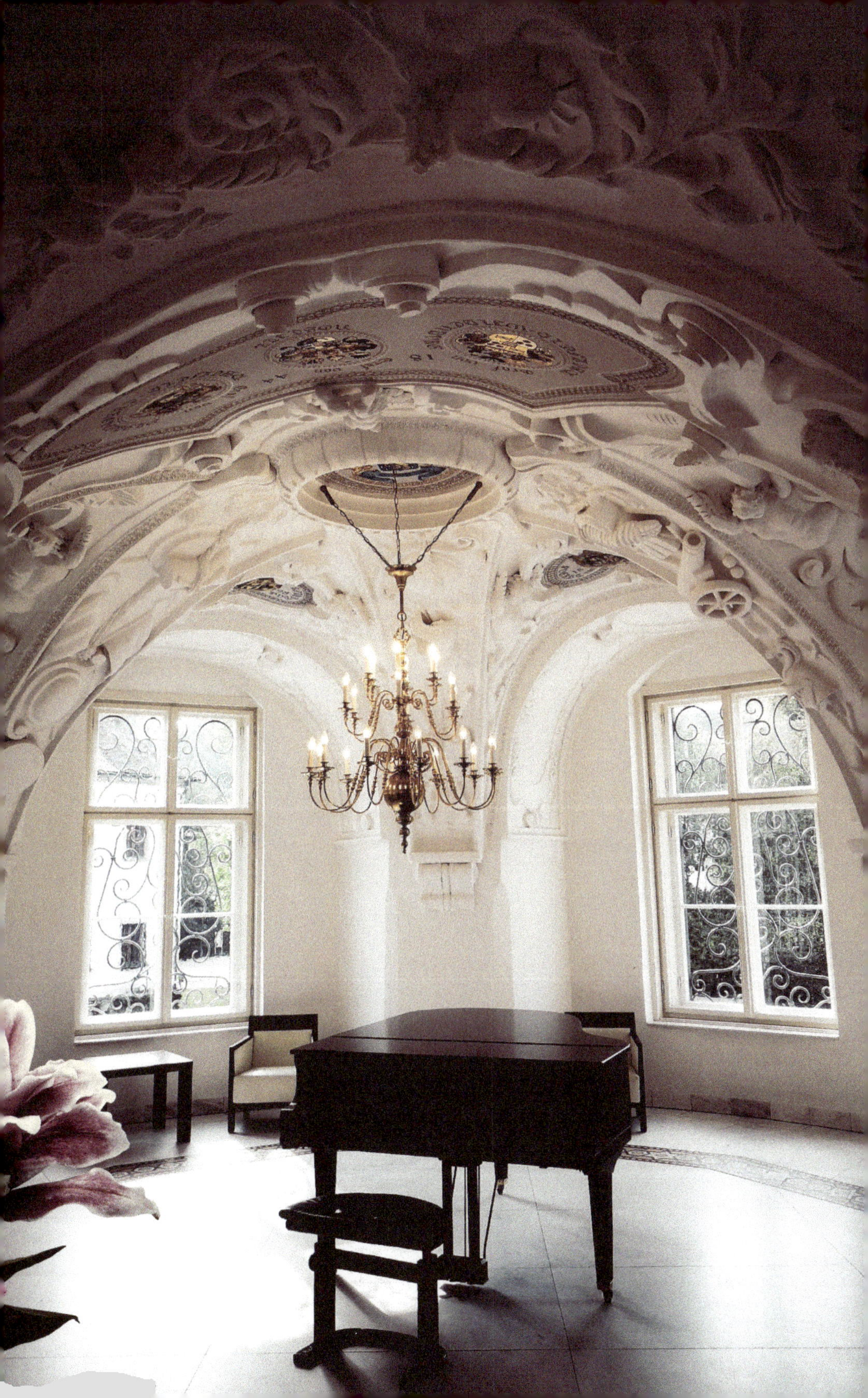

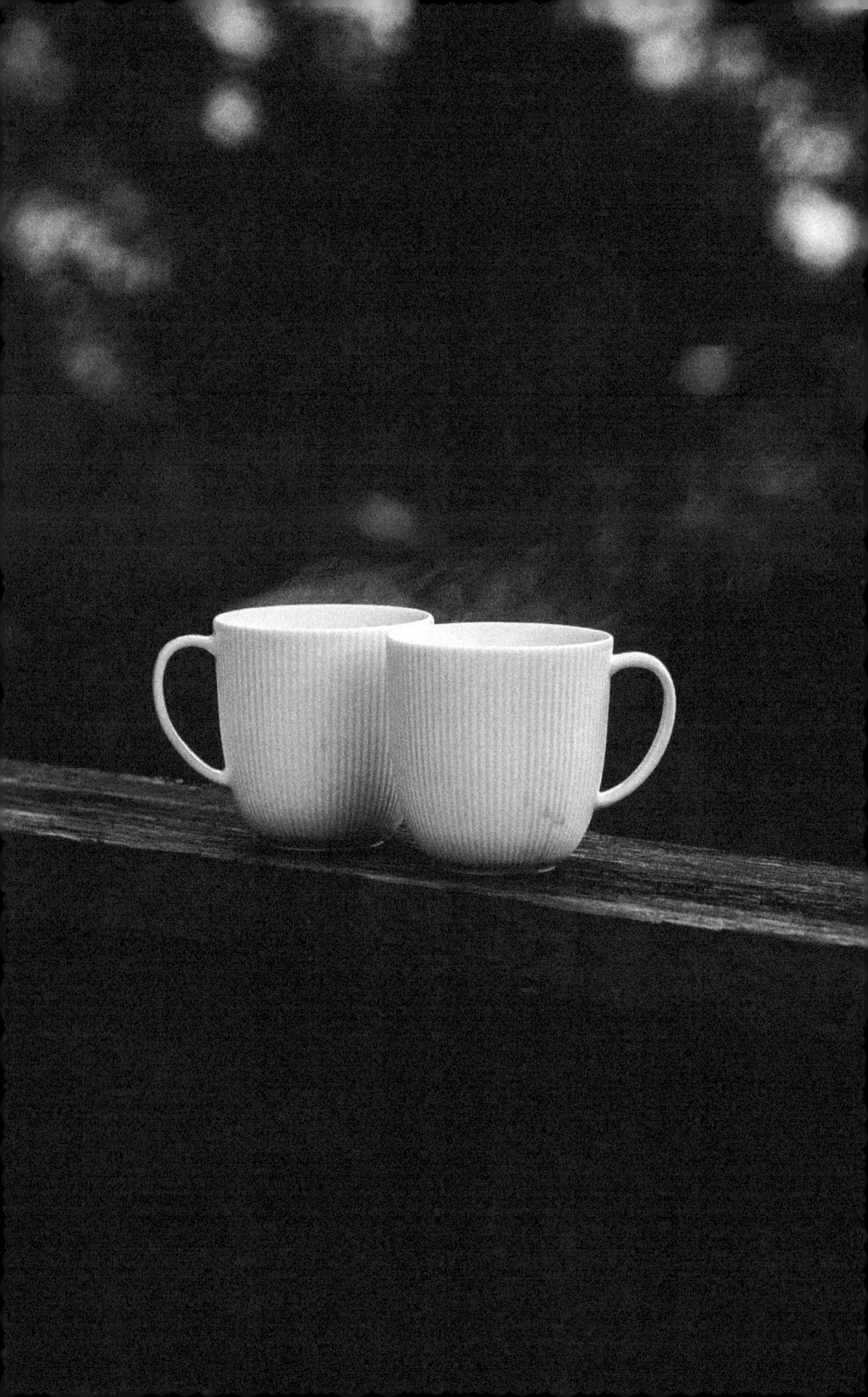

Drenched Thoughts

Dive your face in between my conscious,
use your fingers to spread my *drenched thoughts*.
Make me cum to a conclusion
I never want to finish.

Omnipotent

My paradigm, I tell the wind about you,
hoping she would be so kind and carry to you moments
within a gentle breeze that coaxes your ears
with a gentle psithurism
that holds my deepest of confessions.

I bathe my bare feet in between mothers shorelines
while holding her hand within the sand,
transferring conversations enclosed in an orphic current,
optimistic that she'll find her way to your littoral.

I channel the omnipotence of our moons gravity
and empty the sky's way of navigation
in order to entwine your finger within constellations.

I pluck the colors from opalescent sunsets
and preserve them in my pockets
hopeful to hand deliver them to you
rearranged and wrapped in a bouquet.

I'm interwoven within the liberal arts of your love,
consistently studying the silhouette
of the most requested subject
that I can never get enough of; *Us.*

XIII

MAMZEL MARIE

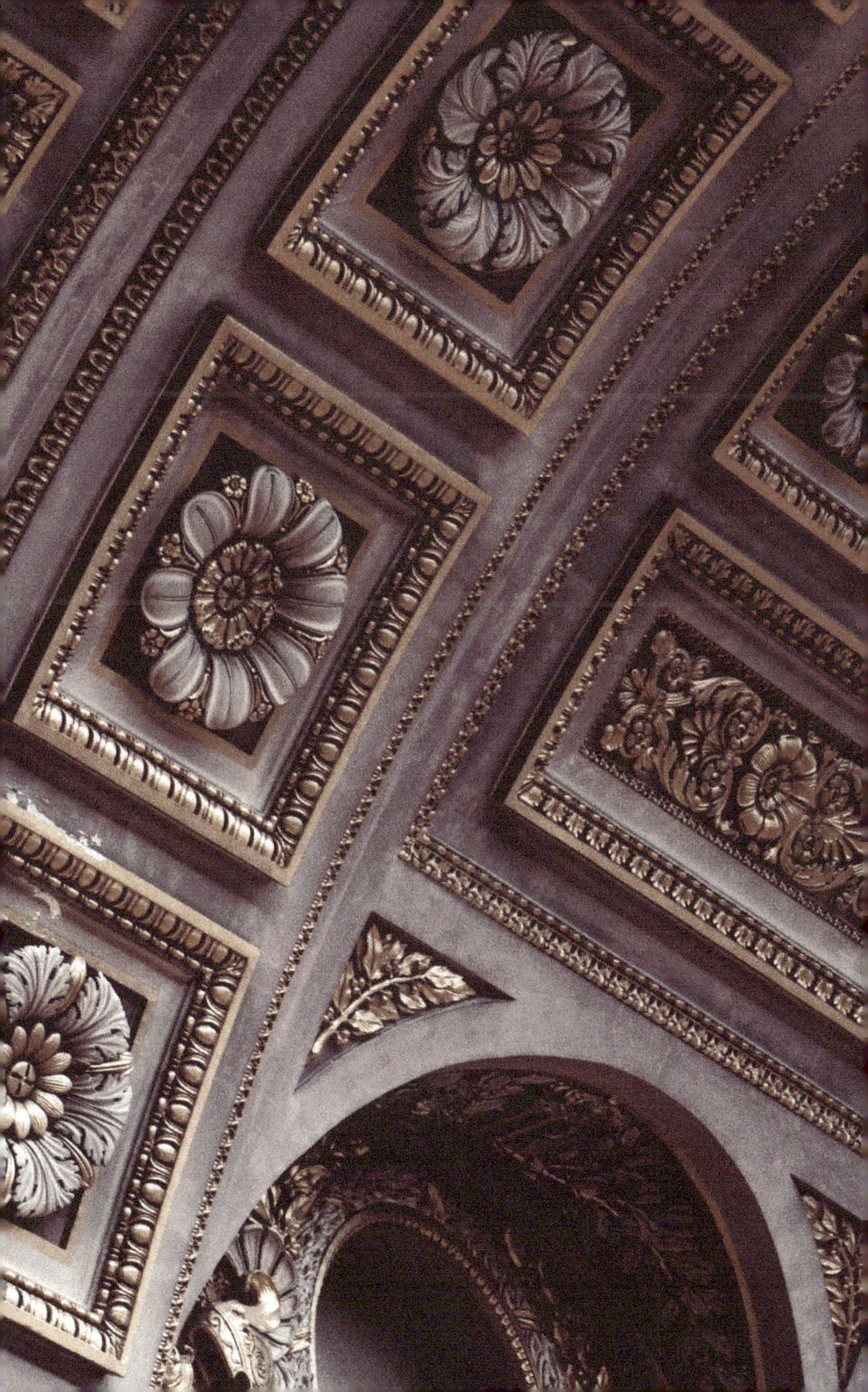

Idiosyncrasies

For the woman that this is all for, just know that even with all of these pieces and every artistic creation that will naturally follow for you, I still feel as if I fail at articulating all the love that I have for you well enough, but I will continually do so, unfailingly. The moment you entered my life, and the time that has passed within the years until this very second, my love pursues to fervidly bloom for you. You have moved my soul in ways I never knew had a direction. Falling for you has been like accepting a dance I never thought I'd willingly stand up and walk to the dance floor for. The rhythm of your heart and warmth within your souls melody is like RnB in the 90s. Home doesn't need an address, it is within a person, and you are that for me. Home.

I'm in awe of you everyday with all that you are,
the culmination of all the little things:

- From the way that you think and how your whole body becomes a vessel of energy the moment you're mentally stimulated, especially when you start creating music.
- The way your voice becomes soft and tender when you feel safe and taken care of.
- The depth that you reach when you get invested into your passions and how you articulate new interests when you speak.
- I love how I know that you can't have Pico de Gallo on your Chipotle order because it has tomatoes and it'll make your acid reflux react.
- I adore how you love extra honey in your tea in your designated tea cup.
- I love how I buy two separate chocolate flavored bars

because I know you don't like caramel even though I do, so I make sure to get you your Kit Kats to be safe.
- I love how you are always enthusiastic to watch scary movies at night even though I'm terrified, but I feel safer because you're by my side.
- I cherish the peace you bring when you run your fingers through my curly hair.
- The glow that you emit when your follow your skincare routine with your aloe and vitamin E.
- I praise how you check the boxes in your planner with a heart so you have tangible verification of the tasks you've completed within the week because it makes you feel accomplished and productive.
- I love how you leave your bobby pins and hair ties in random places of our home because I know walking to the jar is too exhausting for you, so I get to put them back for you when you need them again.
- I hold dear how I get to fold your towel identical to mine because you hang your towel on the shower rack completely different.
- I'm thankful to have your voice on repeat by listening to the songs that you've written about me.
- I'm devoted to learning more about your culture because it brings me closer to you, so I have no problem going to the Korean super market to get all of the ingredients to your favorite meals with your mom on the phone to guide me through the process to ease your homesickness.
- You're worth writing down the names of the mountains your parents took you hiking when you were a baby, so I can take you back one day.
- I respect the way you sit in stillness, even in the distant days.

So, as you continue to read, just know that I see your radiance in everything, even in the most quotidian things that others would call mundane. I'm in love with every ounce of you and all the idiosyncrasies that you are. I'm proud to love every inch of your portfolio, and not just the whole put together picture, but the pixelation and discoloration that comes with the development process.

Thank you for these years of trusting and allowing me to see you in your most vulnerable forms. Out of all the lifetimes I could have met you in, I'm so glad it's this one, and even when this lifetime ends, I'll meet you in another.

You bring to life the depth of human experience.

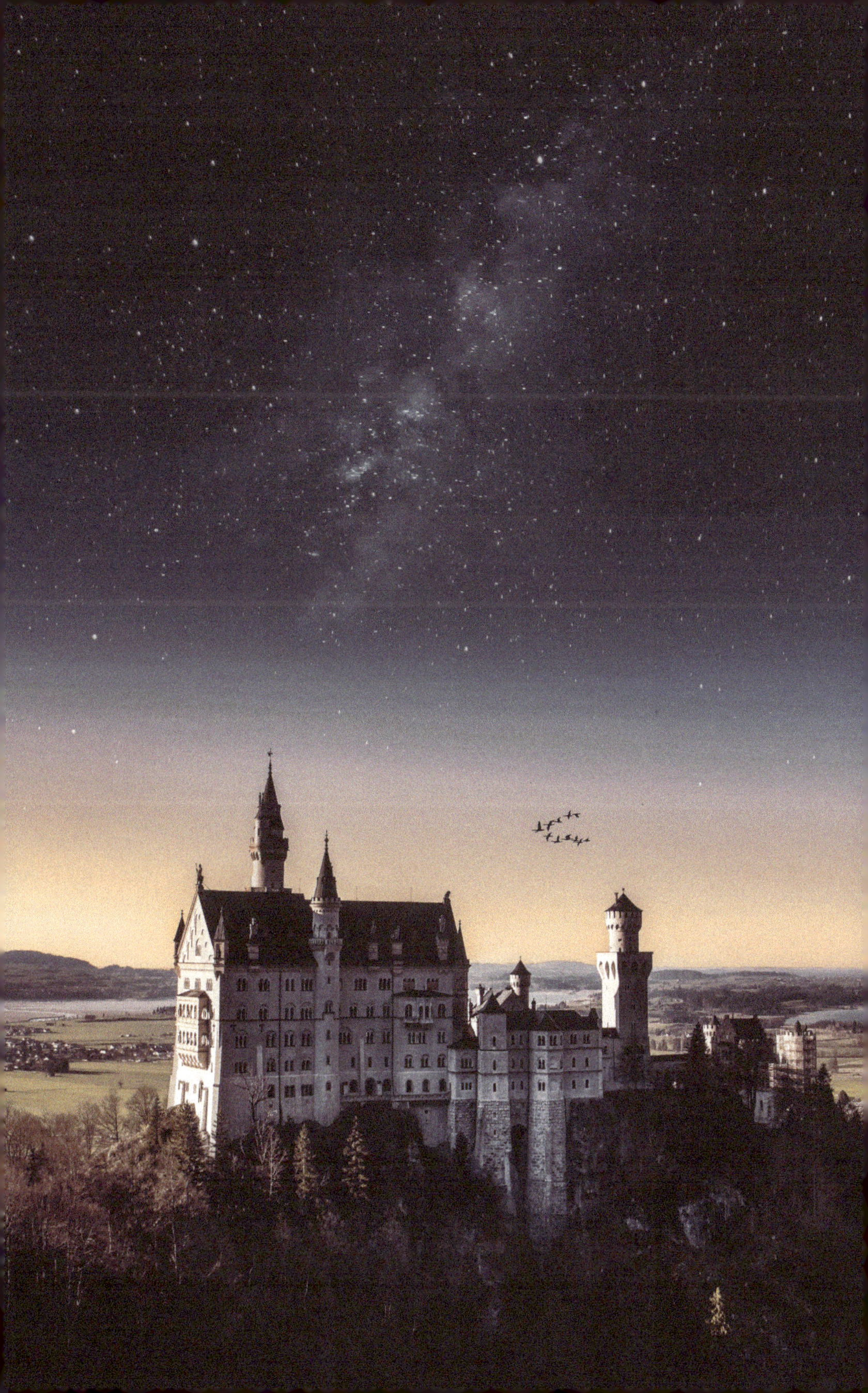

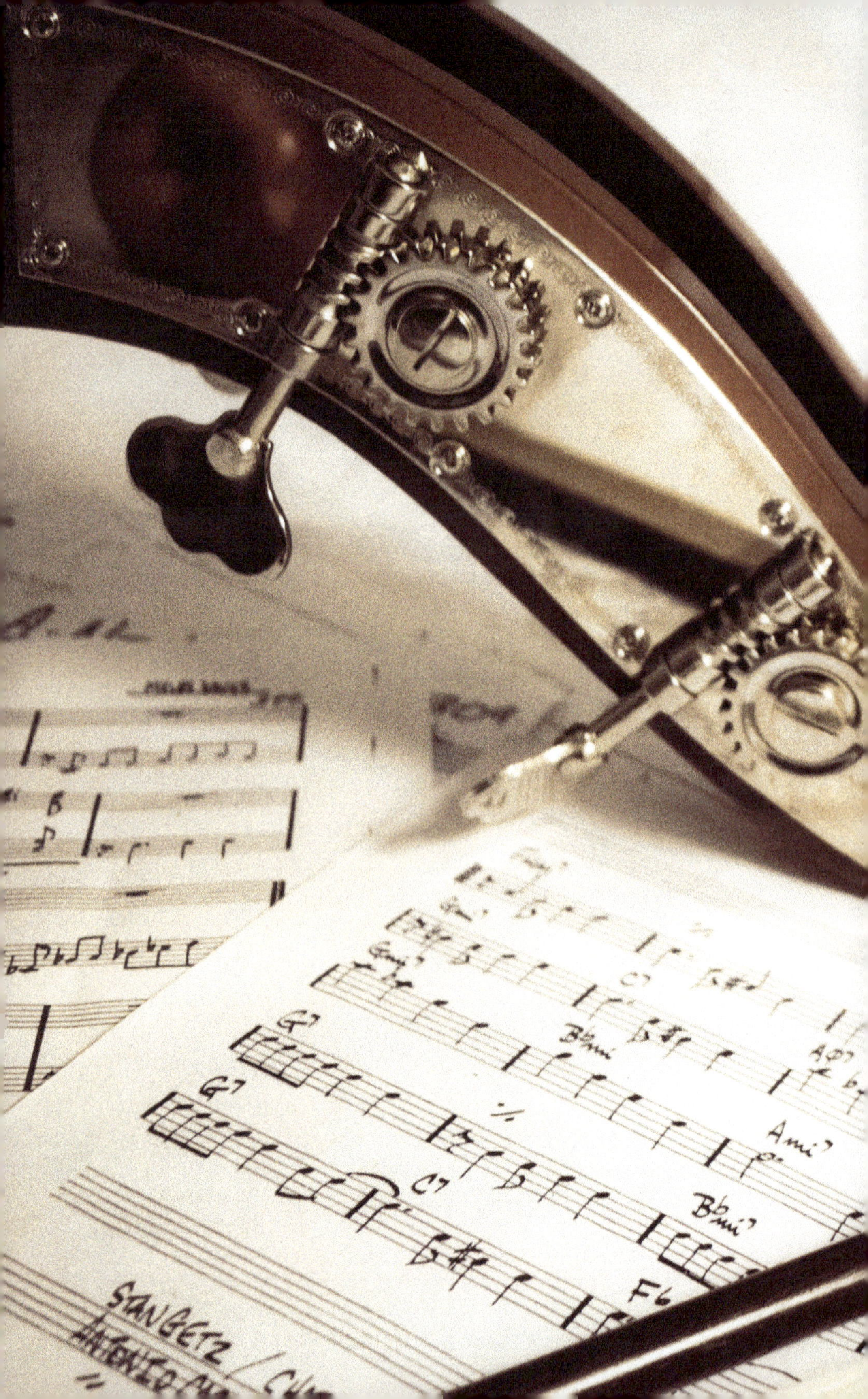
STAN GETZ

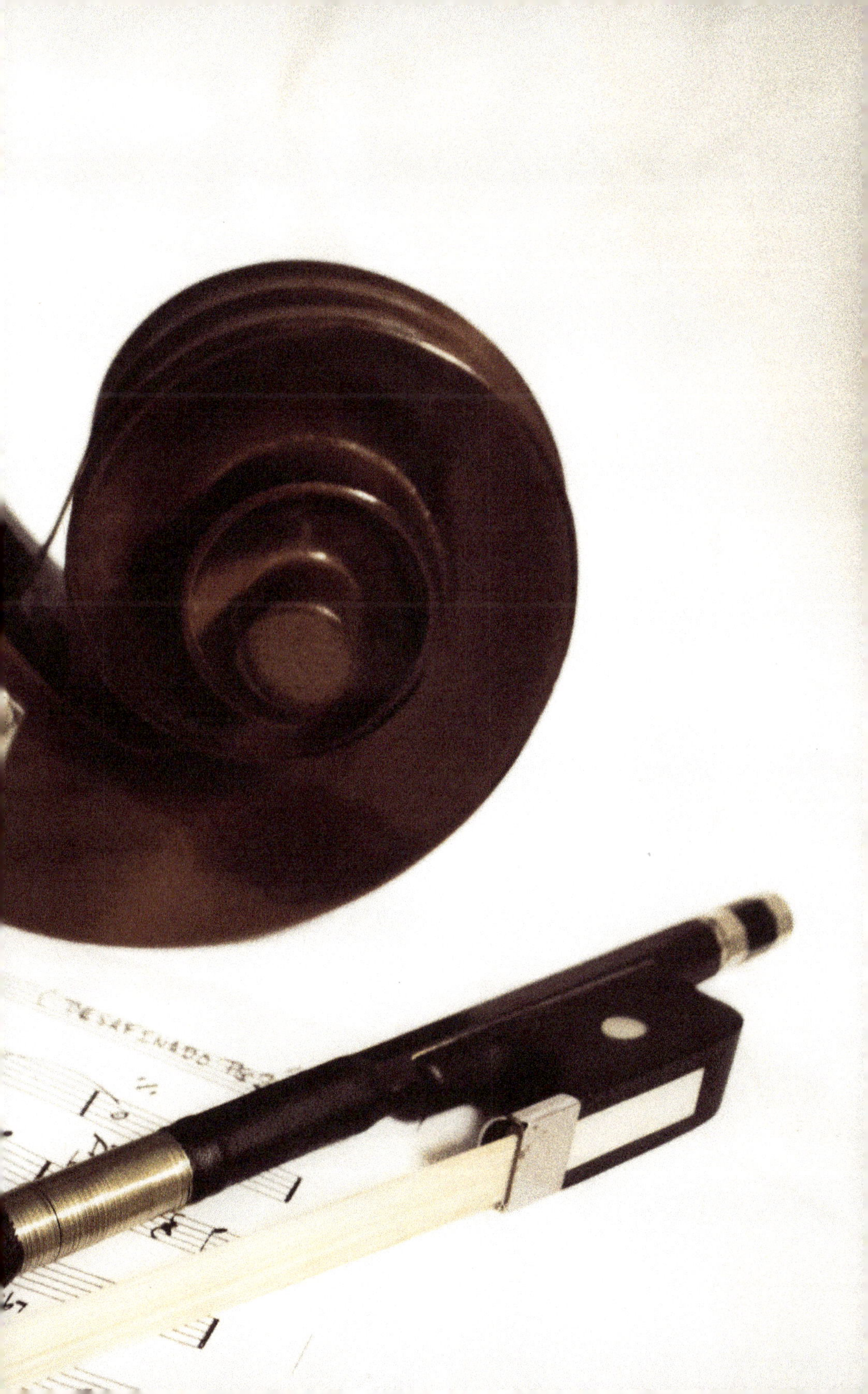
DESAFINADO

Point of View

I wish you could see the way that your own shadow
carries a distant echo
sending a frequency only I've known -
our own morse code.

How you hold untold conversations
from your mouthful of words
as they slip between each breath.
If only you were capable of hearing the cadence
that you speak keeps us both in sync.

To witness how your transparency
creates thorough Baroque portraits
with architectural visions painting stories
in between every blink.

The way your promises leave proof of safety
in the security of imprints
with your footsteps acting as guidance
in ways I never knew had a direction.

I wish I could show you
my *Point Of View* of You.

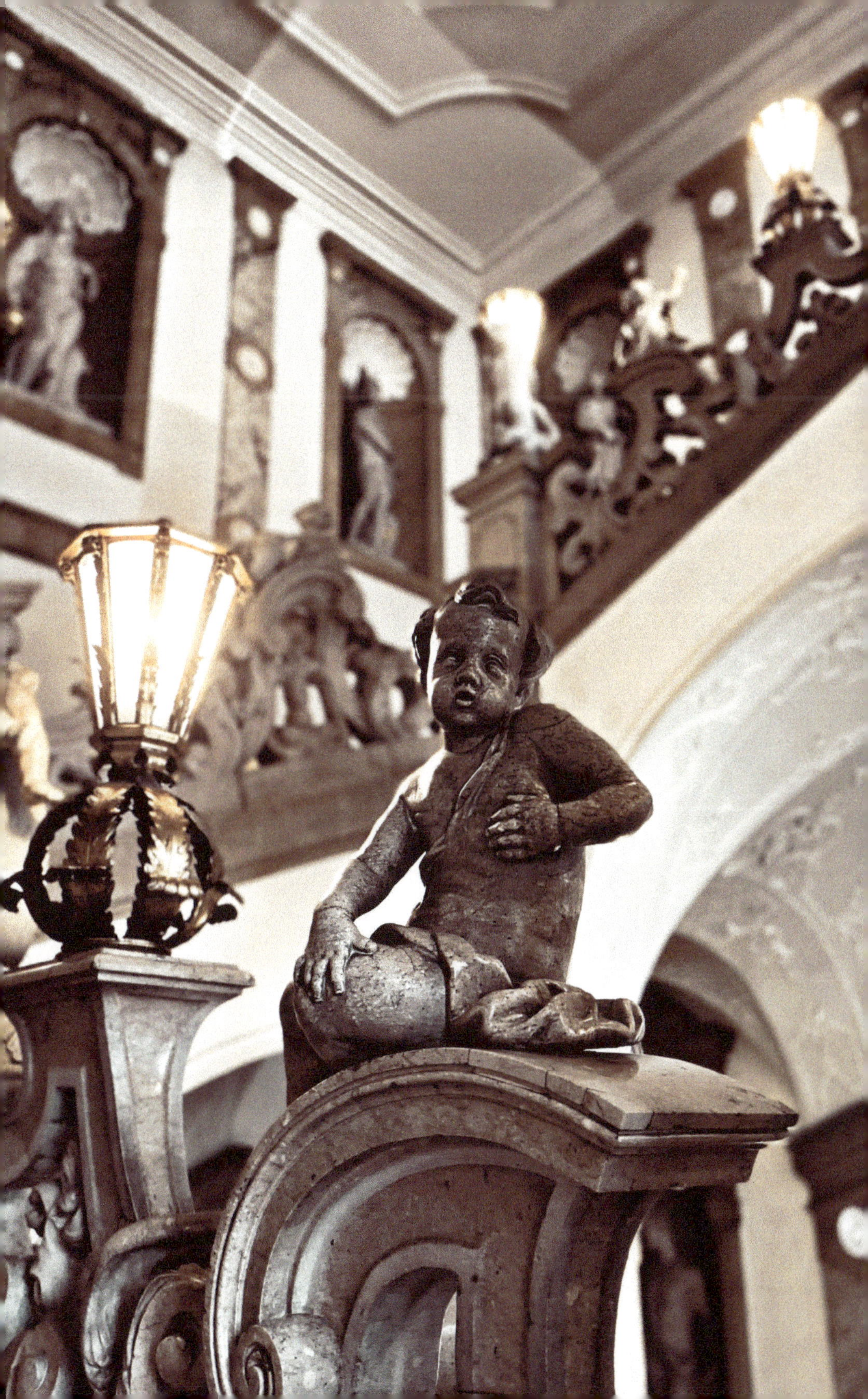

MATVRA ATAS
VIRTVTE ET FORTVNA
DEDVCENTIBVS
SISTITVR

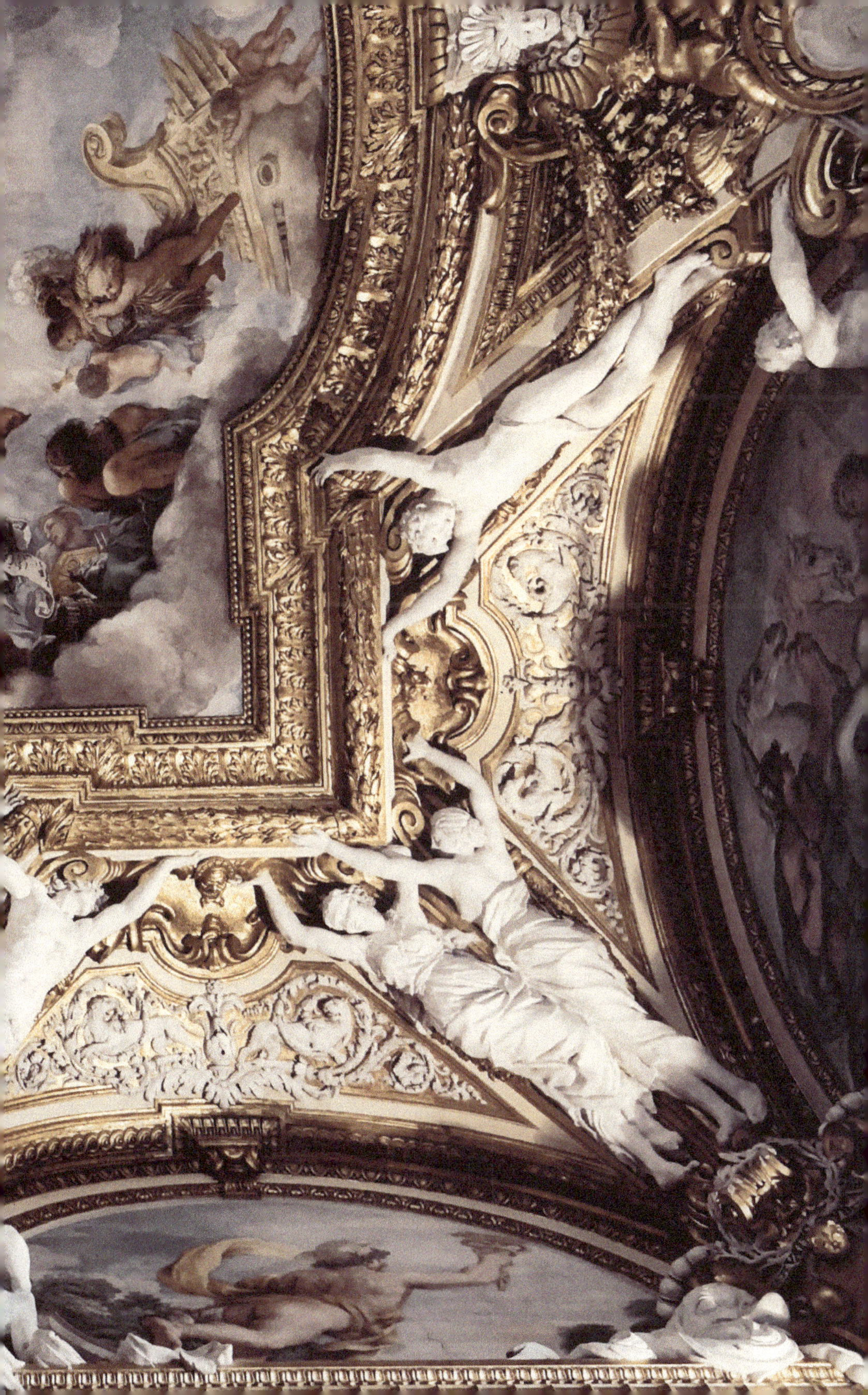

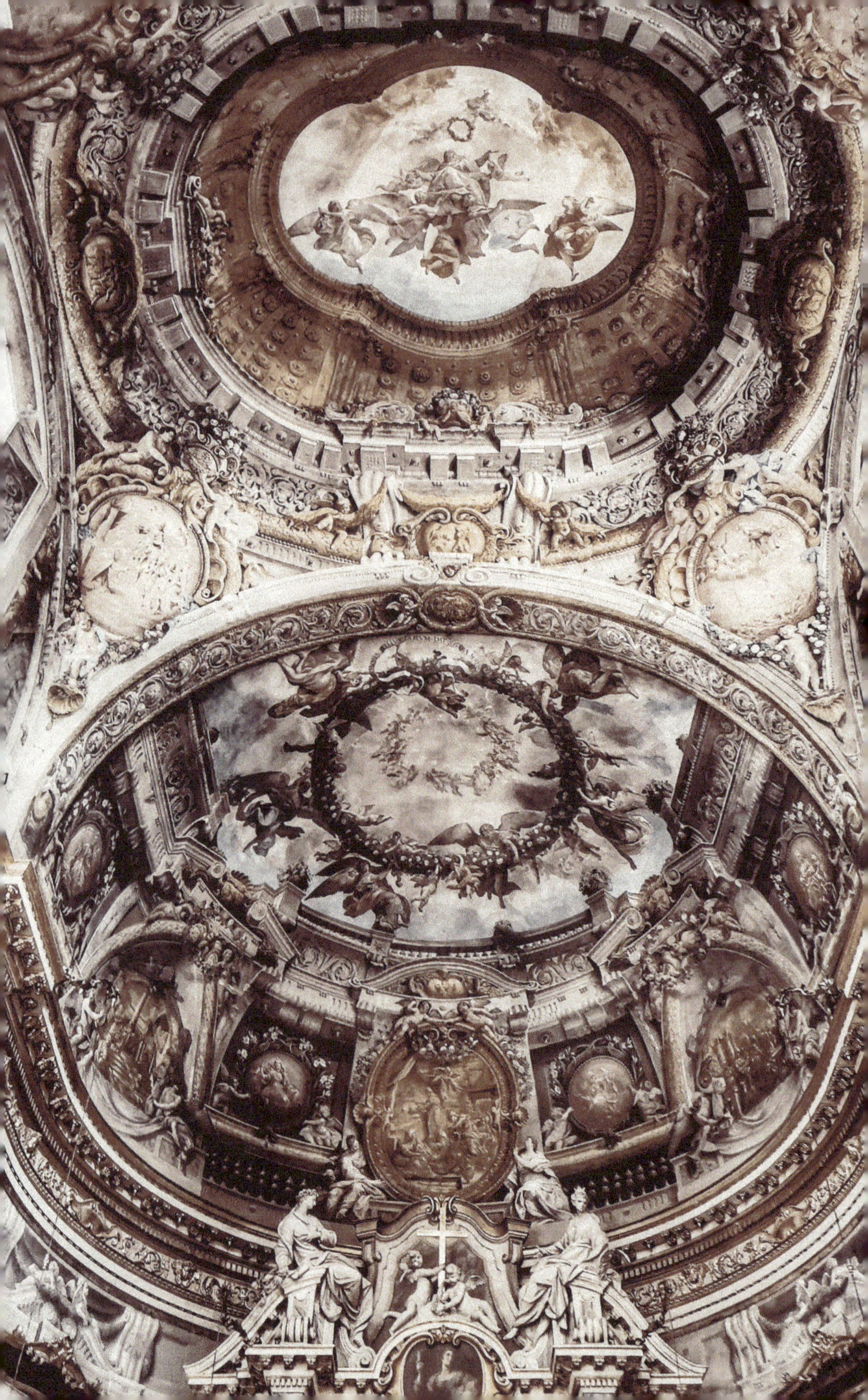

Language of Water

Mastering a new tongue, experiencing new tastes
feels like an eternal cascade,
a melting glacier.

Writing in the language of water
is realizing a stream never carries
a flow that holds irrelevance.

I refuse to speak to you in such a manner
that words can feel redundant,
and images can't hold catalysts.

I refuse my words for you to feel anything less
than vessels full of perfumes,
veins carrying sounds,
and arteries holding atmospheres.

Malibu

Who knew that *Malibu*
could become jealous of the way
that I turn all of my attention towards you
as opposed to her tempestuous waves
or her mountainous views.

What she failed to realize
is that I would rather bathe in a *tide*
filled with the depth of your eyes.

How I would prefer to sleep in your sand
as I learn to count each granularity
within your capillaries
that sits in the palm of your hand.

How I favor becoming immersed
within the intimacy of experiencing the currents
capsulated in God's greatest creation,

— a Woman.

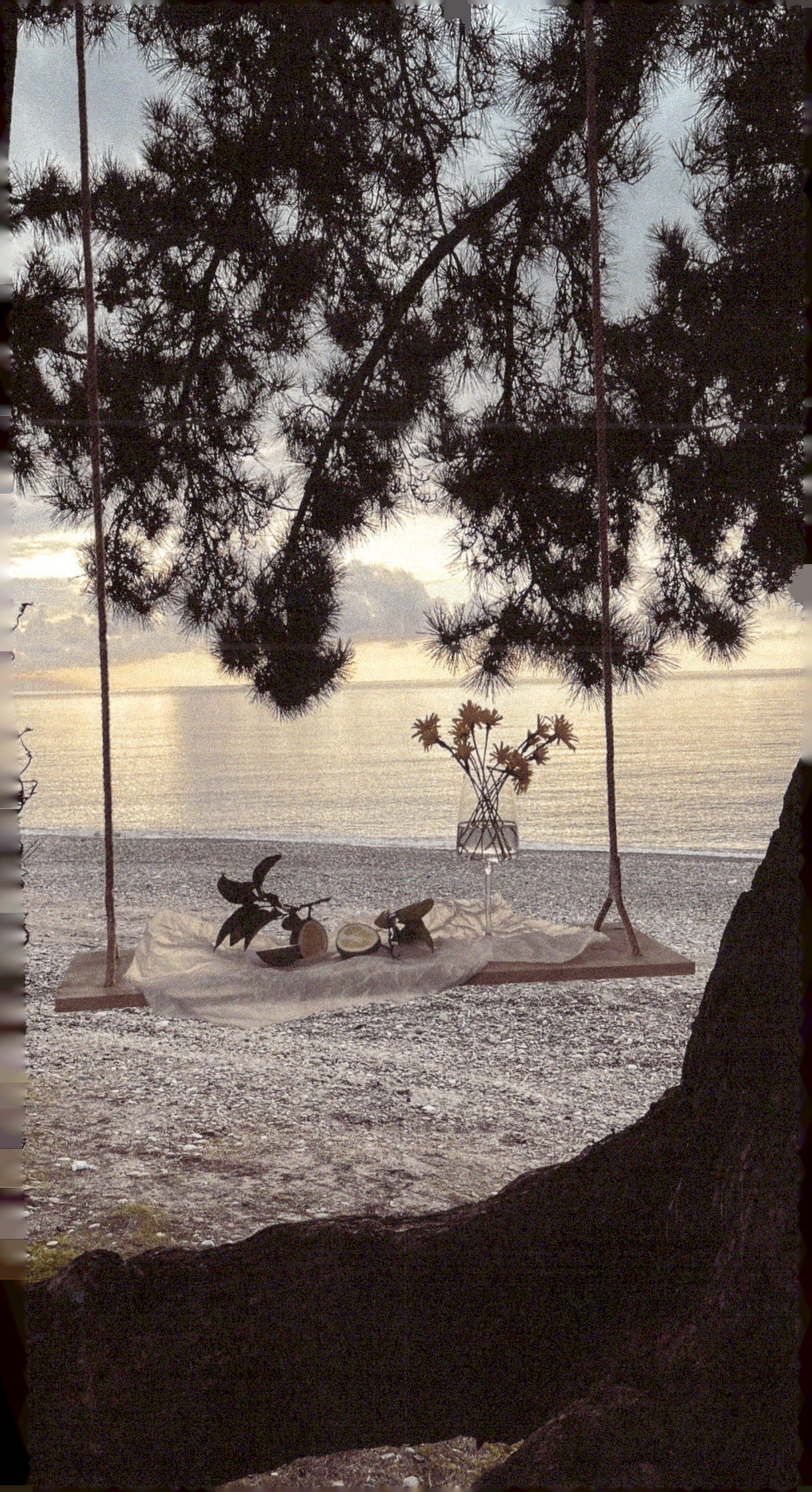

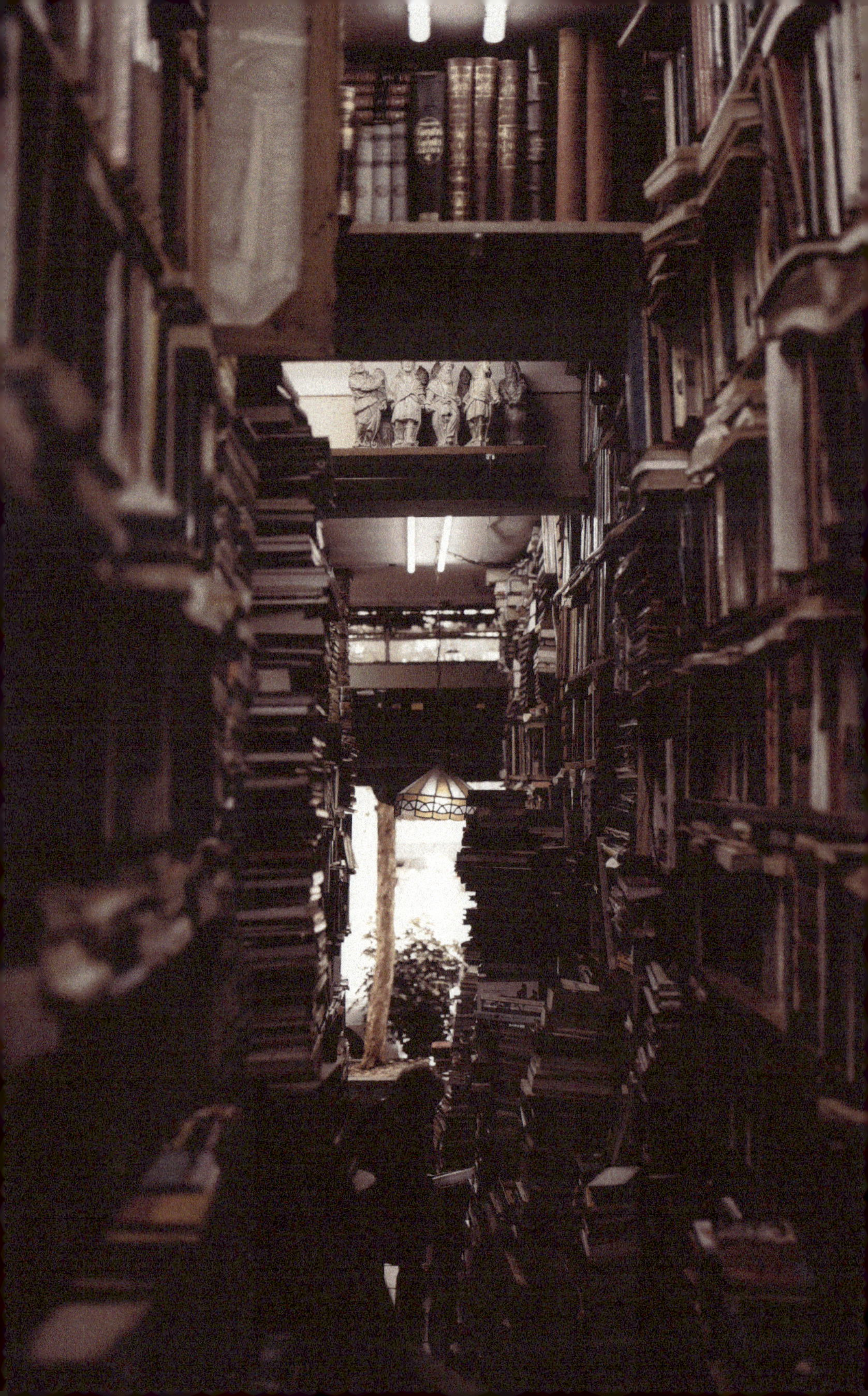

Shakespeare

Why does her love make me want to write in such
a way that it would make Edgar Allan Poe
& Maya Angelou blush?

Is this what *Hozier's muse* felt like?
Does this equivalate to *Shakespeare's intensity*
when he would write?
This is anything but *A Dead Poets Society*.

w

The way she holds *lips of currency,*
- otherworldly.

The way she embodies imagery
that leaves my palms
drenched in syrupy nostalgia
and *coffee stained book sheets.*

Her existence refreshes ones memory of Earth's divinity
that ripens the *air of petrichor,*
a fresh ice-kissed autumn breeze,
and rustling of the leaves.

There's not a single cosmo inside of me that could ever be
satisfied with the thought of her trace not being on me.

Ethereal

Her luminosity reminds me
of Southern California sunlight.

Her name melts off my tongue
like falling snow in the winter.

She is ethereally memorized
within my mind.

Eternally embraced by art like a pressed flower
in-between paper and words printed in my pages.

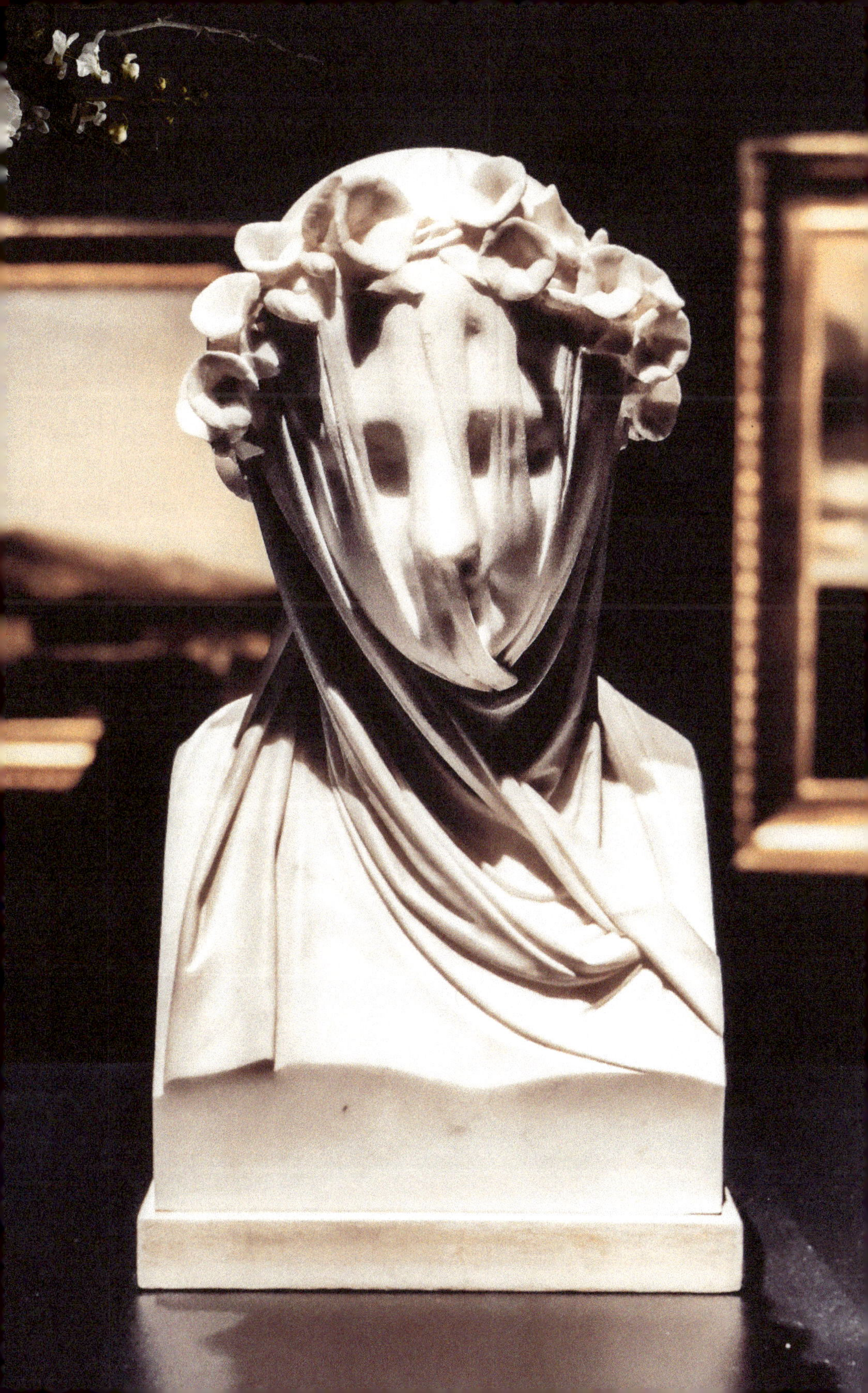

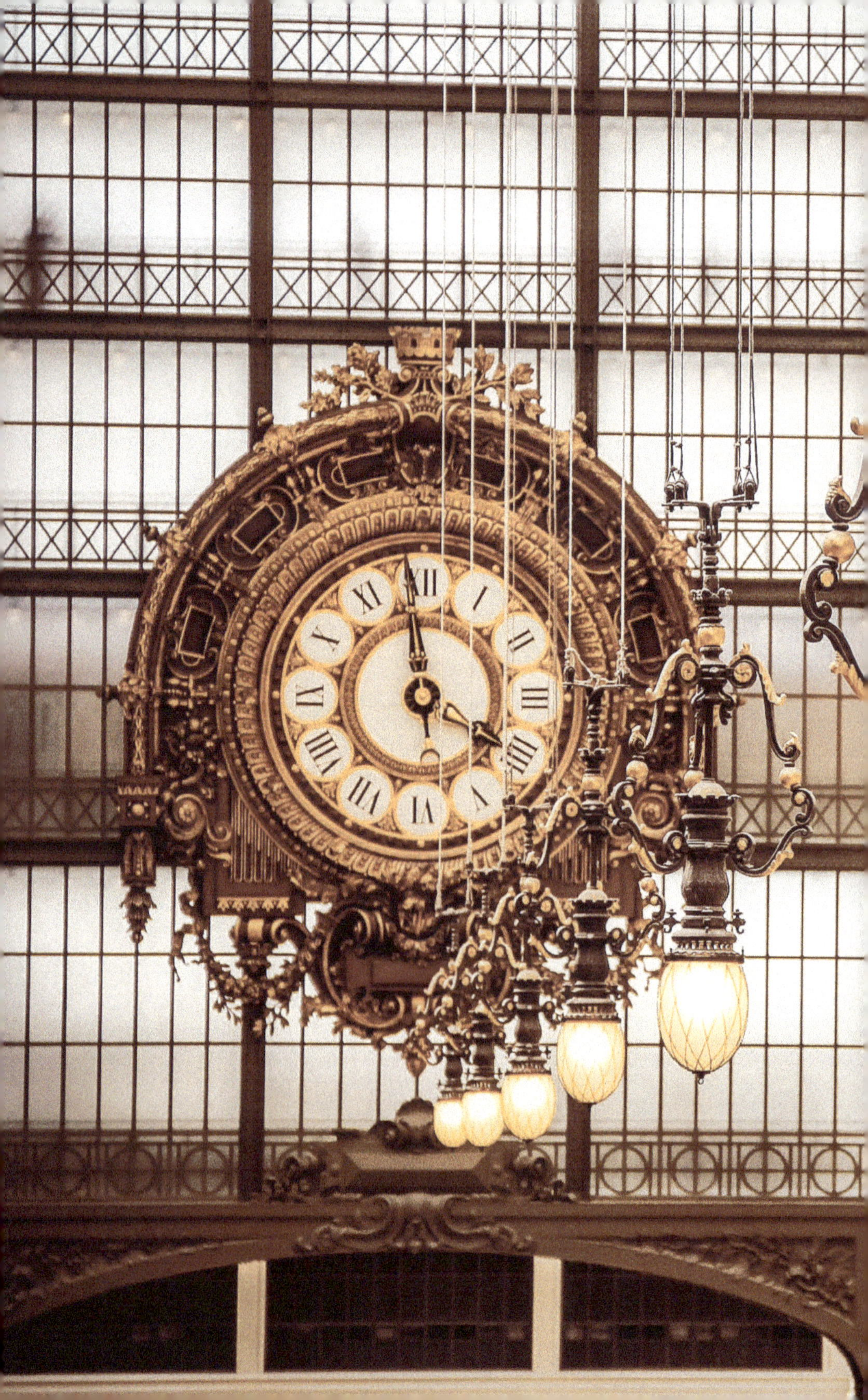

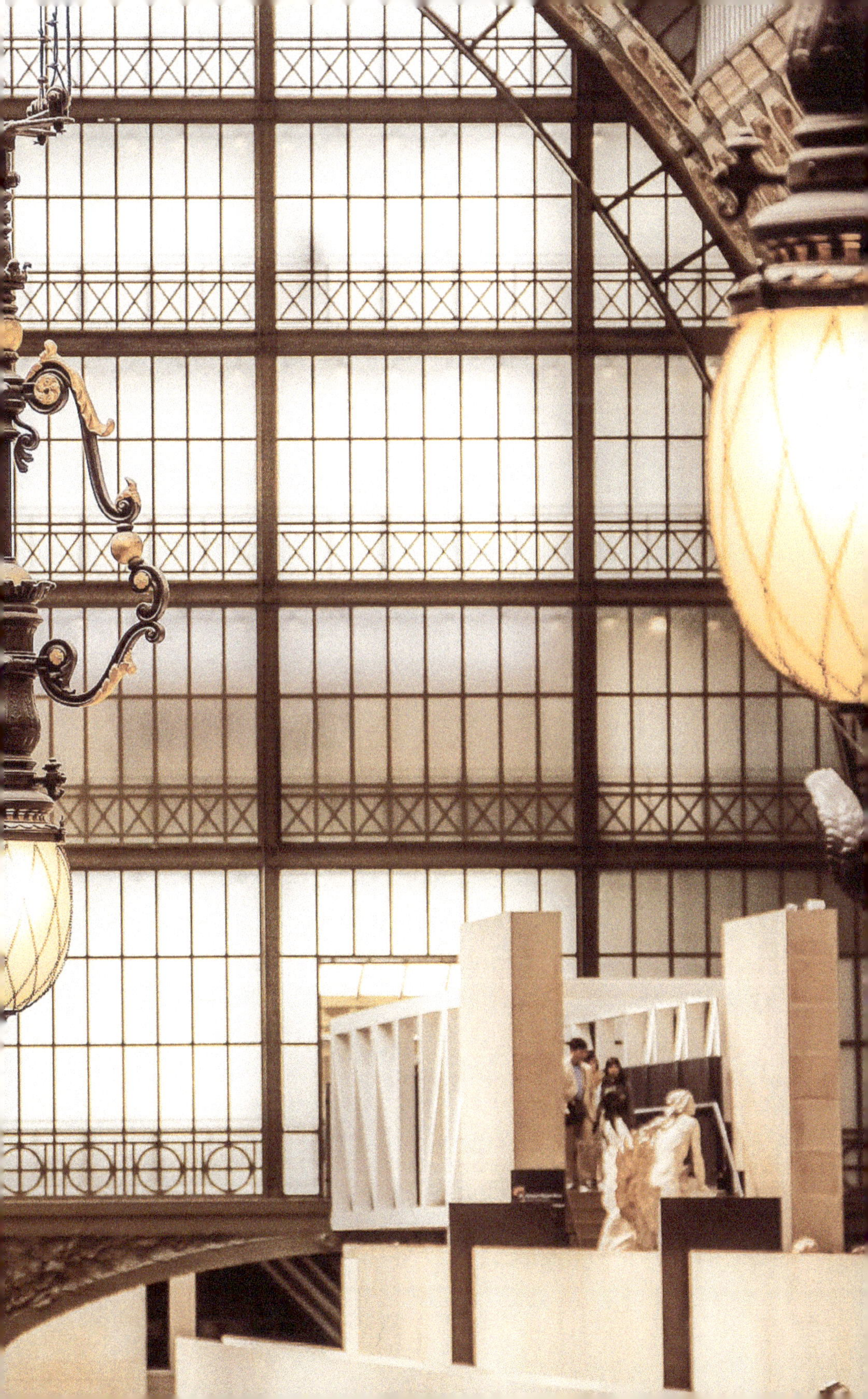

64
thought that the evil
deep with him whose
the garden-plots in the
man's duties allowed.
by a middle-aged woman,
well-trained creepers
200
120

ETCHING OUT A HELPING HAND. 65

...'s disposition was always to take the
...de of any picture. Perhaps the many
... trial and hope deferred had helped to
... thus, when she had known but one
...rce of comfort, and the only light in the
...me had been the dutiful stepson who had
pro...sed to be her staff and comfort, and bade
her be of good cheer. Now his failure had
seemed to quench all the light, and throw a
gloom over everything. If her steady Mark
fell, who could stand? and what could she do
with a family too young to earn and still bound
to attend school, all save Ruth in service,
whose wages as school-room maid were not
more than needed for her own clothing;
though since Muriel Helmdale had interested
herself in Ruth, she had learned to make
up many an article of dress for the little
ones at home.

E

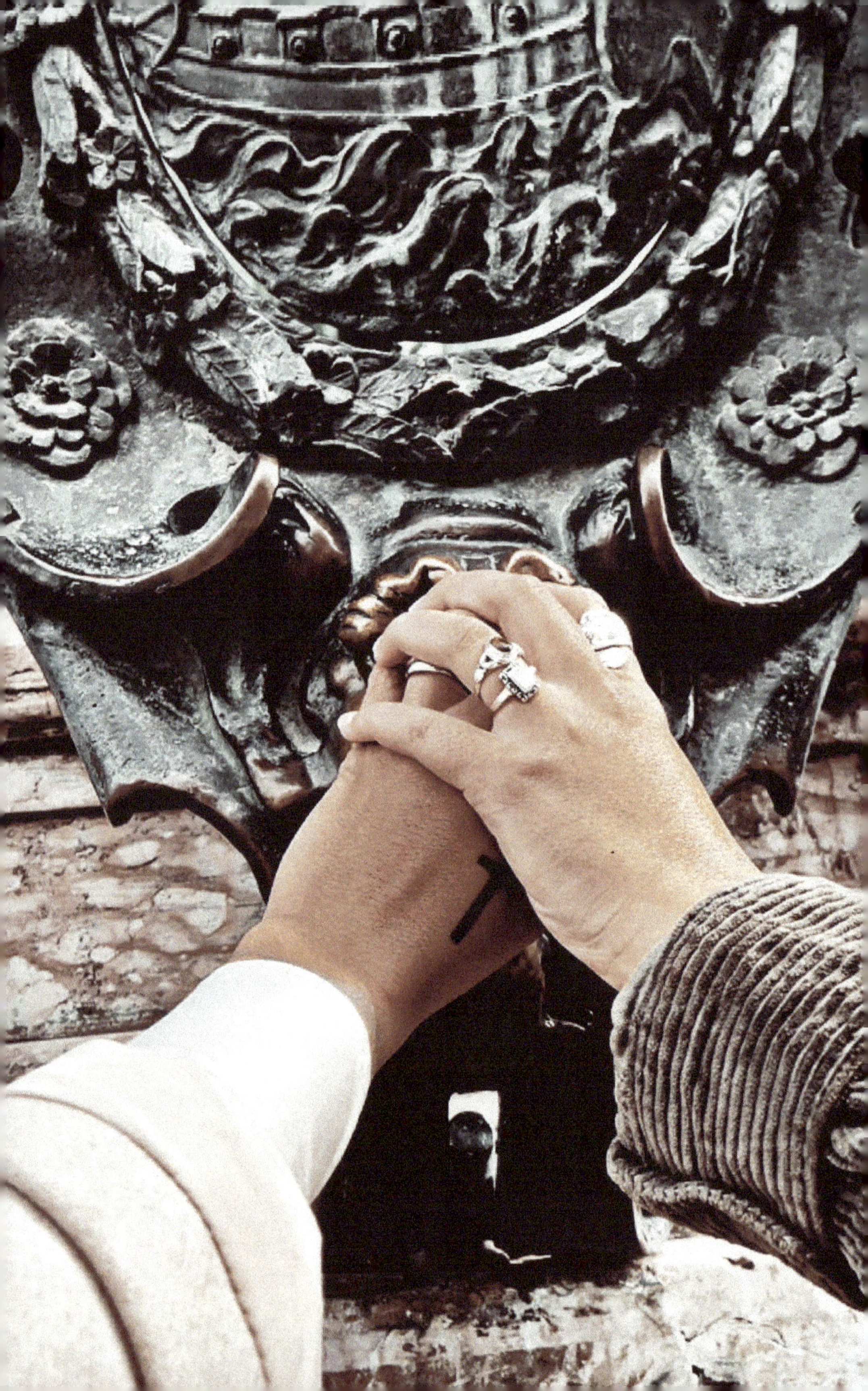

Priceless

I don't desire or demand the things
that others can easily gain accessibility to.

I fall for the *priceless* things.

Like our *hands dancing*
once they become intertwined,
or your *honest eyes*
when they become interlocked with mine.

Magnifies

I've found that the right type of love
intensifies your sight
rather than making the eyes
become blind.

- It *magnifies*.

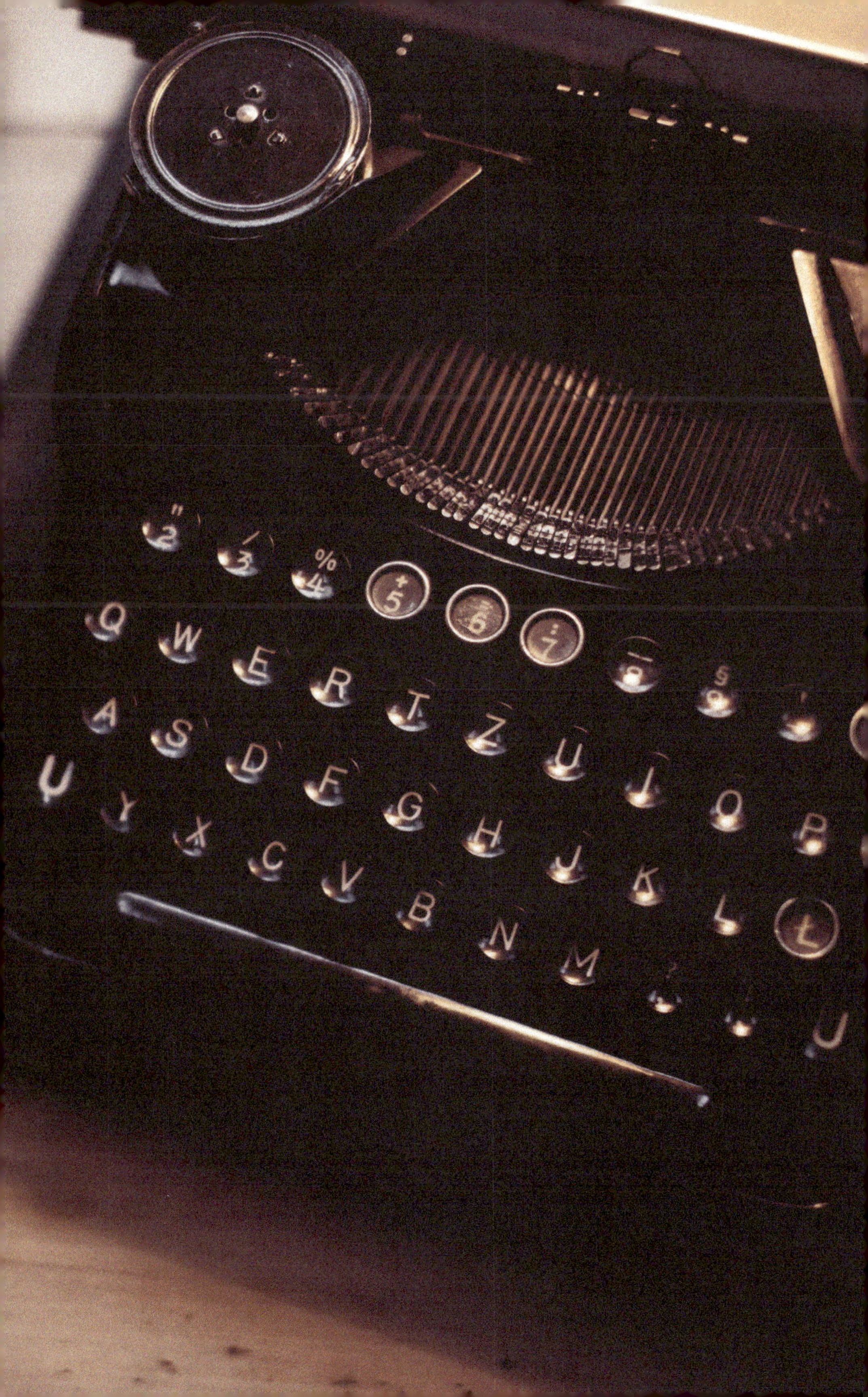

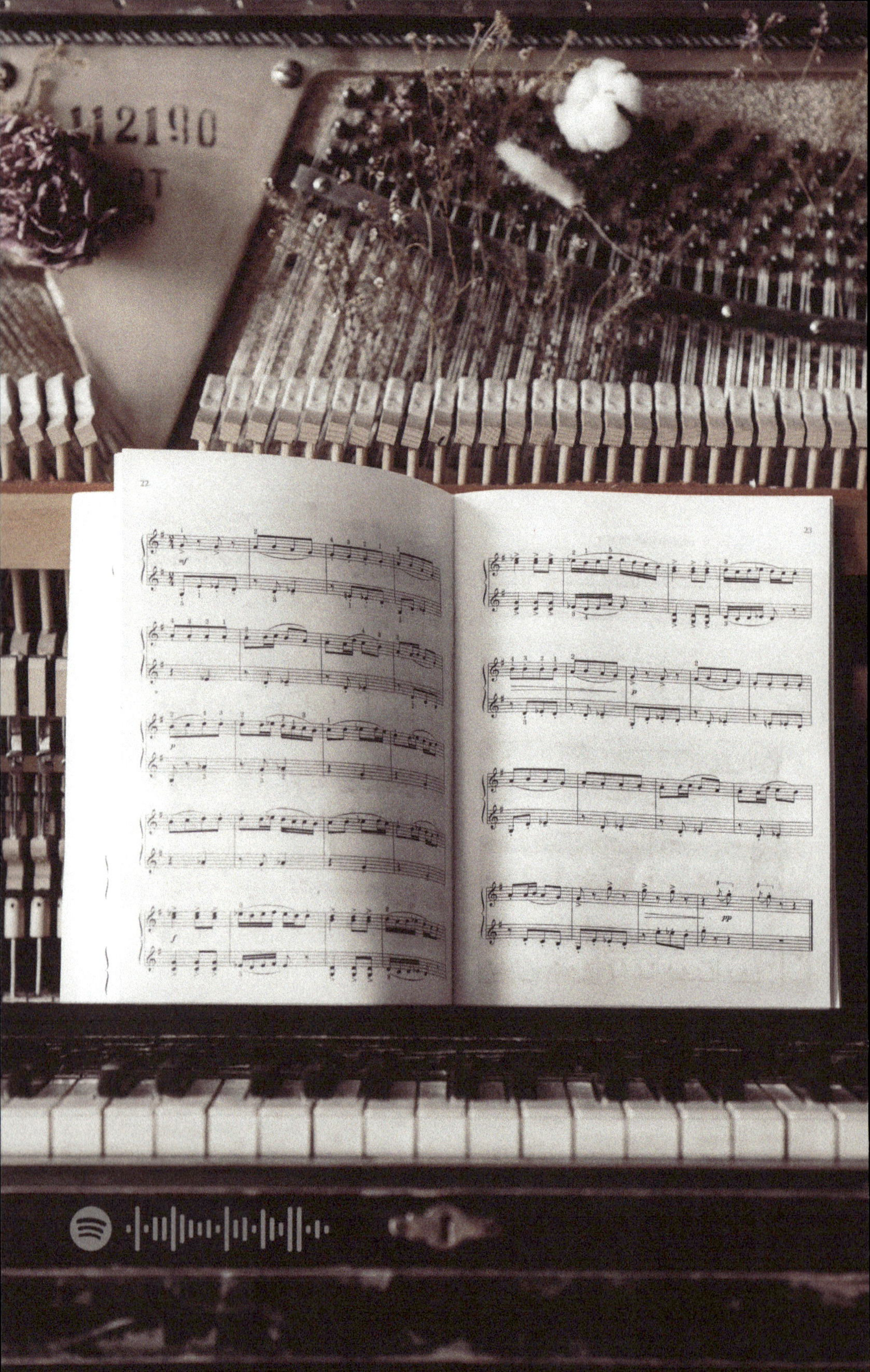
112190

Sonata

My beloved Sonata,
my musical composition:

"If you were an instrument, you would be the violin."

Allow me to deliberately clean in between
every delicate fabric within your strings,
dedicating my hands to handling your body frame
with such adorn intricacy.

With me, to worry will become a distant memory
as my eyes memorize and lionize
your favorite piece to complete
to keep you at peace.

Main Topic

You've become the main topic of conversation
within all parts of me.

Who knew shoulders could talk?
How they whisper for your head to lay on me again.

Discovering the way that lips
can carry an intimate vernacular
within a kiss - *intensity.*

How my hips can overflow with thirst
and call for your anatomy
from just one drop of your femininity - *dripping like honey.*

The way the palm of your hands
can touch my face like a familiarity - *reaching.*
Eager to capture the heat of vehemence
within fingertips - *emphasis.*

Who knew that energies could learn to enunciate.

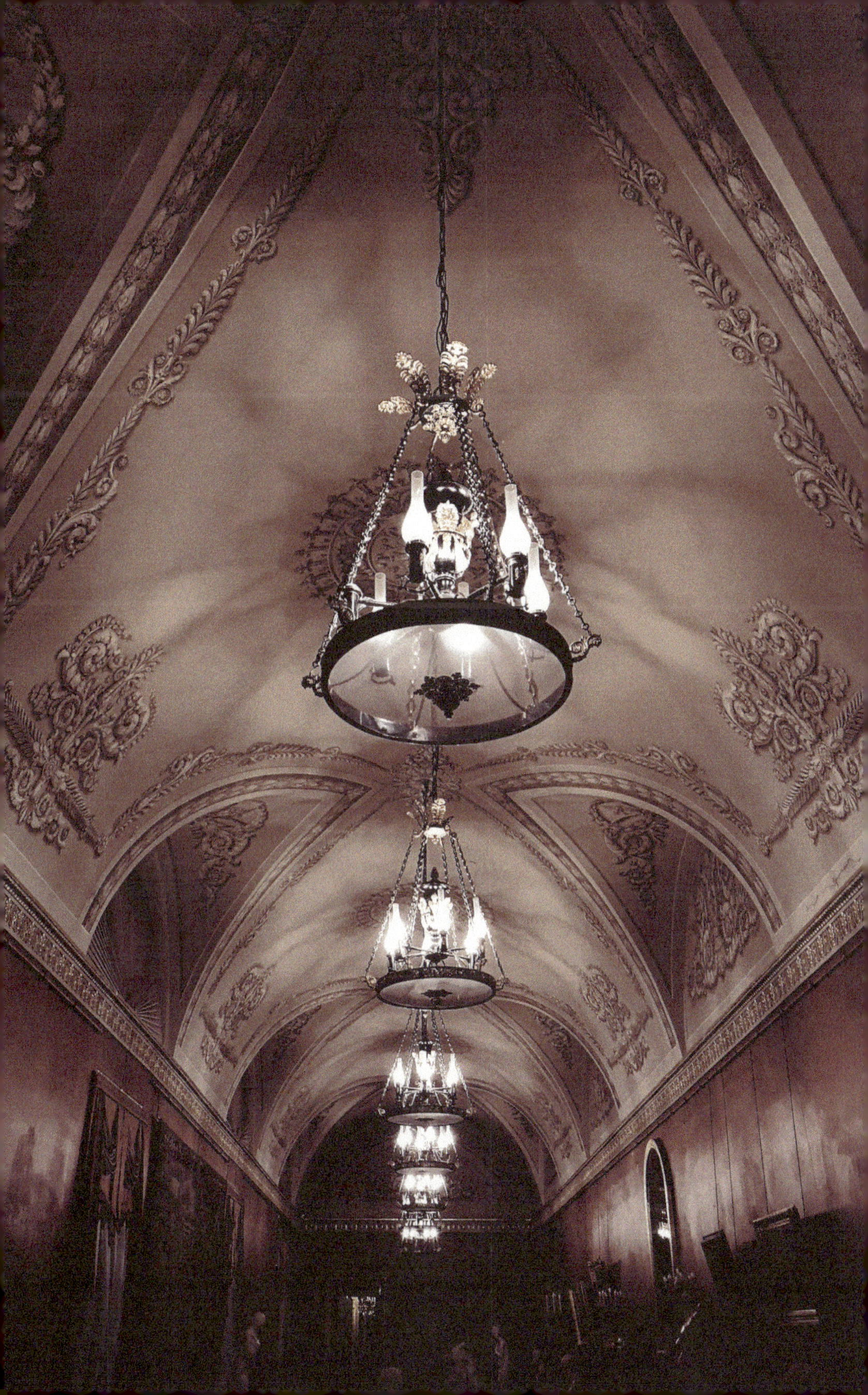

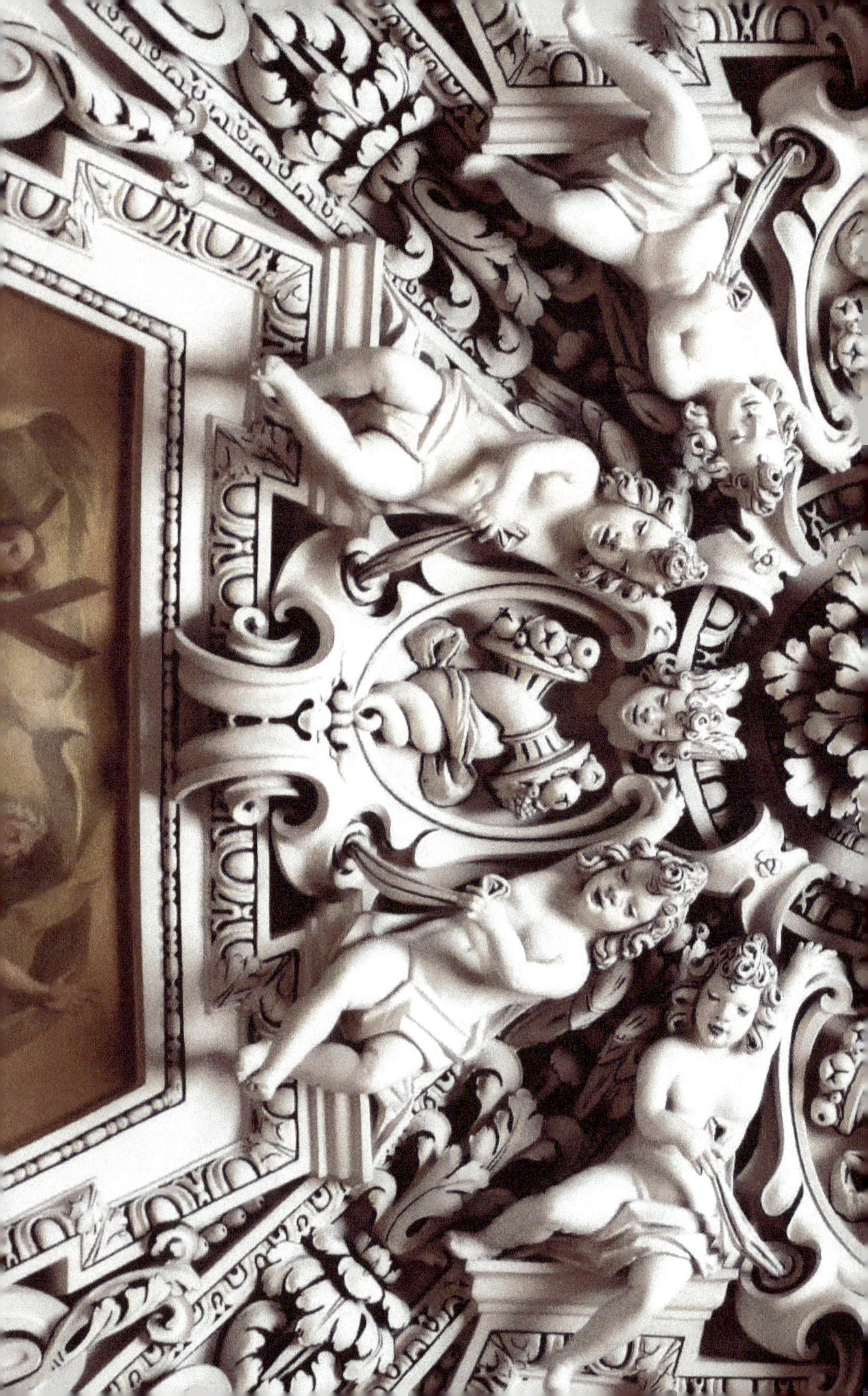

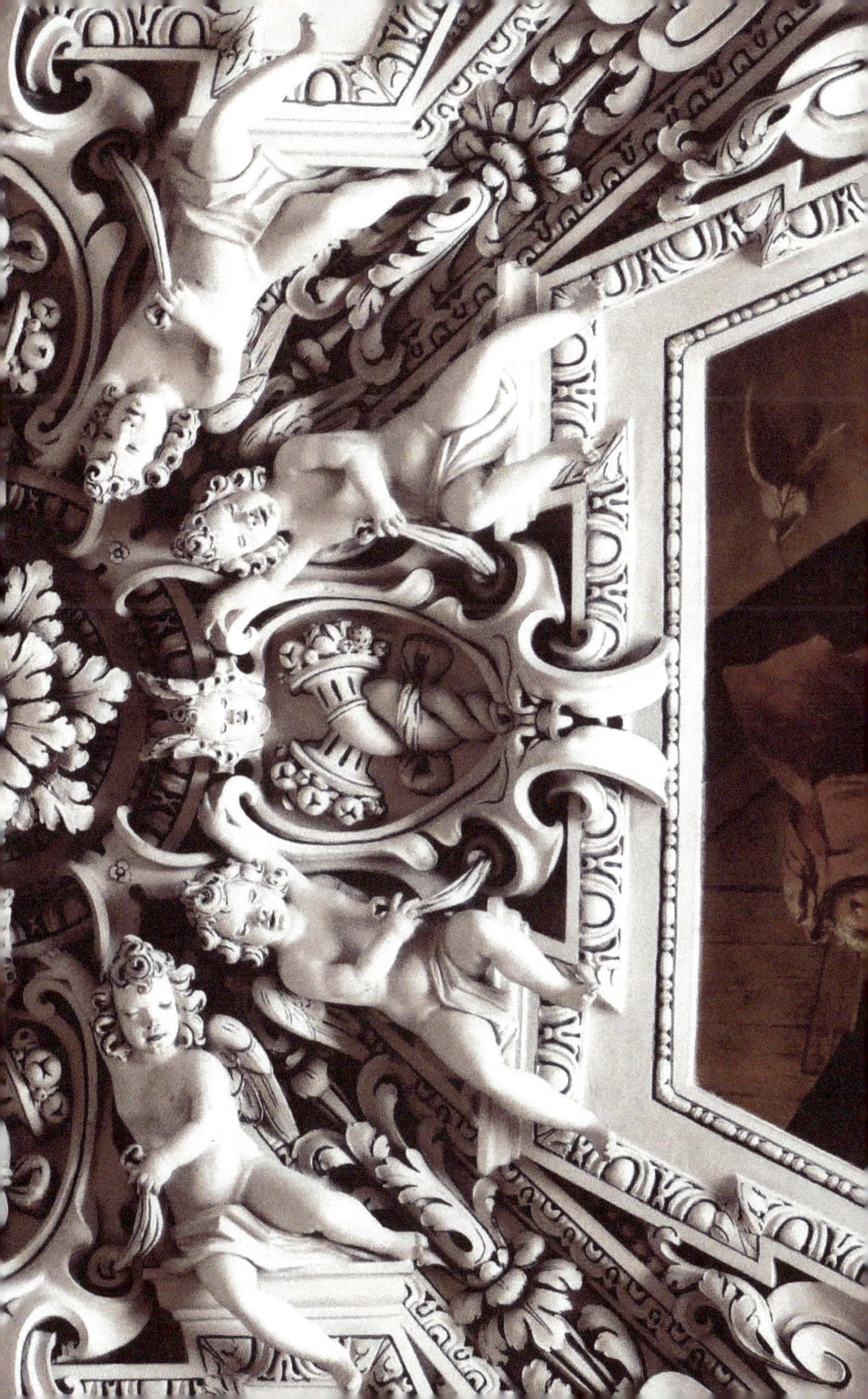

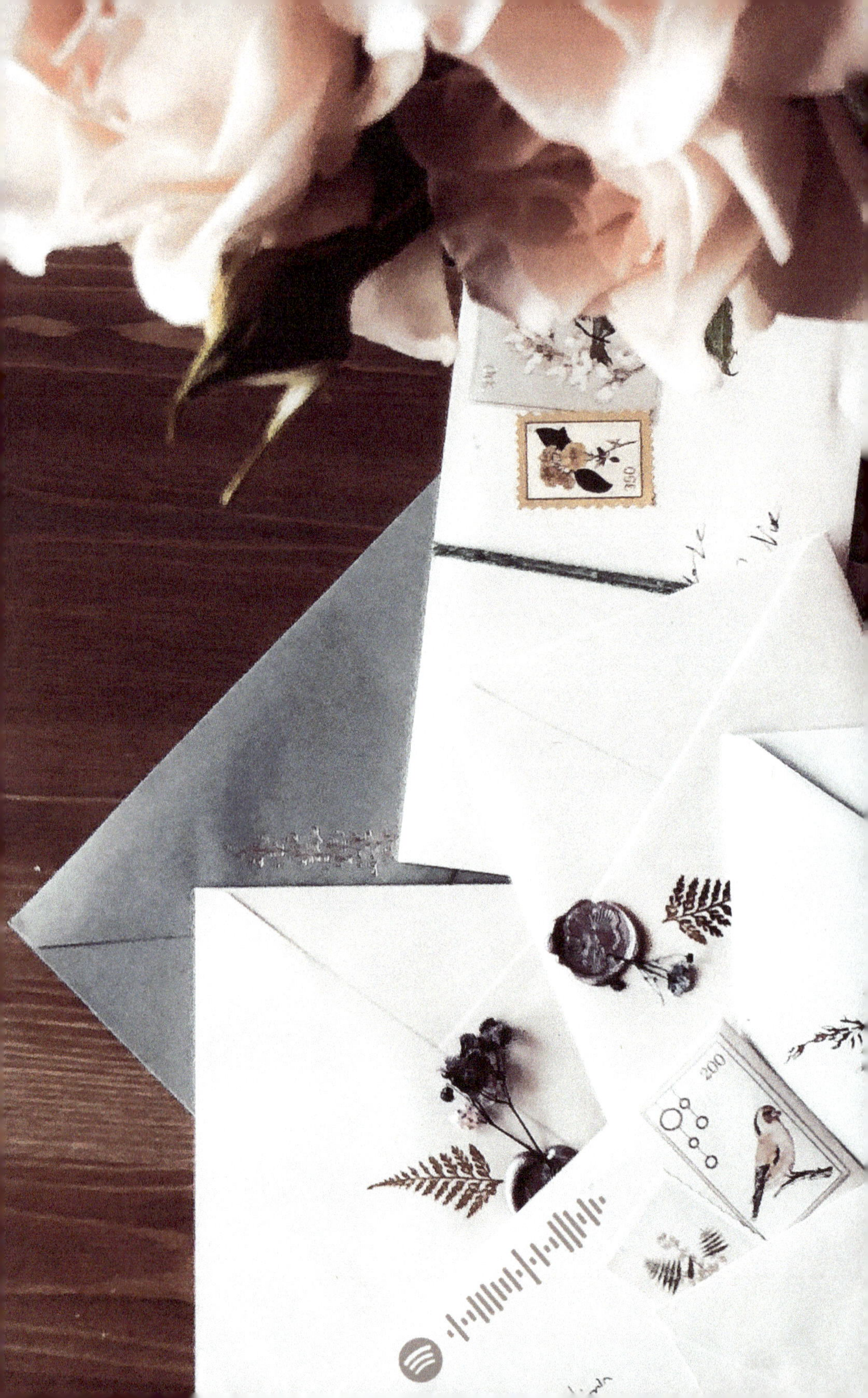

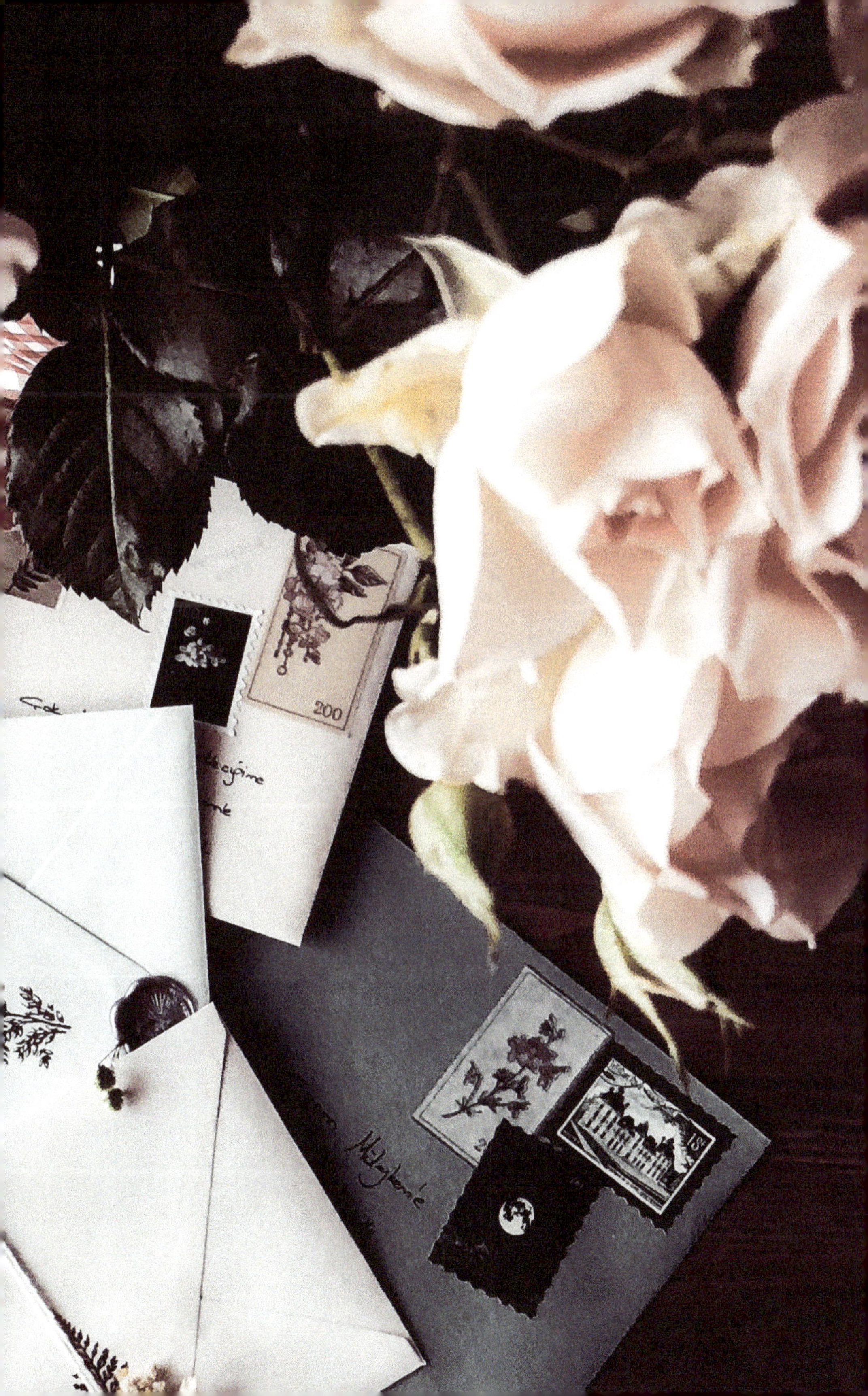

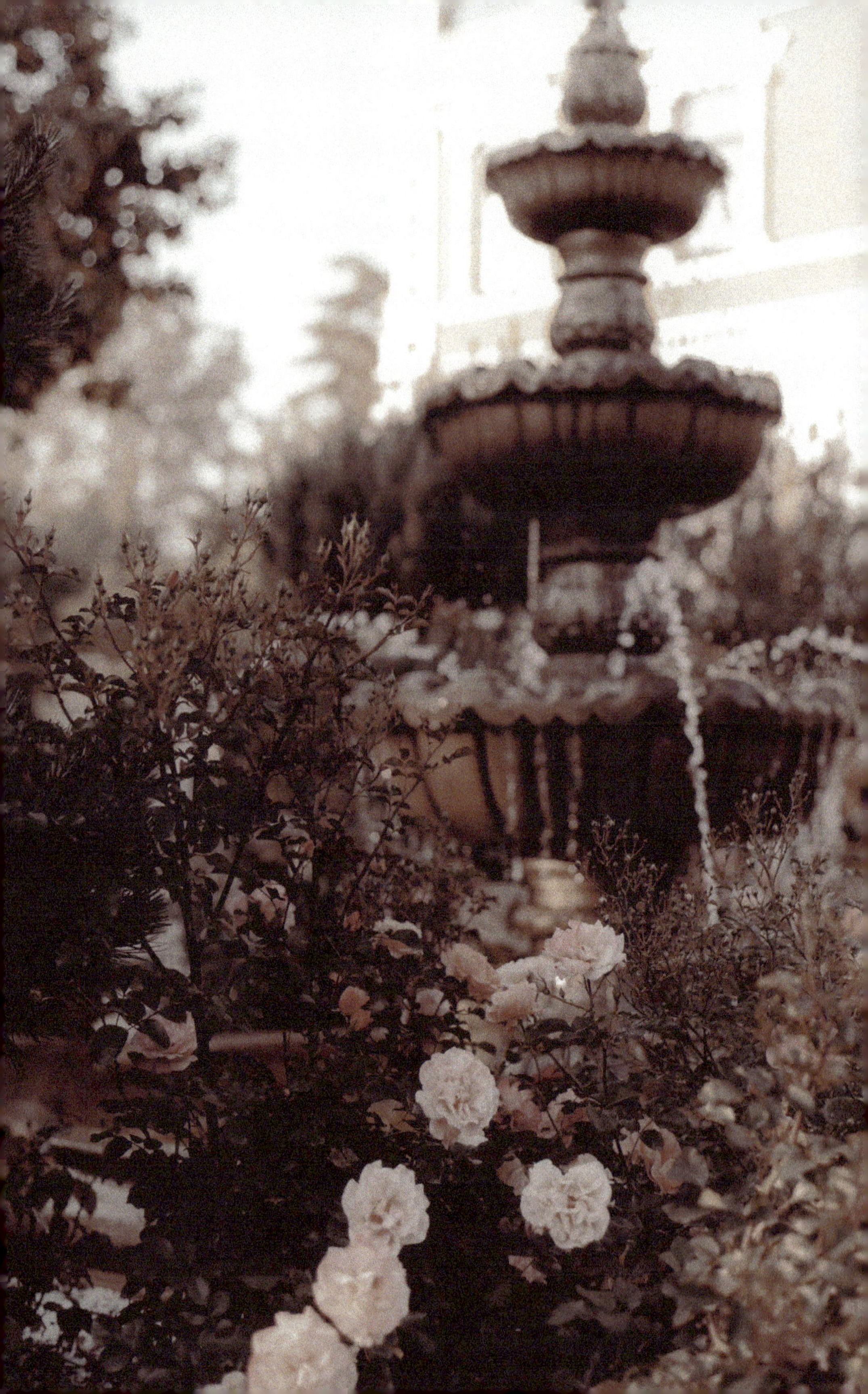

Liquid Matter

Her *liquid matter*
s p r e a d s eagerly all over
my yearning chest.

F L O W I N G.

Drowning my focus
within her essence
from our sensual mess.

C L I M A X I N G.

Feeling her breasts
colliding with mine - flesh on flesh.
Witnessing alignment of our breath,
welcoming her love with a safe space to rest.

I N T I M A C Y.

Emotional Oasis

Gravity bends under the weight of her orbit.
Staring in her direction with the upmost adoration
is an unconscious decision, I never question it -
My *emotional oasis*.

Her quintessence, drenched in potency
carries into a conversation
without concern for dilution.

She is an *artist's* favorite freehand image.

An *interior designers* favored aesthetic decor,
the type that I adore.

A *sculptors* prized marble material
used for ideal creation.

A *musician's* best lyrics in the chorus.

A *seamstress'* most prized silk.

Unique in every way, she is the perfect illustration
with our love story being my favorite *sapphic*.

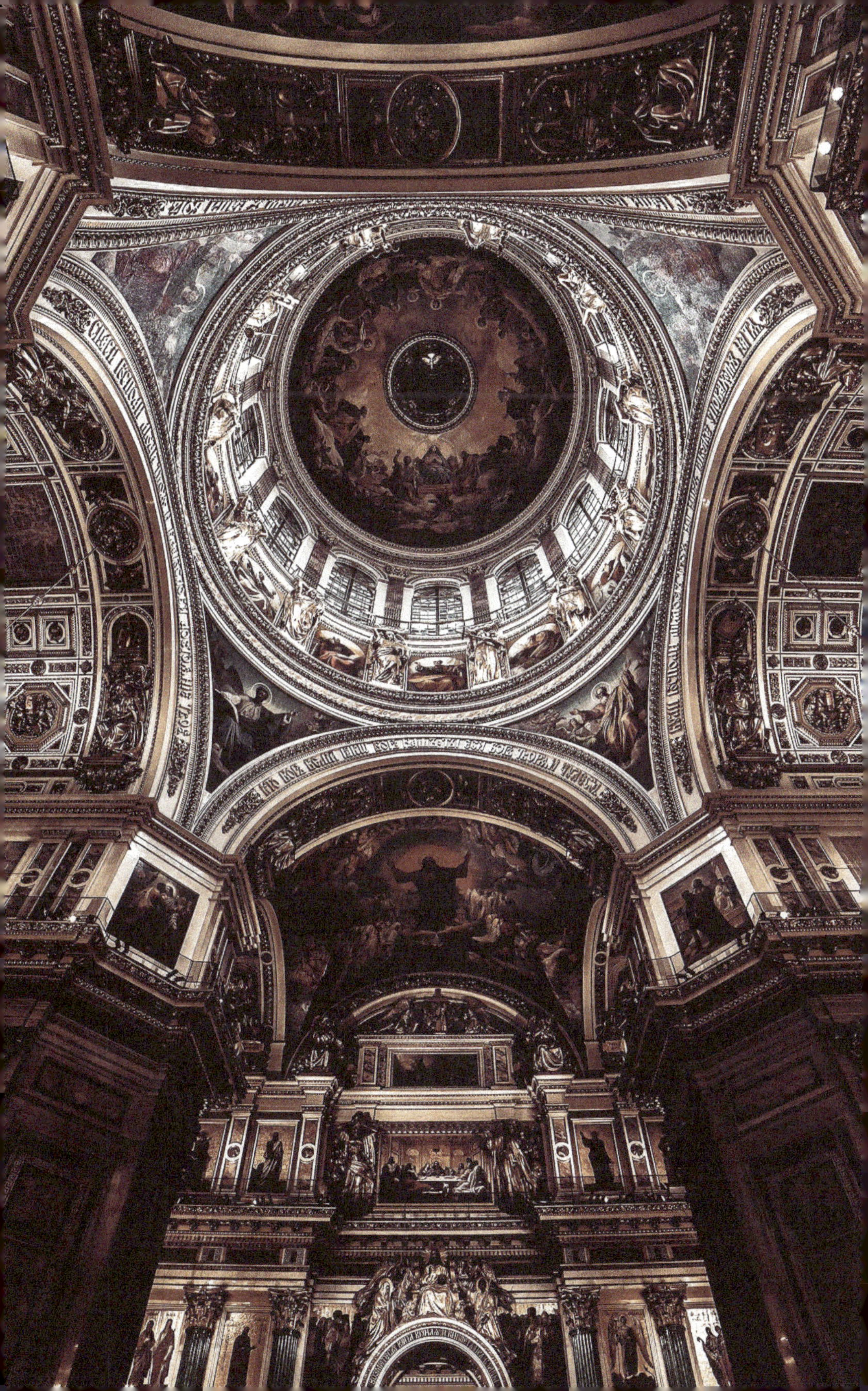

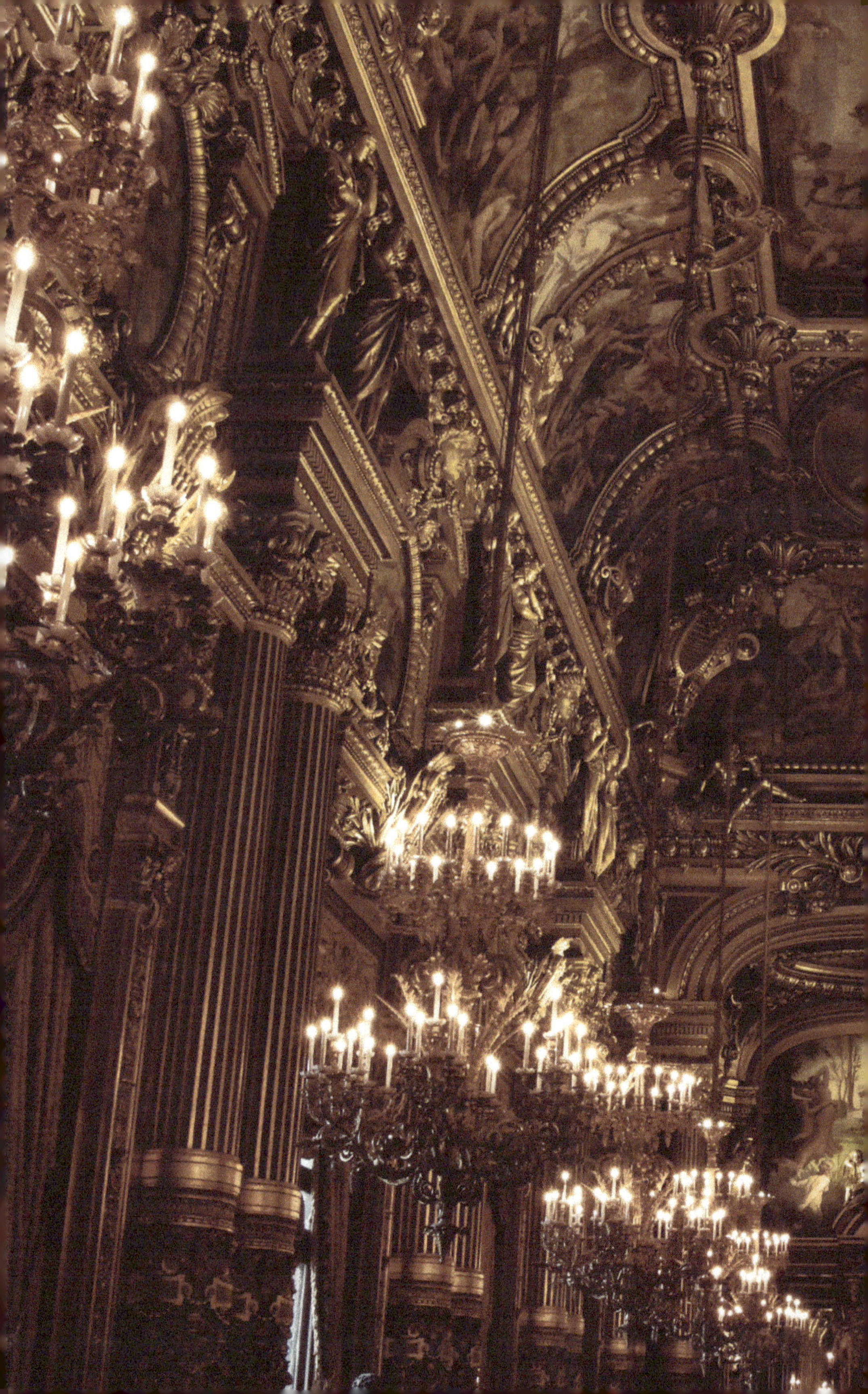

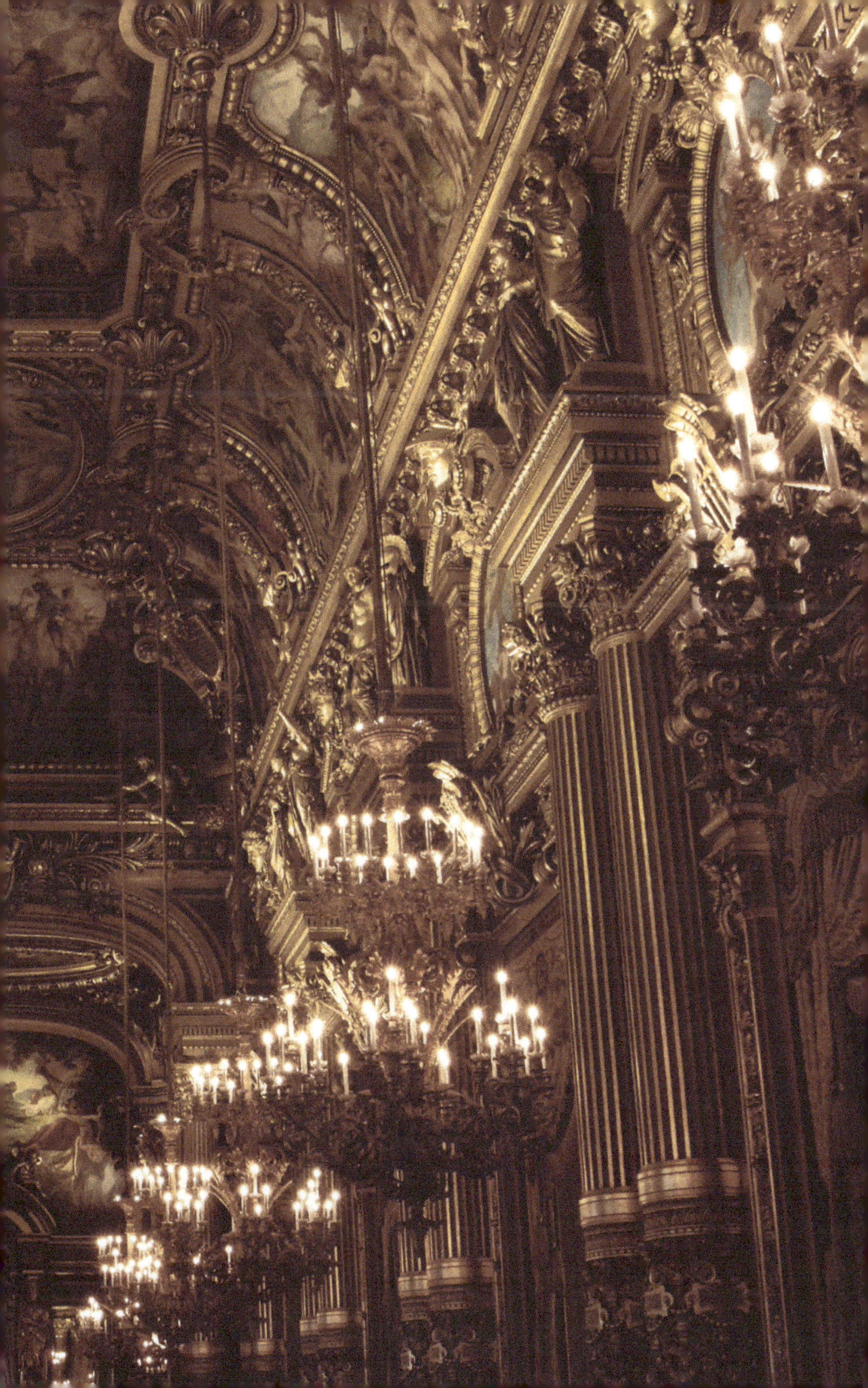

Heirloom

"How much do you love me?"

My dearest,

You would gape in disbelief at the enormity
of what I'm about to admit.

If it were up to me,
I'd empty the oceans and have you tally
every speck of sand that remains on land
after the water has evaporated.

I'd ask for you to count every human heartbeat
that has echoed since the wake of our existence.

I would bend time to savor one more second with you
and beg God to make the sun never pass noon.

You've given me words to plant seeds that harvest hope,
and now my tongue speaks in roses.
I wear your love like heirlooms.

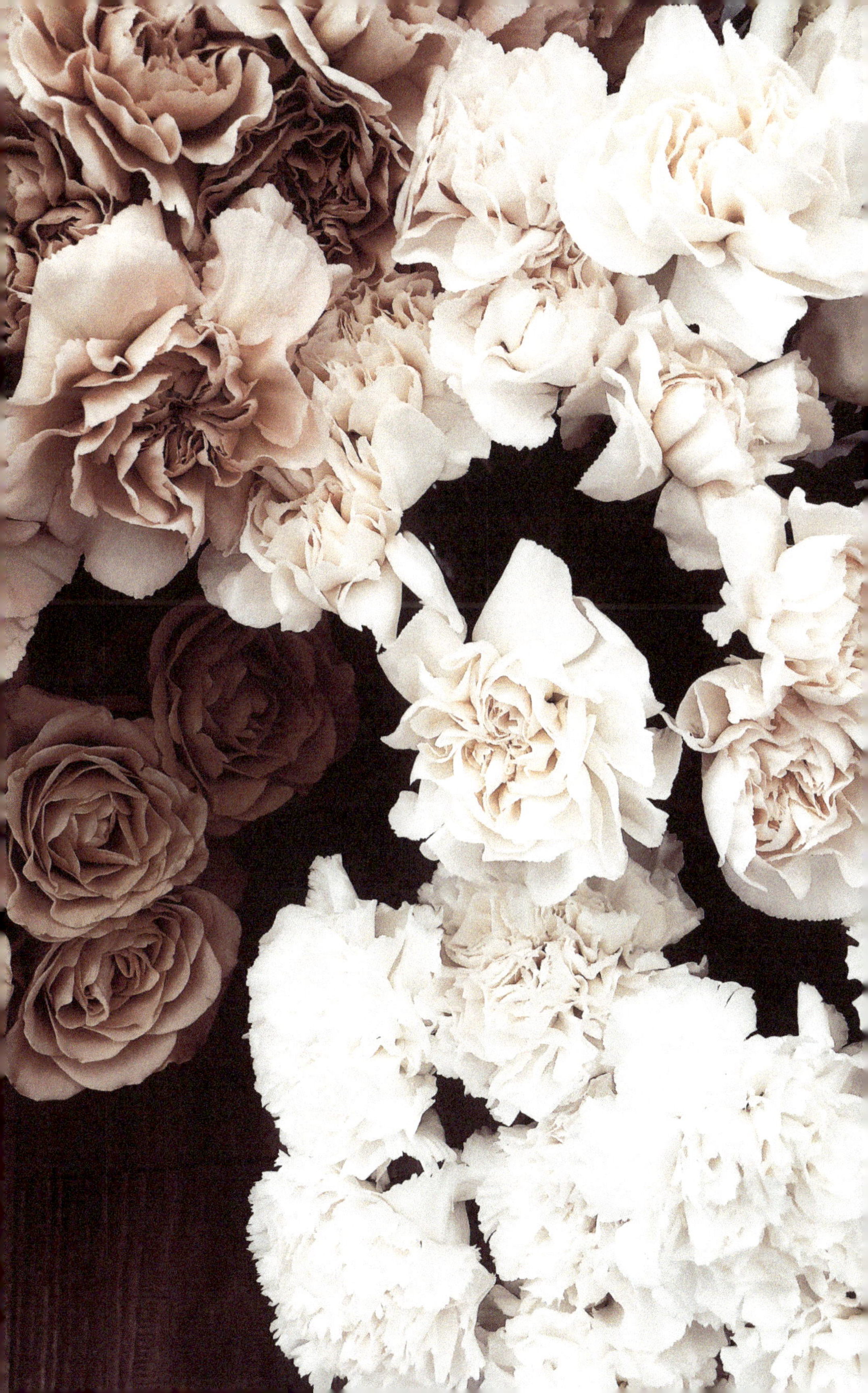

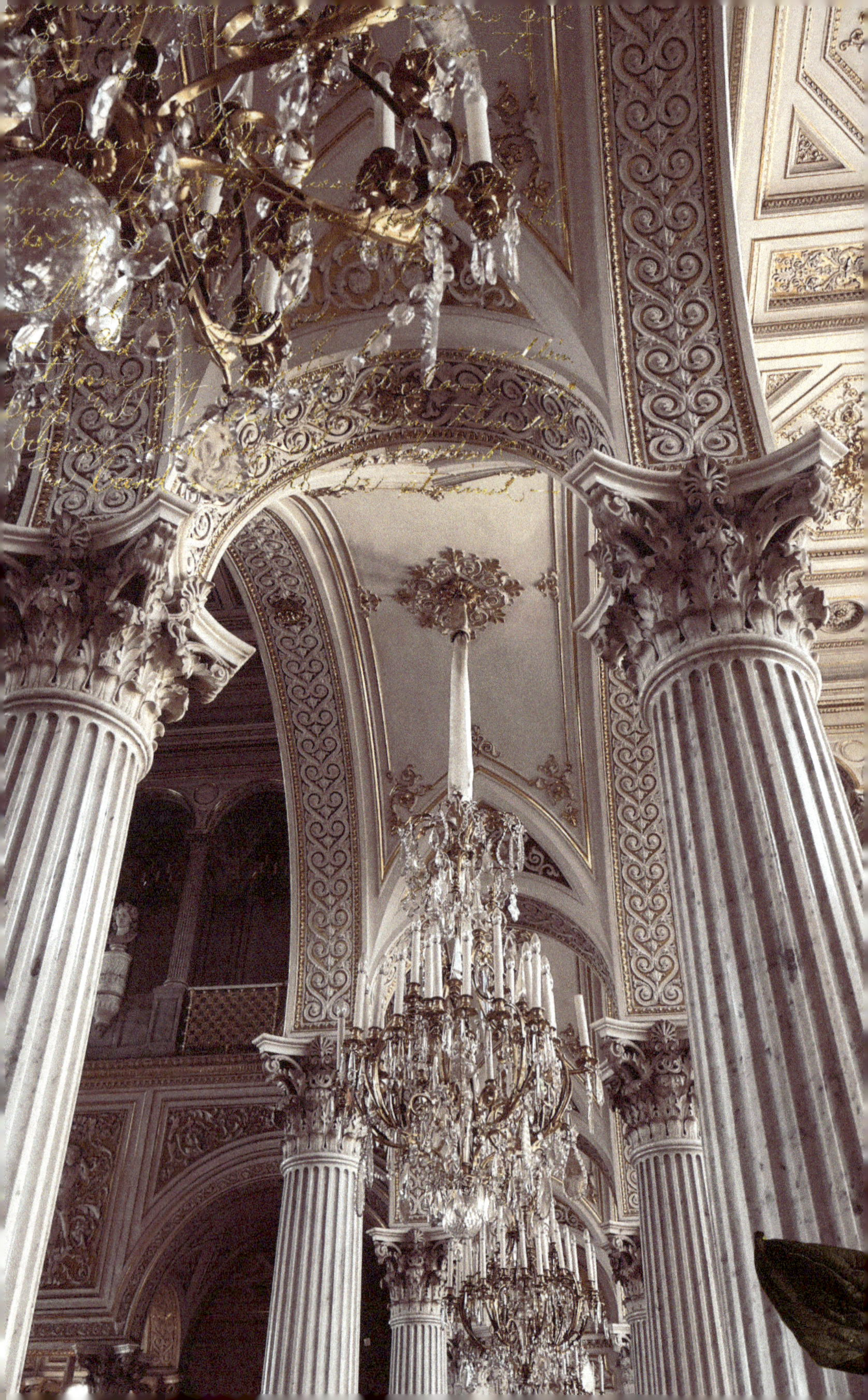

Chords of Harmony

My essence rests with serenity
as her emotional oasis
holds my coat of anxiety.
Her aura drips in nourishment - depression repellent.

Thoughts of her are my most treasured souvenirs.
My mind floods with recollections
from the impact of her presence
with her laughter as my favorite echo - ethereal.

Mind of an instrument,
allow me to fine-tune any adjustments needed.
Your voice holds *chords of harmony*
with hands that *stroke my strings of passion*
at the highest concentration.

Stimulated soul replenishment,
eyes overflow with gratitude from each conversation
as I fall for her mind of a Gemini.
Clutch onto my breath of security
as we choose to continue to walk in sync
with reassurance of each other's gravity.

Hold onto me,
my chord of harmony.

*Strings of Passion = Heart strings

Breath of Nostalgia

My fresh *breath of nostalgia,*
the moment our auras touched
your presence woke me up.

A familiar soul
with possible past time relations
composing our instant connection.
Your warmth carried a safe presence
permeated with positive body language,
where have you been all this time?

Sometimes I question if this is real life
because I cried watching you play your piano tonight
and I'm terrified of how fast time flies.
Is this the price of being alive?

I look at you, and my anxieties minimize,
hearing your voice is one I've come to memorize,
but, having earned the privilege
of comprehending the depths of your benevolence
is my internal highlight.

My fresh breath of nostalgia,
closed eyes miss too much,
more time with you, could never be enough.

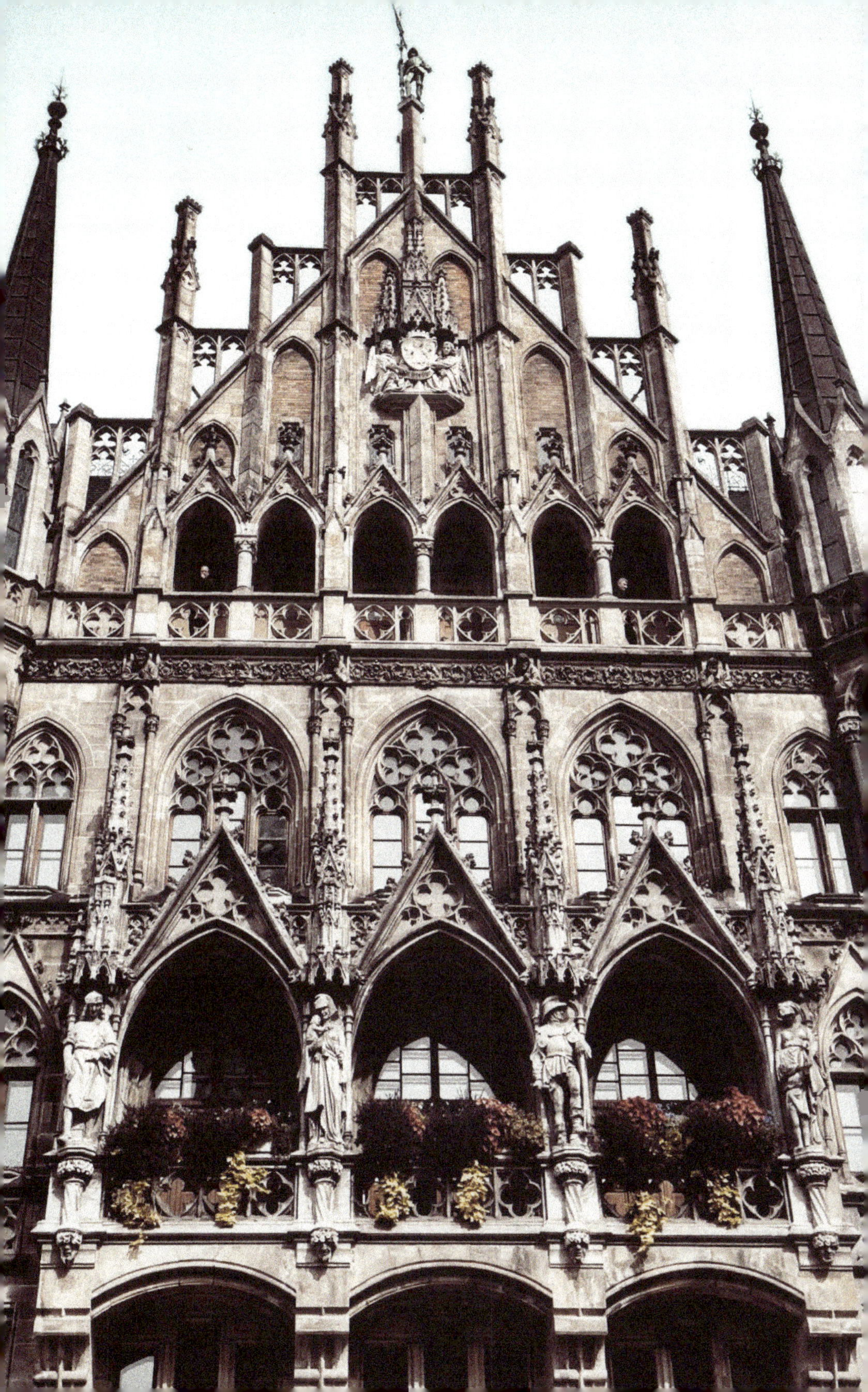

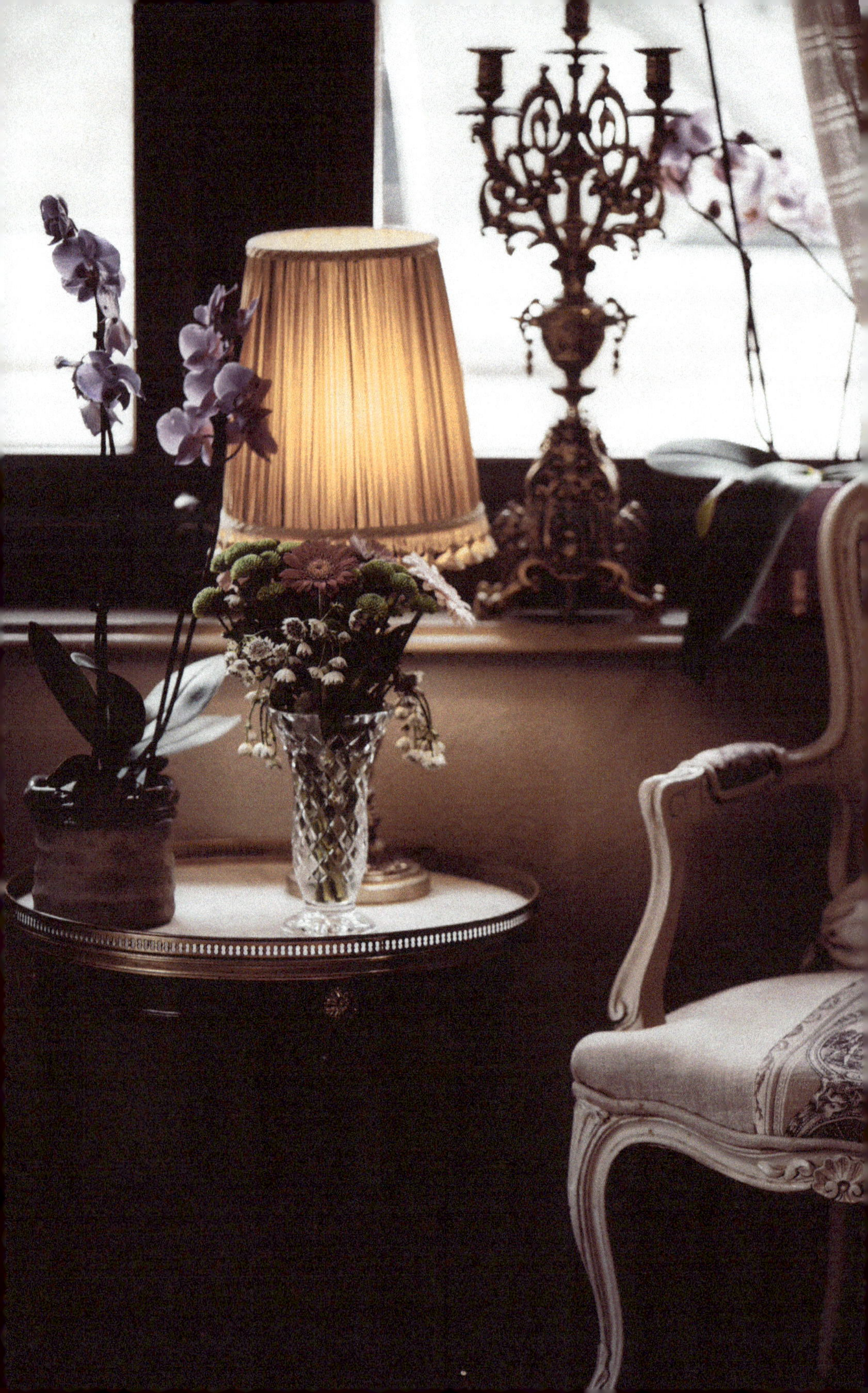

Varnished Horizon

"She is half of my soul," as the poets say.

Possessing the kindest of eyes
behind her circular bifocals,
with an *iris* filled of *varnished horizons*
and metaphorical images I've attempted
to bring to life for ages.

Splendor swollen *lens'*
in your evergreen gardens
saturated in passionate handwritten conversations
in both light and darkness.

Even our oceans
fail to comprehend the amount of depth
your soul holds.

КАРЛ МАРКС
ФОРМА СТИЛЬ ВЫРАЖЕНИЕ
А.Ф. ЛОСЕВ
БЫТИЕ ИМЯ КОСМОС
А.Ф. ЛОСЕВ
А.Ф. ЛОСЕВ
Clavicles describe an 'S' curve
just medial to the
Chest is broad & thick
flaring of the lower ribs
of the ribs not particularly
visibly or to palpatation. Sternum

А.Ф.ЛОСЕВ
ИСТОРИЯ АНТИЧНОЙ ЭСТЕТИКИ
А.Ф.ЛОСЕВ
ИСТОРИЯ АНТИЧНОЙ ЭСТЕТИКИ
АРИСТОТЕЛЬ И ПОЗДНЯЯ КЛАССИКА
А.Ф.ЛОСЕВ ФИЛОСОФИЯ. МИФОЛОГИЯ. КУЛЬТУРА
А.Ф.ЛОСЕВ СЛОВАРЬ АНТИЧНОЙ ФИЛОСОФИИ
А.Ф.ЛОСЕВ
А. Ф. Лосев Высший синтез
ИСТОРИЯ ЭСТЕТИЧЕСКИХ КАТЕГОРИЙ
А.Ф.Лосев Страсть к диалектике
А.Ф.ЛОСЕВ
А. ЛОСЕВ Критика платонизма у Аристотеля
А.Ф.Лосев

Designer Sex//Divine Feminine

Her figure is encapsulated in opulence
and here I am,
falling adrift as I gaze for a minute
in the upmost veneration before I ingest
what sits deep within her lips and drips down
in between her polished inner thighs
like sweet, melted molasses.

We have designer sex in the morning,
luxury foreplay in the evening -
moonlight bathing,
sounding expensive when she's moaning - tongues dancing.
Making love to my name in her mouth when I go south.
Brief intermissions meant to tend to her breasts
as they swell and harden before I please the rest,
lover girl tempo *fare l'amore, mi amor.*

Respectfully, I'm losing all of my self respect
the moment her lips hit my neck.
I apologize, allow me the honor to be a gentle woman
and clean up my intentional mess
so we can come and reset
for you to *cum* for me again and again and again.

Nudity is nothing new,
I've made love to her conscious completely raw and bare
before I ever dared
to strip off any cloth attired layers.

Her figure is encapsulated in opulence
and here I am,
fully immersed within her *divine feminine.*

Warmth of Conversation

Mental stimulation flourishes each interaction
as I discover the infinite salience of you
within the *warmth of our conversations.*

I find myself yearning for our minds
to close in on the distance
to reach a harmonious interaction; homeostasis.

HISTOIRE DES PLANT
sont nettement incurvées dans le bouton.
diploséméné- ou quelquefois formé d'un nombre
supérieur à dix ; fait qui s'observe aussi çà et là dans
proprement dits. Il y a au contraire appauvrissement

us le bouton.
d'un nombre
çà et là dans
uvrissement

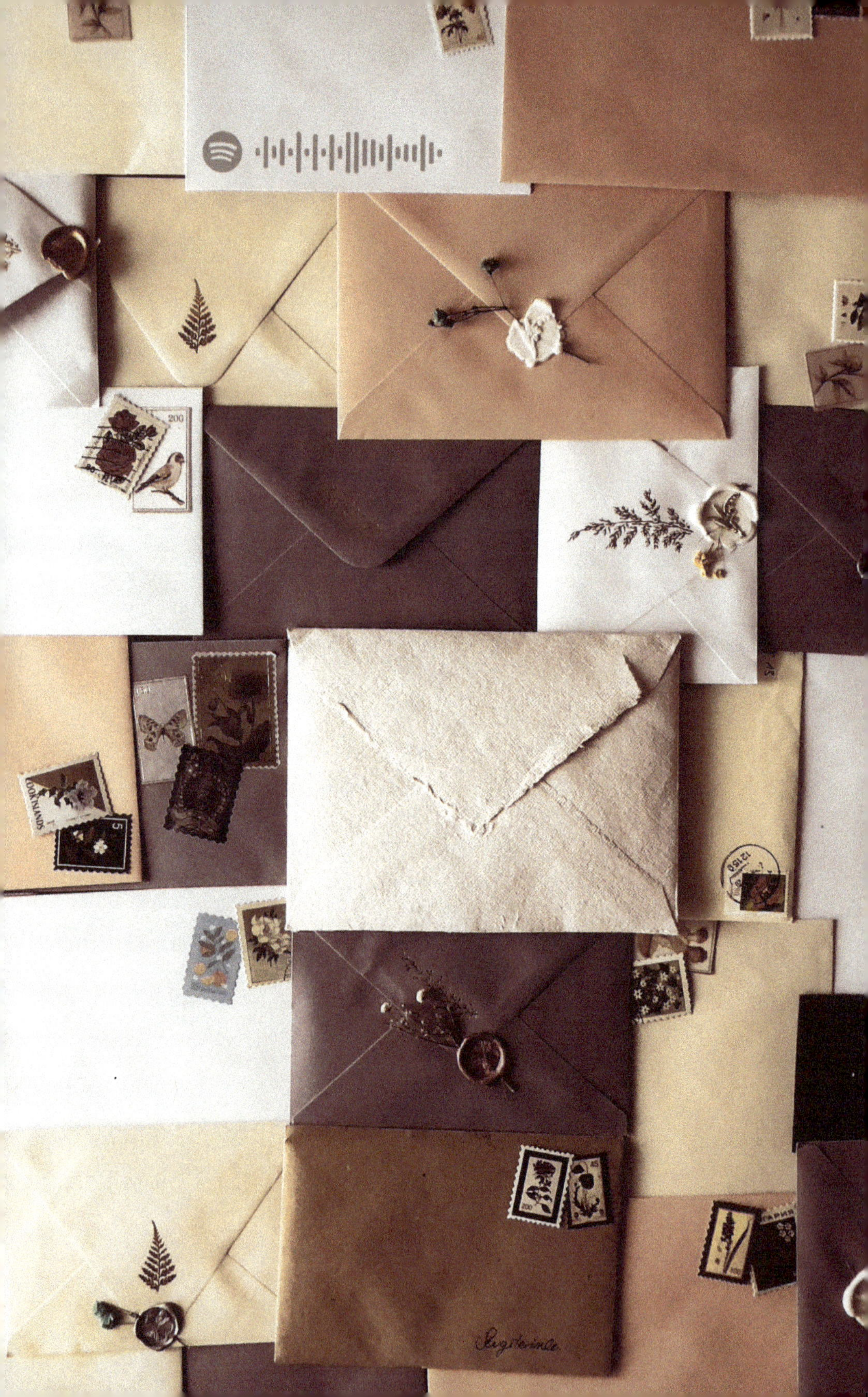

Coat of Anxieties

I've never met a woman so understanding,
one who carries a profound delicacy when she speaks to me
with words that bear the ability
to sooth my anxious tendencies.
My lover, who lifts me of my hefty coat,
and coaxes me to release all my perturbations to the floor
the moment my soul steps in the door.

I admire you, my Honeybee,
the way you glisten with spirituality
and how your intelligence within emotional maturity
brings endless clarity and rationality
to arduous conversations
despite my difficulty with emotional regulation
towards my fear of abandonment.

I'm working on it.

She guides me back to our baseline,
and suddenly trepidation subsides
the moment we interlock our minds.
I'm not perfect, and she knows it,
yet, she reels me back in with our foundation
to save me from drowning
when I've gone too far into the deep end
even though it's not her responsibility,
but here she is anyway, reminding me of our *big threes.*

Her gentleness,
her God-given patience,
her warmth encapsulated within fingertips,
I could never take this for granted.

Hold my face in between your hands again.

Amorist

I sit secluded in thought,
glued to the same position for hours in admiration
as I warmly add inordinate amounts
of the most divine pieces of literature
that has touched the deepest parts of my veins
and remind me of her to my Pinterest board
in hopes she feels the crescendos of my love.

I sit inspired and in awe, as a Poet,
to articulate every fiber of her being into a novel,
persistently committed to loving her
grandest of museums and quietest of hallways.
Call me an Amorist for I write with ardor,
searching for synonyms of my most treasured words,
meticulously placing punctuations,
separating stanzas to match my tempo and tone
so she is familiarized by my spoken mannerisms
in hopes of piecing together a new piece of her, for her.

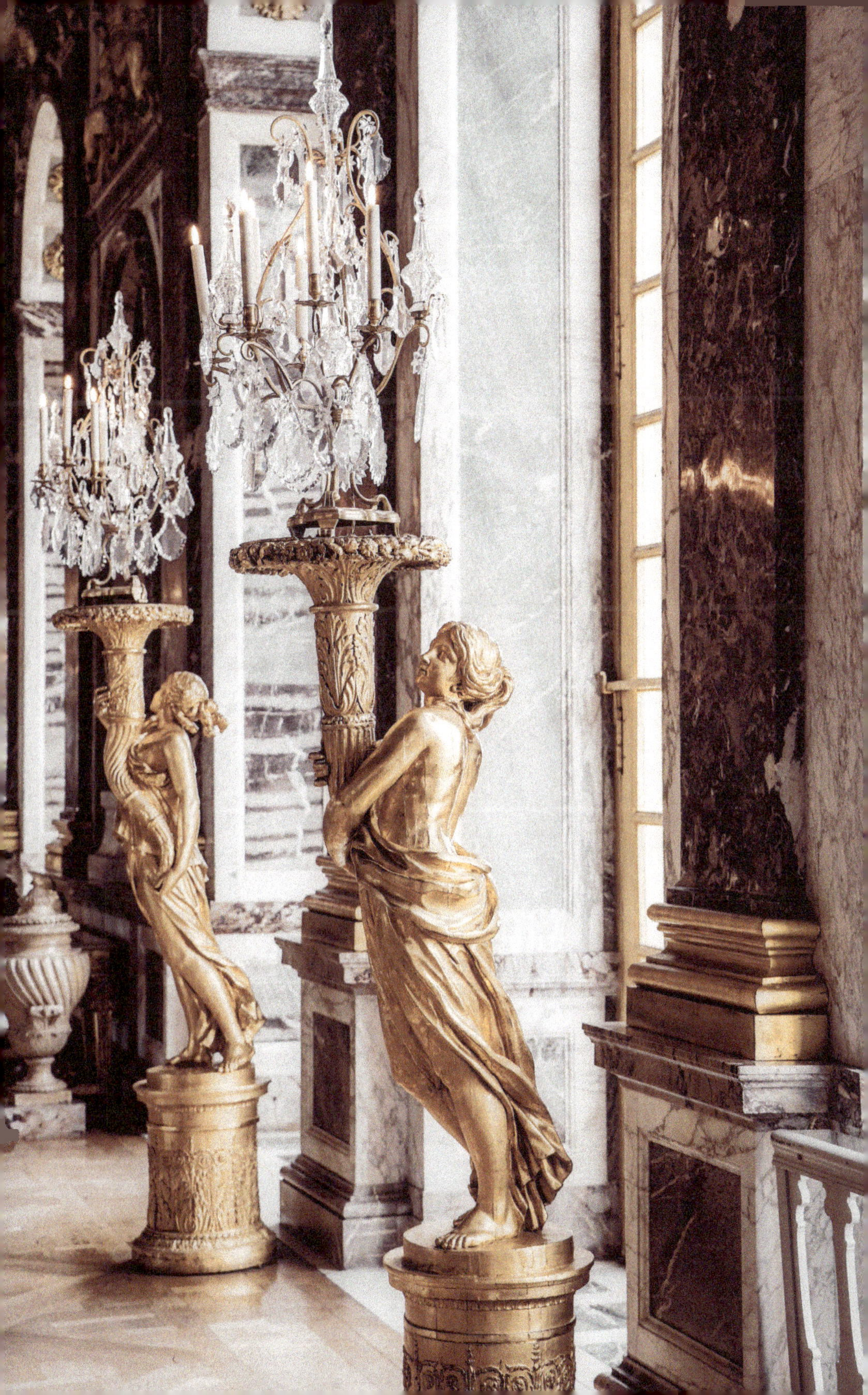

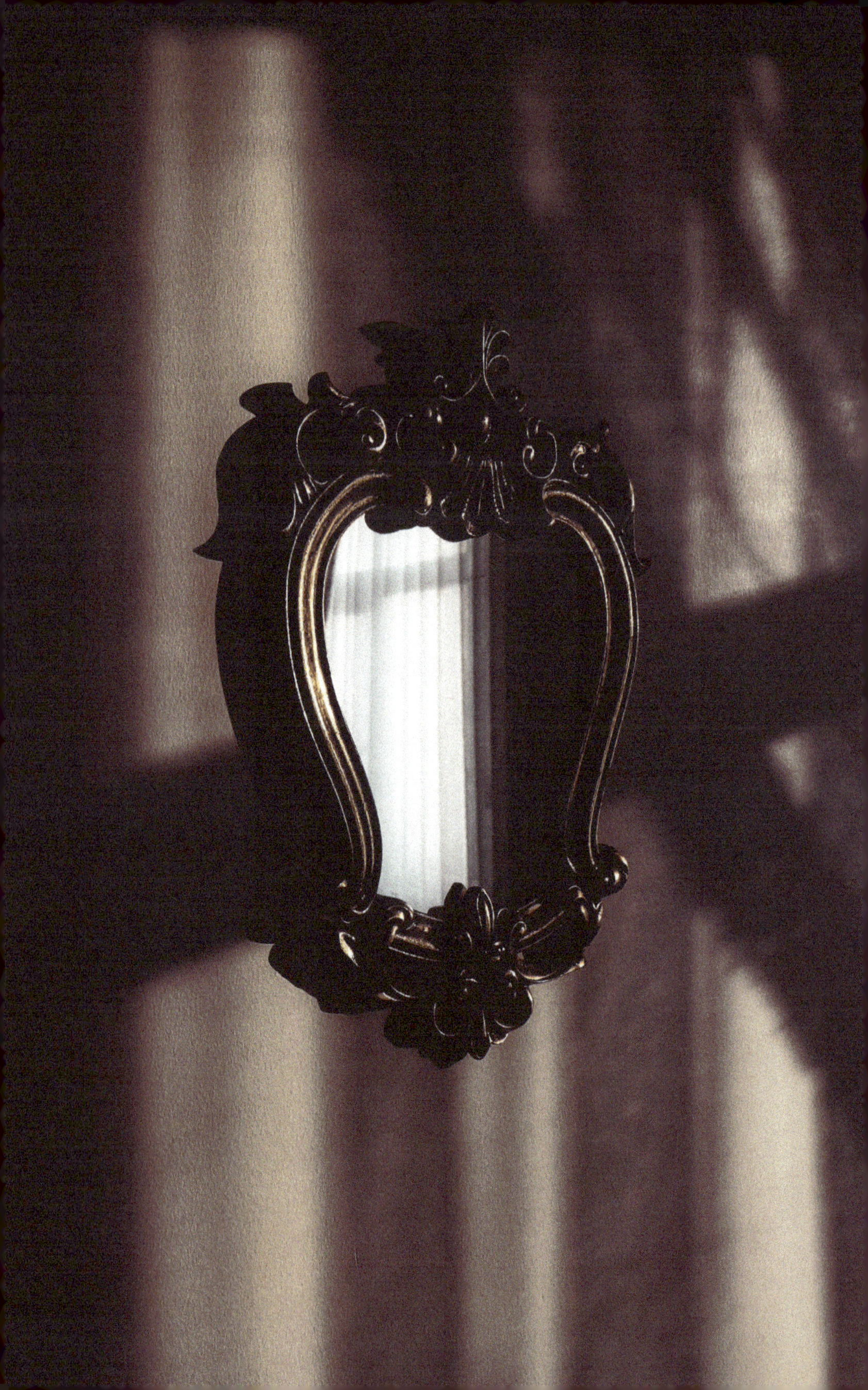

Haptic Memory

Even in silence, her presence is bountiful,
her haptic memory follows me.
WANDERING.

Reminiscing of how my body effortlessly
falls asleep beside her being,
surrounded in content as I sink into her arms of safety.

Recollecting the euphonious rhythm of her heartbeat
as its tempo communicates a steady conversation to me.
SERENE.
Sensations between our intertwined hand link,
exploration of our electric filled lips,
memorializing her hands passionate stories onto me
as my face is caressed by her palms and fingertips.
Emotions flood me at the thought of it.

The heat of fresh water dancing off of our skin
as we shower, I lose track of the hour.
I can stay in here for hours.
Kneading shampoo and conditioner into her scalp
as I routinely kiss her shoulder,
massaging body wash all over each other,
washing out her hair,
into her soul is where I stare.

Her aura could grow flowers,
and inside me, she planted a garden.
I'll protect our harvest no matter the season,
I promise.

My constant,
do you remember me?

Call me an Amorist for I write with Ardor.

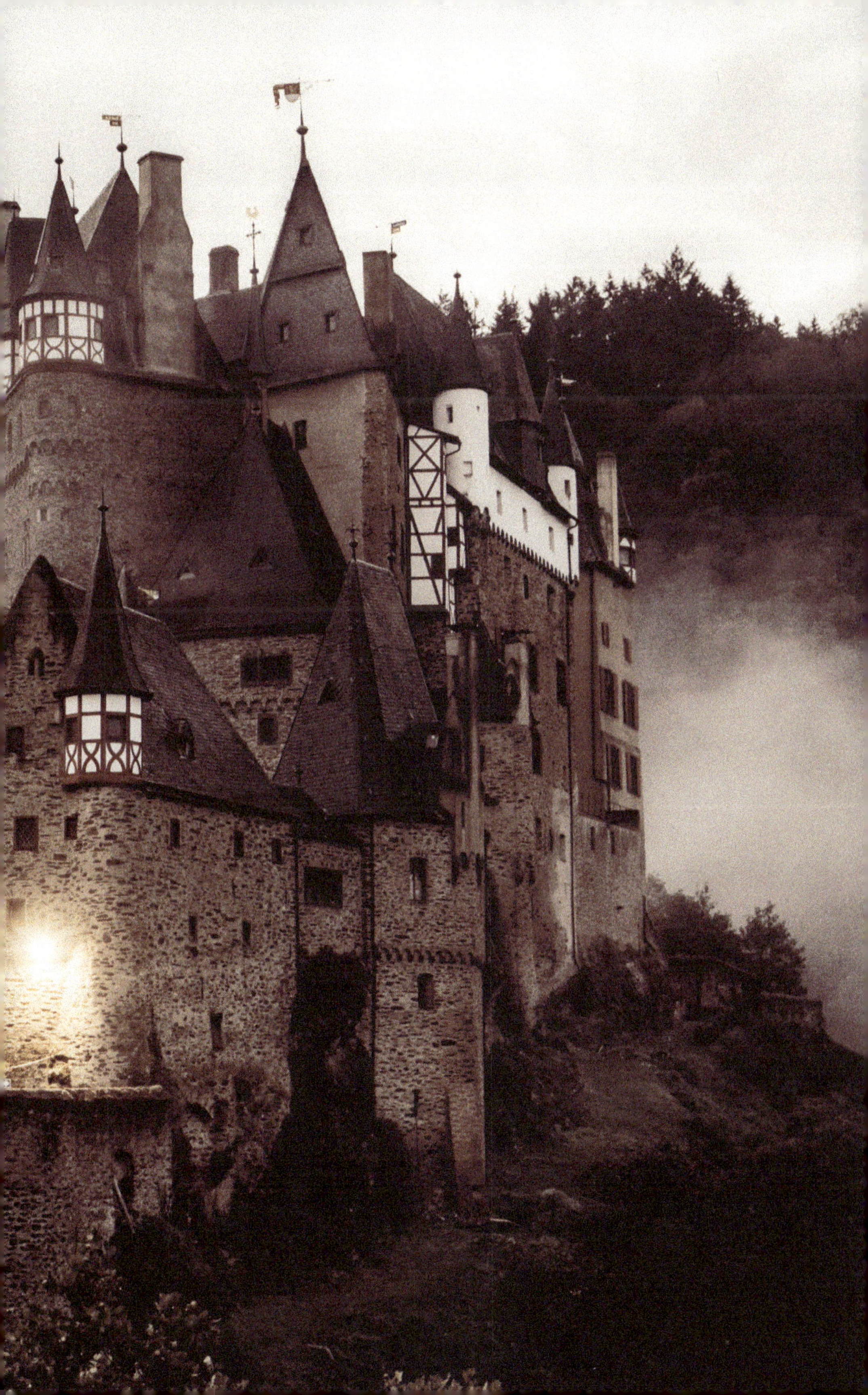

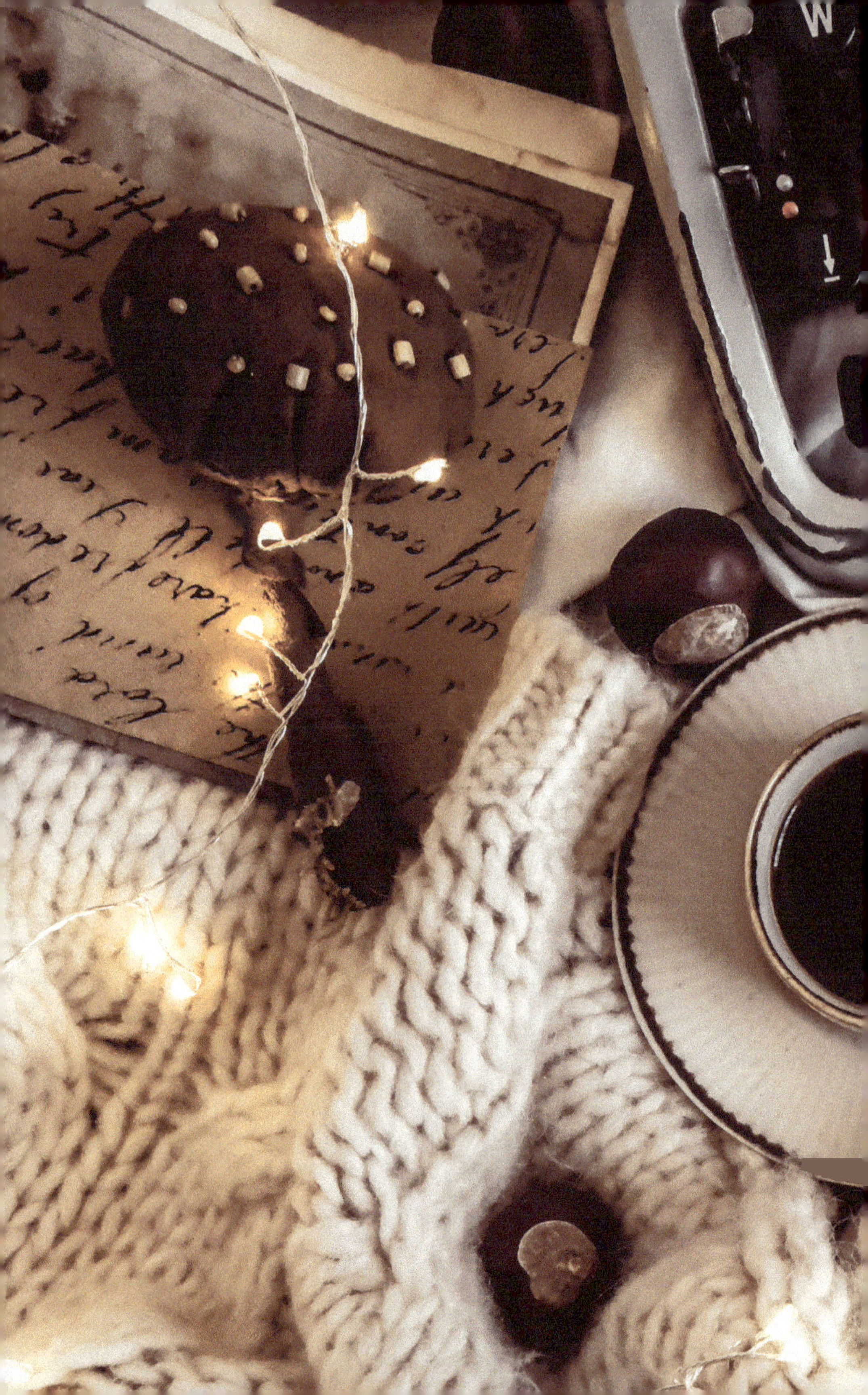

The story of a fabulou

There was Ring Lardner—During the Twenties, he was one of America's most original, widely read and quoted writer/humor... author of "You ...iend and ...tt and ...vis, ...othy Parker and ...ties.

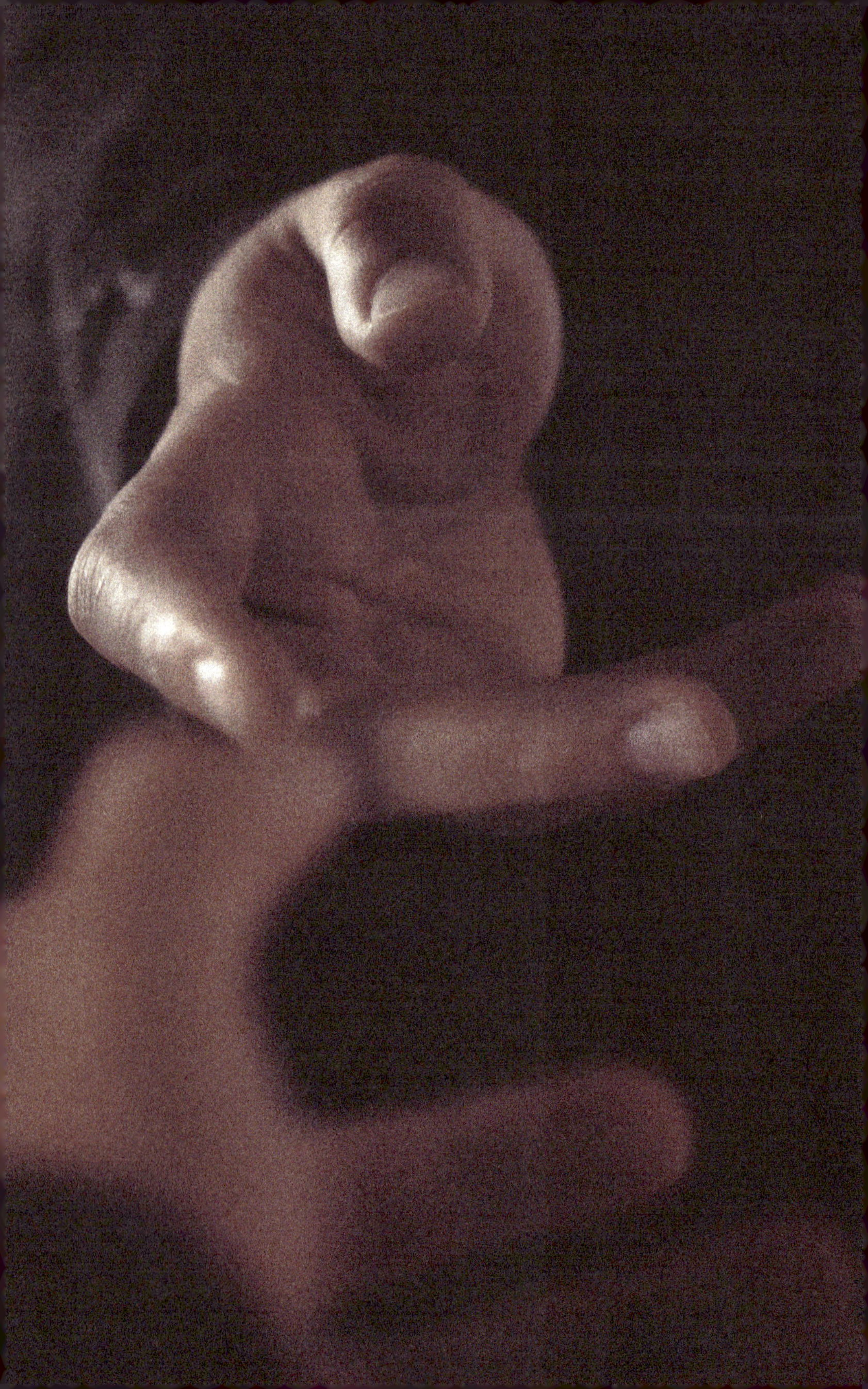

Afterword

To love a woman, the right woman, is to experience the greatest depths of not only them, but also of yourself. Learning to confront your triggers, working through your trauma, addressing the most damaged fragments of yourself to avoid projection, and taking accountability for what has yet to be resolved within your own inner turmoil. To love a woman, it takes passion, understanding, communication, comprehension, trust, healing, and so much more. With that, I have so much more work to do. I'll make us proud.

To M, my best friend, family, my missing piece, my love, the woman who this is all for, I hope that you feel me, and see yourself through all of this. You will always have this book as a tangible reminder of how much I adore, love, and respect you. I pray that your ambition guides you to the greatest and highest self that you strive to be and that you reach every goal you set your alluring mind on. I'll continue to be here with you every step of the way for as long as you want me to be, *being available only for you*, working on ourselves separately, but together, as we always tell each other. My loyalty is reserved only for you. I hope you find your way back to me. I love you.

-A.

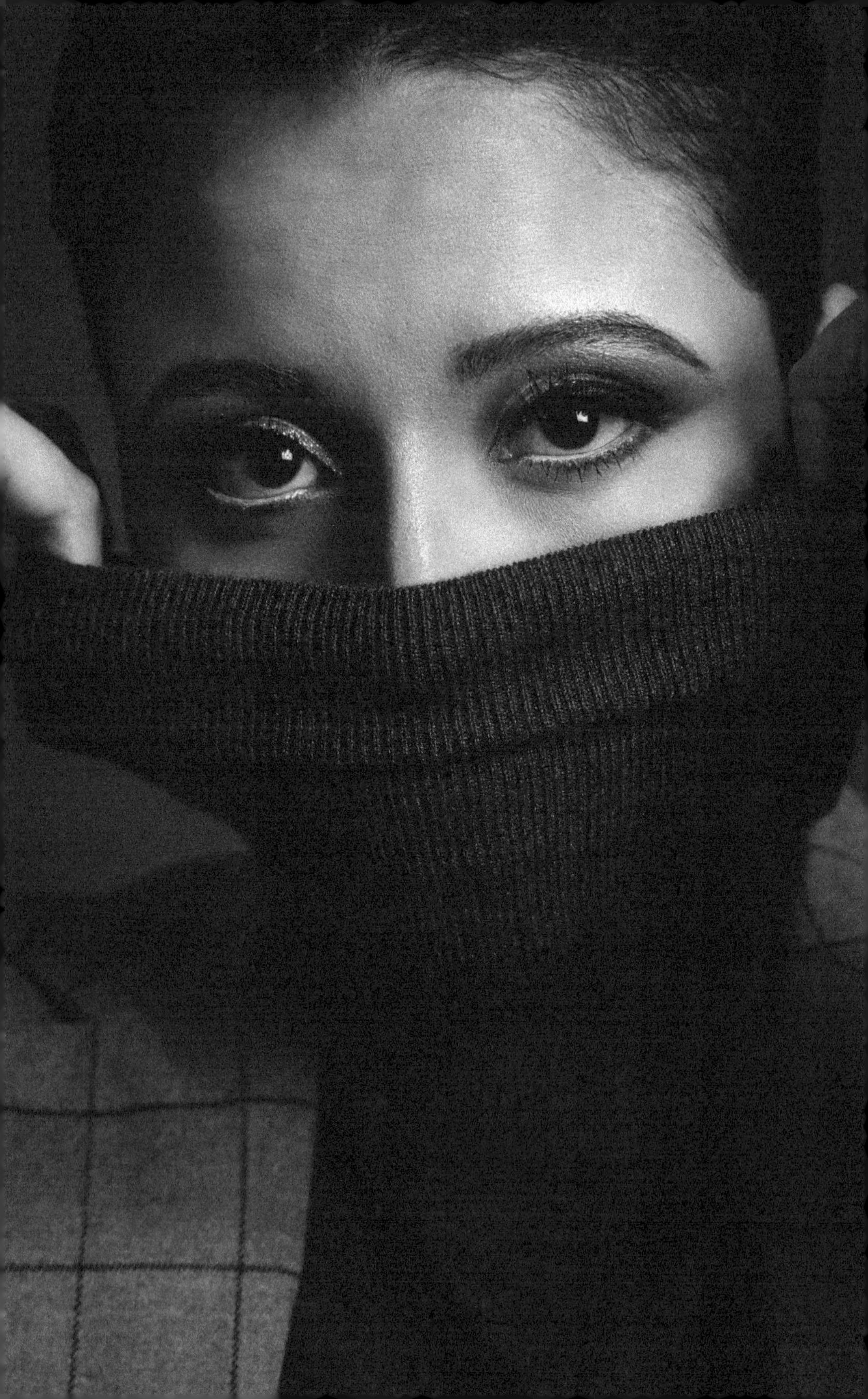

About the Author

Angela Solis was born in sunny but severely drought-stricken San Bernardino, California in April of 1998. She is the eldest of her four siblings.

As a writer, she is known for writing rhythmic poetry, and her unapologetic bold take on love and life around her. She is also a dedicated spoken word artist where her poetry is available on all music streaming platforms She is a full time online college student at Southern New Hampshire University, and is in her final year of study for a Bachelor of Arts degree in English with a poetry specialization and a creative writing sub-concentration.

When she is not writing, you will find her traveling the world with her best friend, having mimosas at a new brunch location, having her own concert in the gym, sleeping in the sun like a lizard, at the beach, or obsessing over finding new matching outfits for her children. She has two beautiful fur babies, her four-year-old daughter, Luna, an Australian Cattle Dog/Pit Bull Mix, and her two-year-old son, Oliver, an American shorthair cat.

Also by the Author

Albums

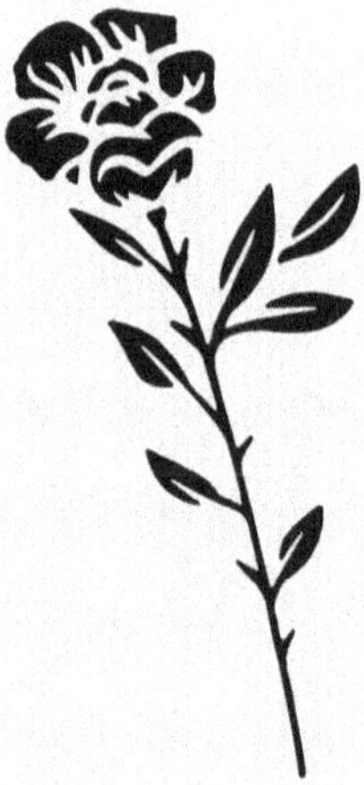

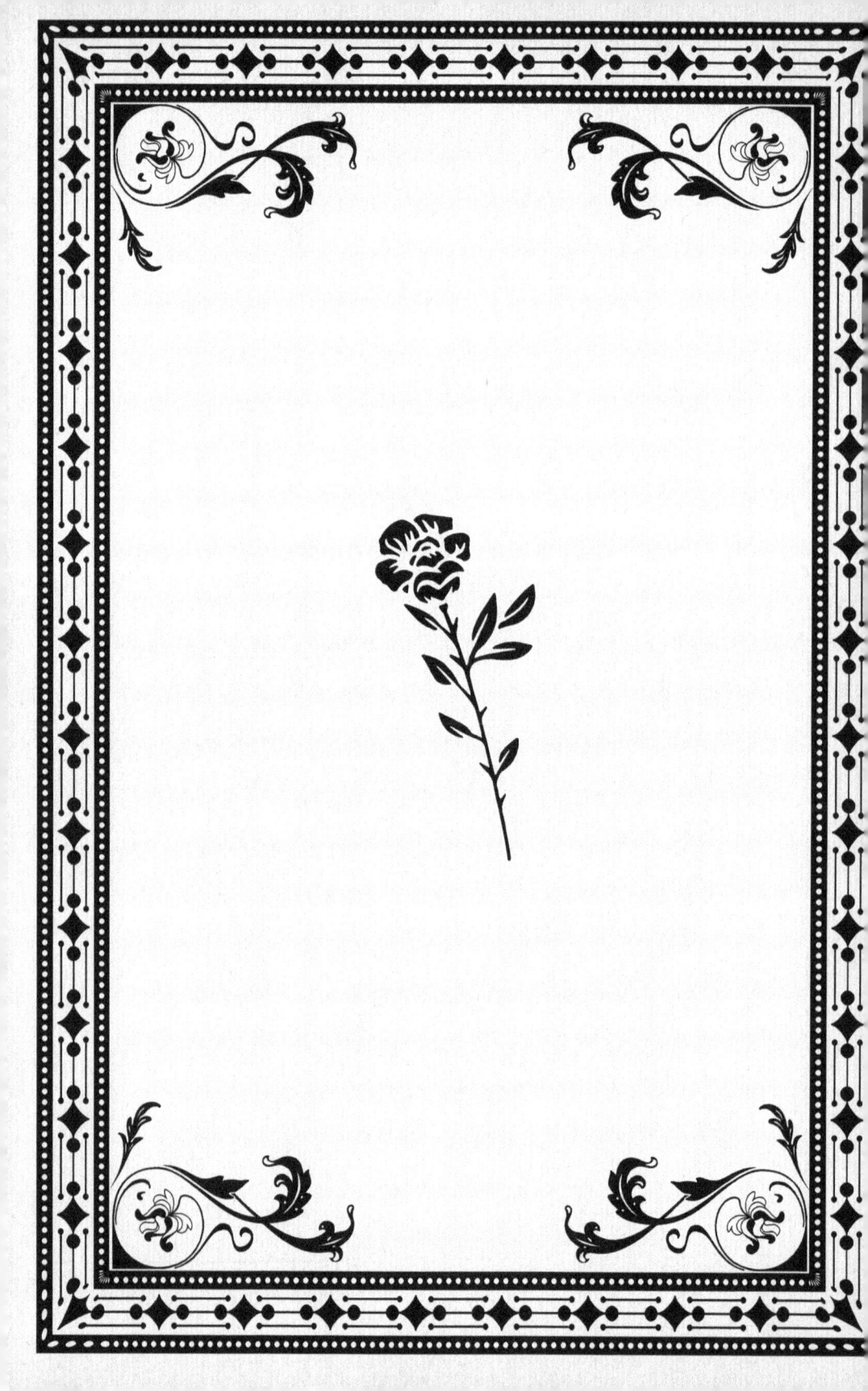

Divine Femininity

Divine Femininity

a collection of poetry about her
from my point of view

Manic.

Singles

Shakespeare

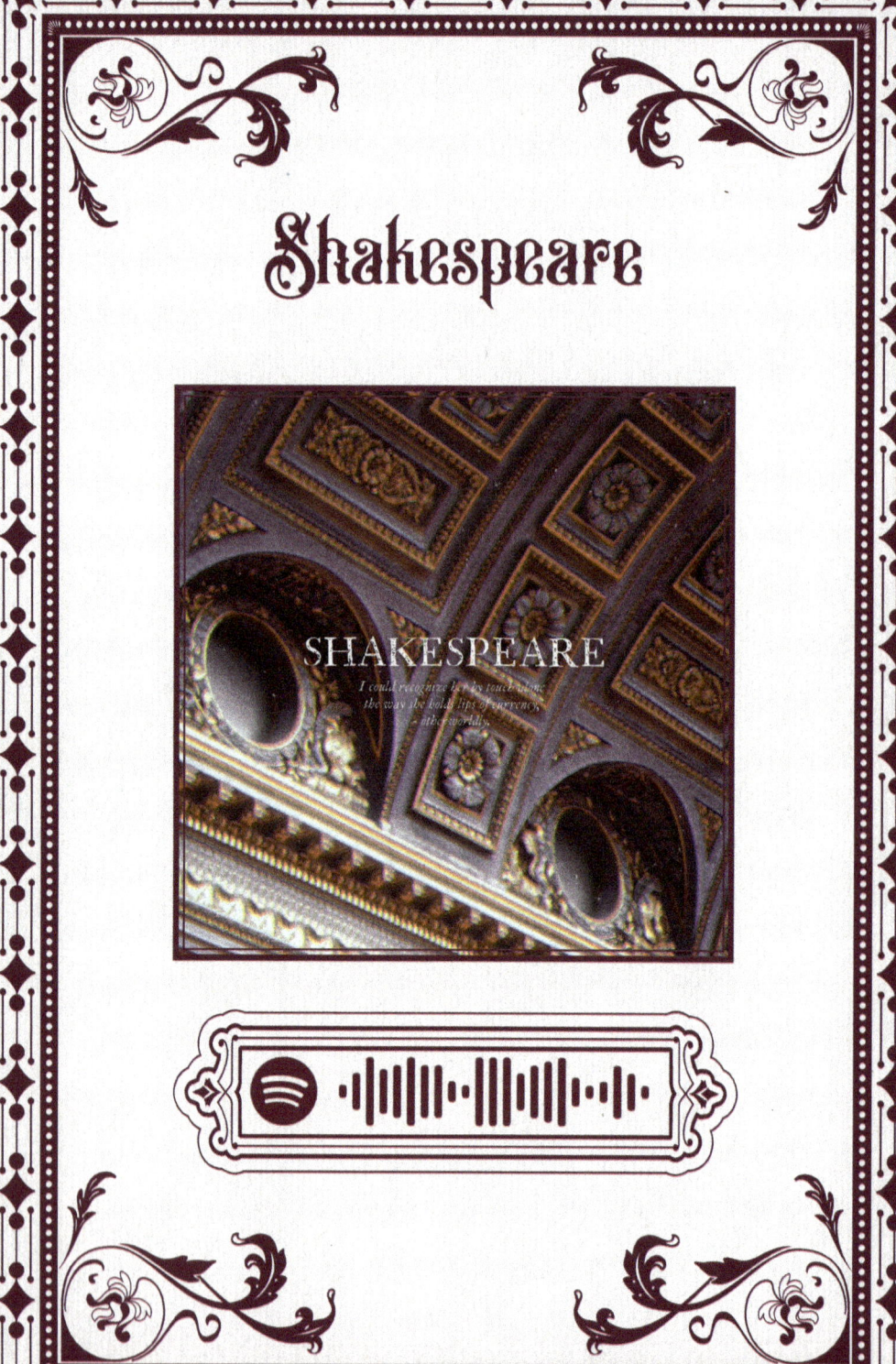

SHAKESPEARE

*I could recognize her by touch alone,
the way she holds lips of currency,
otherworldly.*

Intricate Mind

INTRICATE MIND
*deep soulful eyes, when it came to her,
she caught me by surprise*

Language of my Literature

Timeless

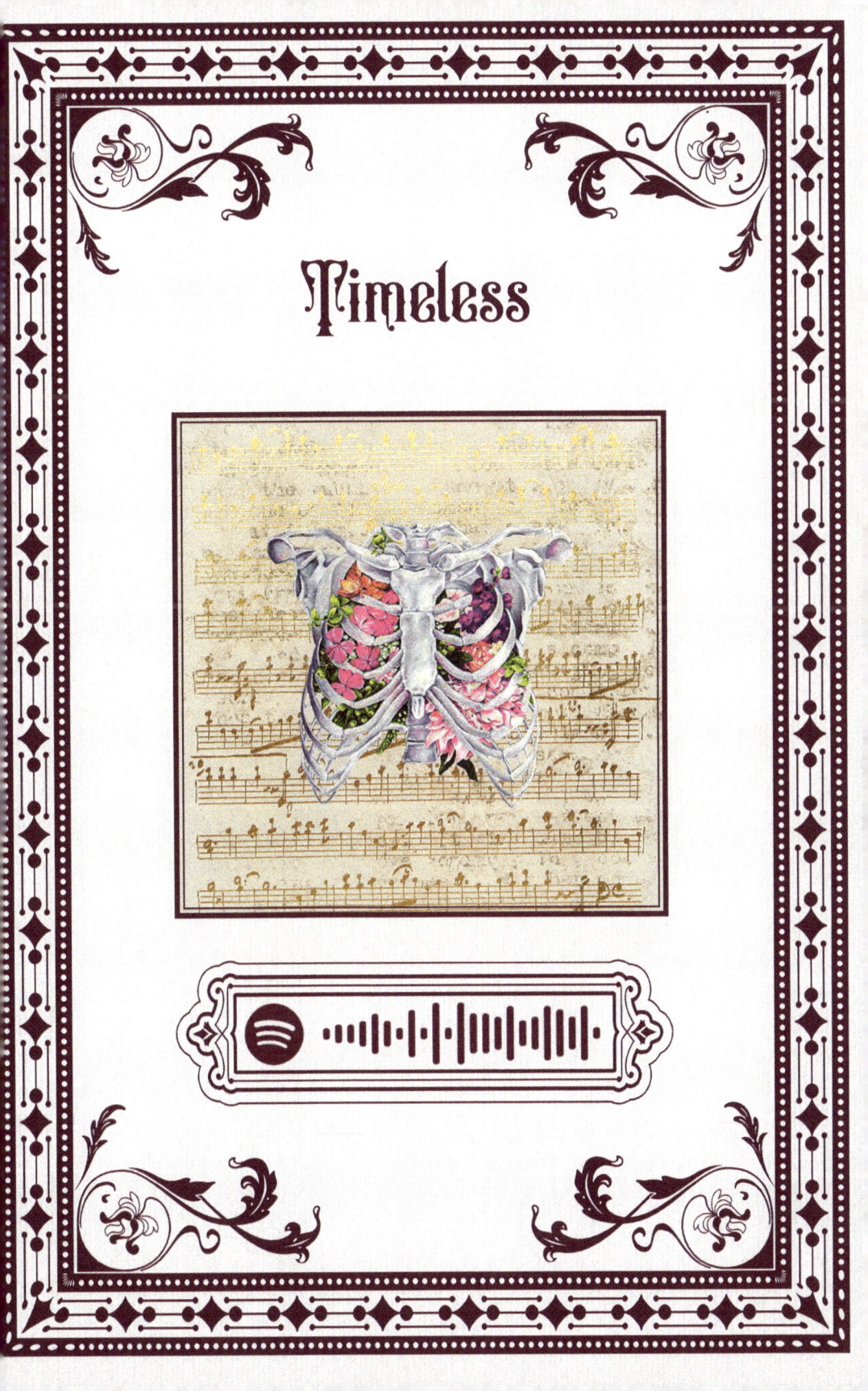

Brown Eyed Girl

BROWN EYED GIRL

ANGELA SOLIS

Melancholy

Melancholy

ANGELA SOLIS

Other Books

Amazon Rating & Reviews

★★★★★ 5 out of 5

6 global ratings

MANIC. is a collection of poetry that takes the reader on an introspective psychological conflict between the familiar ease of existing in pain, and the need for fighting one's way to restoration.

Within these pages, you are allowed to be a passenger to Angela's own inner journey. This book's existence itself is a testament to the ongoing battle of demolishing the stigma of mental health - focusing intently on the tireless battle between the thoughts to end your own life with your own bottle of prescribed medication and the insatiable zeal that motivates you to keep fighting, each day, just to see another sunset and the smile on a loved ones face.

You have the rare opportunity to see inside a poet's heart, mind, and soul as they spend months braving depths, processing the past, living boldly in the present, and making vows for the future. May you find a quiet place to let these words soak into your bones, may your mind and soul be transported by her narrative, and may you close this book with the understanding that you are not alone.

Manic.

RELEASED: APRIL 9, 2021

Amazon Rating & Reviews

★★★★★ 5 out of 5

36 global ratings

What Lies in the Wolf's Heart is a debut poetry collection that takes the reader on an emotional journey of both trial and triumph. It seeks to encompass as many stories as possible through multiperspectivity and connecting with each individual on a soul level, reminding them that no one is truly ever alone in this life. Written from the heart, these poems touch base with universal themes, including but not limited to mental health, self awareness, love, depression. Above all else, this heartfelt book serves as a voice for the voiceless.

What Lies in the Wolf's Heart

RELEASED: DECEMBER 27, 2019

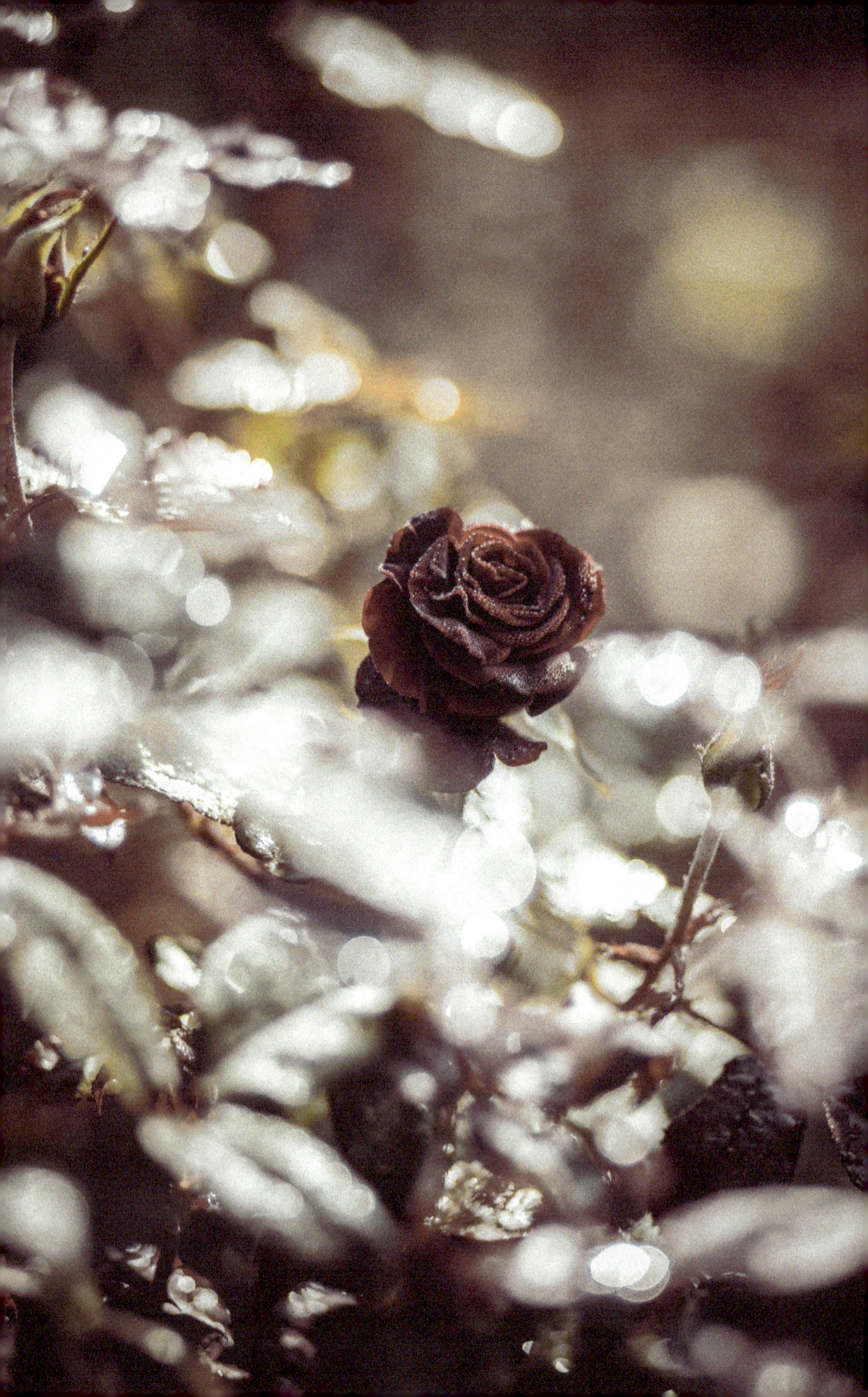

Scan for more poetry by
Angela Solis

For my
Artist

I love
you —K

Ingram Content Group UK Ltd.
Milton Keynes UK
UKHW052129270423
420867UK00009B/55